WHO
WE
ARE

WHO
WE
ARE

A PORTRAIT OF AMERICA
BASED ON THE LATEST U.S. CENSUS

SAM ROBERTS

All rights reserved under International and Pan-American Copyright Conventions. Published in the United States by Times Books, a division of Random House, Inc., New York, and simultaneously in Canada by Random House of Canada Limited, Toronto.

Library of Congress Cataloging-in-Publication Data

Roberts, Sam
    Who we are: a portrait of America based on the latest U.S. census / by Sam Roberts.
        ISBN 0-8129-2192-5
    1. United States — Population.   2. United States — Census, 21st, 1990.   I. Title.
HA201   1990k
304.6'0973'09049 — dc20   92-56842

Design by Anistatia R. Miller
Charts, tables, and graphs by Anne Cronin

Manufactured in the United States of America

9 8 7 6 5 4 3 2

First Edition

To my mother, Ethel Roberts,
a source of wisdom and strength
who spanned the century as a sturdy bridge
between immigrant parents
and two new generations of Americans

ACKNOWLEDGMENTS

A book begins with one word: an editor's yes. This book would not have been possible without the encouragement of Peter Osnos and Steve Wasserman of Times Books, who were present at the conception; Dwight Johnson and his colleagues at the Census Bureau, whose patience and guidance were incalculable; Professors Andrew Hacker and Andrew Beveridge of Queens College of the City University of New York, who sagely helped interpret raw statistics and translate them into trends; my generous Times colleagues, in particular Felicity Barringer for her expertise, Anne Cronin for her skillful transformation of numbers into compelling images, and Gerald Boyd for his indulgence; Ruth Fecych, senior editor of Times Books; Paul Neuthaler, my learned editor-for-life; the staffs of the Population Reference Bureau and of American Demographics, who responded to questions; and above all to my loving wife, Marie, and my sons, Michael and William, for their patience and encouragement; and to all the other people who count.

CONTENTS

WHO
WE
ARE

CHAPTER I

WHO
WE ARE

W ho are we? For two centuries, America has taken stock every decade, fulfilling a constitutional mandate and then reaching beyond it to produce a vivid, statistical self-portrait. In 1990, the nation's bicentennial census cost billions of dollars to produce — more than has ever been paid for any other painting by numbers. With a population that had grown 10 percent to at least 248,709,873 people since 1980 (plus 922,819 Americans living overseas), America embarked on the final decade of the twentieth century manifestly beset by doubts about its destiny in the twenty-first.

America, Theodore H. White once wrote, is more of an idea than a place. It is an idea that has drawn together the most diverse population on Earth and one that is becoming more varied every day. Uncle Sam, meet Ms. America. Today, the average American is a 32.7-year-old white woman who lives in a mortgaged suburban home that has three bedrooms and is heated by natural gas. She is a married mother, with some German ancestry, on the cusp of the MTV generation — roughly the thirteenth to come of age since Benjamin Franklin's. She graduated from high school and holds a clerical job. She moves to a new home more frequently than residents of any other developed nation. She is also a myth.

If average is a mathematical mean and if typical is emblematic of that mean, then the United States consists of too many parts to make a representative whole. It is a country of contrasts personified by a quarter of a billion people — including the homeless, whom the 1990 census counted specifically for the first time, and the prison population, which exploded by 139 percent in the decade (and included 2,356 Americans in legal limbo on death row at the end of 1990), though the number of inmates still was outnumbered by the residents of nursing homes. The nuclear family fizzled in the 1980s: for the first time, the number of married, childless couples surpassed the number of couples with children; fewer than three in four children are being raised by two parents; only one in seven families includes a married couple with two children; women, with and without children, began working outside the home and marrying later than at any time in a century; the ratio of divorces to marriages set a record; and the decline in household size halted. The birth rate rose again to what relieved demographers hailed as a "replacement level" of 2.2 children per woman — a rate suppressed by a record 15 million abortions during the decade but fueled, in part, by the surge in babies born to women who had never married. Still, only during the Depression of the 1930s had the population grown more slowly. And only during the 1950s had the population expanded by more people than are expected to be added in the 1990s.

Unlike the Balkans and the Baltics, unlike Western Europe — which took centuries even tentatively to embrace an imperfect union of sovereign states—the artificial political subdivisions that constitute the United States have withstood two centuries of unique civic evolution and wrenching tectonic upheaval. Only once did the fragile mosaic split, but the nation survived the Civil War in the nineteenth century and has endured far longer since that war than the four score and seven years between the nation's birth and the breach. The Civil War's grim legacy, though, is a nation still ambivalent about race, a nation that makes self-interested overtures to the Third World but over-looks a seemingly impenetrable Fourth World in the ghettos of its biggest cities and in its rural Tobacco Roads. Because, in part, of the decline in European immigration, blacks represent a greater proportion of America's population today than at any time in a century.

In 1941, before it was even half over, Henry Luce dubbed this the American Century. "It now becomes our time," he said, "to be the powerhouse from which the ideals spread throughout the world and do their mysterious work of lifting the life of mankind from the level of beasts to what the Psalmist called a little lower than the angels." America dominates the world—those whom Kipling called "lesser breeds without the law"—even more unequivocally at the century's end. The United States defended some countries, defeated others, and fed still more. They returned the favor, but in less proprietary ways. The rest of the world provided America with the immigrants who have made the burrito as ubiquitous as the bagel. America, ambiva-lently, provided a welcome. At no other time in the nation's history have so many people born abroad been residents of the United States. Nor have so many places within the nation seemed foreign to so many others—despite the commercial homogeniza-tion of America that television, faxes, and other forms of instant communication accomplished. The breadth of delocalized mar-keting was typified by the Brooklyn Savings Bank's metamorpho-sis from a neighborhood bank into a national conglomerate with an anonymous name. It merged to become Metropolitan Savings, then finally changed its name in the 1980s to the innocuous CrossLand. Every translucent store enclosure from Michigan Avenue to Main Street is now touted as an atrium. Fortunately for President Bill Clinton, no Big Mac attack need go unrequited for long. *The New York Times* declared the Gourmet Revolution accomplished, now that sun-dried tomatoes, extra virgin olive oil, and microwaveable chicken entrées scarred by faux grill marks are universally available.

But never before, despite previous waves of immigration, has the nation been so diverse. Nor have contrasts between and within regions, while becoming more isolated, been so stark. In the Pacific region, one in five Americans is foreign-born. In a broad swath of the Midwest Farm Belt, only one in fifty is. Blacks made up a majority in 89 of the nation's 3,141 counties, but the census found not a single one in another 117 counties and they accounted for less than 1 percent of the population in 1,400 others. "If you believe that the descendant of an English lord and a descendant of a Polish shtetl are part of the same group, then that group is going to continue in the majority for a long time to come," said Ben J. Wattenberg, the demographer and political commentator who has hailed America as the first universal nation. "Still, there's a big difference between being a 90 percent majority, a 70 percent majority or a 55 percent majority."

Whatever its size, that majority is tenuous. It is hardly homogeneous and it is shrinking. The 1990 census found that whites made up 80 percent of the nation's resident population. Blacks increased 13 percent to constitute 12 percent of the population. The number of Hispanic people climbed 53 percent, to 9 percent of the population. Asians doubled, to account for about 3 percent of the total. Only three in four Americans are non-Hispanic whites (referred to hereafter, for the sake of brevity, simply as whites) although distinguishing Hispanic people as foreign or newcomers seems to defy even history: they settled in

New Mexico before the English landed in Jamestown. Moreover, half of them typically skipped "white" or "black" on the census form and identified themselves as "other." Until the 1970 census, Hispanic people, except for Puerto Ricans in some states, were not even counted as a separate category. In 1990, the census found that whites constitute only half of New Mexico's population. Nationwide, they account for more than 99.5 percent of the population in 60 counties. But in 186 other counties, blacks, Hispanic people, Asian-Americans and other groups that, individually, are still regarded as minorities together have become the majority — suggesting what the nation as a whole may look like around the middle of the twenty-first century.

The nation's complexion changed more starkly in the 1980s than in any previous decade, and twice as fast as in the 1970s. When the 1980s ended, Asian-born Americans outnumbered the European-born. United States residents born in Latin America outnumbered both. Between 1980 and 1990, not only did the share of white children shrink in every state, but an even more striking shift occurred: blacks no longer made up a majority among the nation's minority children. In 1980, one in five Americans identified themselves as having African, Asian, Hispanic, or American Indian ancestry. In 1990, one in four did. One in eight people nationwide speaks a foreign language at home, so many of them that the 1990 census devised a new category — linguistic isolation — to measure households in which all members speak a language other than English and none fourteen years or older speaks English very well. One in twenty-five children nationwide and nearly one in seven in California were isolated in this linguistic limbo. In 1980, two thirds of Californians were European whites; ten years later, only a little more than half were. As many immigrants came through California during the 1980s as passed through New York during the first decade of the century. California is now home to nearly four in ten of the nation's Asians and Pacific Islanders. Nearly two thirds of Miami's residents are

Hispanic. But in New York City, where there are now more Asian-Americans than in Hawaii, an even higher proportion of residents speak a language other than English at home.

New Jersey gained 365,177 residents during the 1980s, but only 2,998 of them were non-Hispanic whites. Its Native American population — or, more precisely, the number of New Jerseyans willing or wanting to be classified as Indians — soared by an astounding 78 percent (although the number who listed themselves as Asian-Indian was nearly six times larger). Since 1980, the number of Americans identifying themselves as Indians rose 38 percent — a reflection, perhaps, of the ambiguous census category, "Indian (Amer.)," which, while it also asked for tribe, appeared on the census form several inches above what for many immigrants probably was the more appropriate designation: "Asian Indian." In 1990, the number of American Indians living east of the Mississippi was ten times greater than the first census estimated. But in embracing a heritage that had become culturally chic, they also abandoned a name that a European had bestowed upon them by mistake. Instead, Indians became Native Americans or, better yet, First Americans. Perhaps more significantly, another group that had even fewer historical or emotional motivations to adopt a country that had savagely kidnapped its forebears from another continent, centuries ago, proudly reverted to an earlier identification: African-American.

From the beginning, America has been a nation on the go. Examples abound. In virtually every decade, except, perhaps, the 1930s, when only about 50,000 immigrants arrived yearly, more people have always been coming into the country than emigrating; and even in the 1980s, most people lived in a different house at the end of the decade than when it began. Fully 80 percent of New Yorkers were born in the state they now call home. But 70 percent of the people who lived in

Florida in 1990 had moved there from someplace else. Florida gained 3.2 million people during the decade, more than twice as many as lived in the whole state in 1950. But that was only about half the number of immigrants, newborns, and newcomers from other states who boosted California's population in the 1980s until it required a record fifty-two congressional seats and had gained a political dominance that no state had wielded since New York in the nineteenth century. Too big, some Californians complained. One faction in the northern counties fantasized about secession from the rest of the state, as New York City had similarly contemplated a generation earlier and as its two most middle-American boroughs, Queens and Staten Island, still do, if ambivalently.

States are a political contrivance of cartographers. Today, the American state of mind is being defined by the suburbs. Jefferson notwithstanding, fewer than one in fifty Americans live on what the census broadly defines as a farm anymore. Instead, despite the remaining vast tracts of sparsely populated land, one fourth of the nation has gravitated to cities or seems stuck there. Fully another half of the nation has made metropolitan areas outside central cities — in other words, the suburbs — the most popular place to live. Ninety percent of the nation's population growth in the 1980s was concentrated in metropolitan areas of a million or more people, and such growth was most rapid outside the denser central cities. The 1992 presidential election was the first in which suburbanites cast fully half of the votes. For the first time, half the nation's population lives not merely in metropolitan areas — by census standards, a low threshold — but in megalopolises of a million people or more. The United States now qualifies for the roster of city-states — those tiny nations, countries with vast uninhabited areas and the industrial giants like Germany and Japan — in which three quarters of the population live in nonrural places. Even Vermont had bestowed upon it the mixed blessing of its first official metropolitan area, though its reputation as the pristine pastures that provide raw material for Ben & Jerry's ice cream was largely undiluted (recalling Harry Lime's dismissive observation in *The Third Man* that after 500 years of democracy and peace, all that Switzerland had produced was the cuckoo clock). But New York, which until as recently as 1960 had been, with Rhode Island, the most urban state, slipped to tenth — tied with Massachusetts and becoming less urban even than California, New Jersey, Rhode Island, Hawaii, Utah, Arizona, Nevada, Illinois, and Florida. The spaces in between are still wide open, but the most urbanized region of the nation is now the West.

As defined by density rather than destiny, there may be no more frontier to tempt the imaginations of Americans. Still, they were lured by employment and other opportunities and by places to which they wanted to return or to retire. Cleveland and Detroit lost population. But Naples, on Florida's Gulf Coast, grew by 77 percent as the West and South surged.

Again, the nation's population center shifted farther west from where it began its journey two centuries ago, near Washington — a city seemingly so far removed from the rest of the country that President Ronald Reagan pronounced it as not a place of "real people." Yet Washington typified another phenomenon that had become all too real, and not just in America's cities: Government officials there have more to fear from random gunfire than from assassination attempts. While congressmen no longer routinely arm themselves to attend nighttime sessions on Capitol Hill, as their predecessors did in the nineteenth century, violent crime bred by poverty, racial tension and greed, and symbolized by the arrest of Washington, D.C.'s mayor on drug charges, focused everyone's attention on the extent of social disintegration.

Materially, the nation's growth was uneven. More households owned three vehicles than one. Many more homes boasted at least five bedrooms than lacked indoor plumbing. But more and more people lived in housing they could not afford. Home ownership rates declined for the first time in fifty years. Crowding increased. Poverty — among blacks, in particular — was no longer a consequence of America's failure to absorb new immigrants quickly enough, as it had been historically, and with the influx of middle-class blacks, Hispanic people and Asian-Americans into the suburbs, society was becoming as segregated by class as by race.

Poverty was redistributed. So was wealth. In 1990, the government counted more millionaires than it did homeless street people, and if all the millionaires had been assembled in one place it would have taken nothing less than the Yale Bowl to hold them. For the first time, three in four Americans were high school graduates, and a growing percentage were granted college degrees. But their economic gains were not always commensurate with their education.

"Life," lamented a character on *Middle Ages*, a short-lived, age-appropriate television comedy whose name evoked a gothic rite of passage, "is the scariest thing there is." Jann Wenner, who a quarter century earlier had founded *Rolling Stone* magazine, gathered no moss in producing another contemporary publication for his peers, titled *Family Life*. "A generation that once raised hell," Wenner deduced, "is now raising kids." Steamy romance novels celebrated parenting as a surprisingly fulfilling by-product of sex. The bulge of Baby Boomers climbed the chronological ladder and they became bifurcated — the younger ones struggling more as the census captured a statistical portrait of Dorian Gray in reverse. For the first time, the census measured labor participation rates for mothers and found that among those with preschool children, a record 60 percent worked outside the home. And those who didn't earned an honorific: "housewife" was summarily replaced by "homemaker." More Americans now work selling goods in wholesale and retail than in actually manufacturing goods for sale; more in finance, insurance and real estate than in construction; more in providing comforting protective services than in catering to leisurely recreation and entertainment. Twice as many people work for government as for themselves.

Even the vast trove of vital statistics accumulated by the Census Bureau and its sister agencies cannot realistically produce a composite American, though. We know that the number of college students studying Japanese tripled, that black teenagers were six times as likely as white ones to be fatally shot by someone else but half as likely to take their own lives with a gun, that the number of births to unmarried women soared about 75 percent over the decade, and that a major league baseball player's average salary more than quadrupled — from $144,000 in 1980 to $598,000 in 1990. Couch potatoes rejoice: 67,000 people were injured by exercise equipment in 1990, or about twice as many as were injured in accidents involving television sets. But no formula can find the average of diversity. And numbers alone, however valid or vivid, lack invaluable context.

In 1890, America's centennial census proclaimed "a century of progress and achievement unequaled in the world's history." But can a nation with the highest homicide rate of any developed country persuasively argue that it is so much more civilized at the end of the twentieth century than it was at the beginning? Does its self-congratulation at absorbing new immigrants — in contrast to Germany, for example — suggest hypocrisy, given its undiminished obsession with race? Has it forgotten that an icon of political oratory — the traditional family — is a mid-nineteenth-century phenomenon fashioned by the Industrial Revolution and historically most prevalent among the white middle class? Who, as America nears the millennium, will broker the economic and cultural differences that are recasting the country and dividing some groups of Americans even as they bring others together?

As the 1990s began, network television, the validator of popular culture, briefly replaced *thirtysomething* with a successor series for the fortysomething generation: *Home Fires*.

"I want things the way they were," said a character on the series.

"The way they were when?" his wife asked.

"1978," he replied.

Current events now devolve into history so quickly that nostalgia can't keep pace. So much is mist. Even 1978, hardly a halcyon time, seems like a simpler era — viewed from a decade punctuated by the Mariel boatlift from Cuba, the highest unemployment rate since 1940, the highest poverty rate since 1965, the election of the first black mayors of Chicago and New York, the appointment of the first woman to the Supreme Court, the boom on Wall Street and the subsequent crash, the first decline in life expectancy for blacks while the expected life span for whites increased, forecasts that AIDS would become the leading killer of people 25 to 44, and as the 1980s closed, the birth of an American who raised the number of new infants that year to its highest level since 1964. During the last half of the twentieth century, the United States elected a Roman Catholic as president for the first time, nominated the first woman candidate for vice president, and then began the final decade before the millennium by electing a presidential ticket of Baby Boomers that personified the first post-Depression and post–Second World War political generation. The unofficial anthem at the 1992 Democratic National Convention, Fleetwood Mac's "Don't Stop (Thinking About Tomorrow)," suggested that thinking nostalgically about yesterday is no longer enough.

In 1992, the Republicans convened in Houston, a city that epitomized the shift in population and political power to the South and West, the spirit of entrepreneurship, of technology and of American know-how. That spirit had earned the city's name a footnote as the first word spoken from the Moon as Neil Armstrong immortalized his first step into the lunar dust with a garbled metaphor. By convening in New York that same year, though, Democrats returned to their roots. They risked the taint of an immigrant garrison, in part, to make a point: Now that it had saved the world, the nation had to save itself; insecurity and instability were universal (more than one civic booster in New York reminded visitors that the murder rate was higher in Houston), and if some people looked and lived differently from others, this, after all, is America, where what counts most is Who We Are — people who embody an idea and an ideal that is more important than place.

CHAPTER II

WHY WE COUNT

A merica's bicentennial census was conducted by 520,000 workers, or more people than General Motors employs worldwide. The government spent $2.6 billion to tally the nation's vital statistics, or about $1,040 per person counted. Tens of millions of census forms from 3,141 counties, 23,435 places, 49,961 census tracts and 6,961,150 census blocks were microfilmed, tallied, computerized, shredded and then placed in warehouse vaults in Jeffersonville, Indiana, an Ohio River town that gave its labor, but not its name, to producing Louisville Slugger baseball bats, where they are to remain until the year 2062 — considerably longer than the statute of limitations for most crimes, but long enough to guarantee that, barring a medical miracle, the vast majority of respondents to the 1990 count will have died. The answers were scanned by lasers, digested by computers, massaged by demographers and finally regurgitated onto compact disks, tapes and tens of thousands of pages of charts and tables that paint a compelling statistical portrait of who we are and where we stand.

During the 1980s, the nation's population grew by 9.8 percent; the world's by 19 percent. As the world population explodes toward 6 billion, the United States is home to fewer than one in twenty of the planet's people. Even that proportion is shrinking. The nation ranks third or fourth (depending on how the former Soviet republics are counted) in human mass, but is losing ground. The population of the United States is projected to double in about nine decades. China's may double in five decades and East Africa's in only two. The United States is politically predominant and militarily supreme, but only sixth in infant mortality and life expectancy. Its largest city is the fifth biggest on the globe (but boasts a roomy 11,000 people per square mile compared to 248,000 in Hong Kong). Yet for nearly a century, Americans have fueled the world's richest and most productive economy. And, like no other nation, the United States has been repeatedly reinvigorated by immigrants.

The twenty-first decennial census is a massive if imperfect snapshot of an amorphous moving target. It is an idealized, computer-enhanced composite of what the nation's founders had in mind when, in Article I, Section 2, of the Constitution, they mandated that Americans hold up a mirror to assess their growth every ten years so that their representatives and direct taxes would be "apportioned according to their respective numbers." Even then, the mirror was concave. The Solomon-like Founding Fathers were themselves responsible for the first contrivance when they foreshadowed the new nation's obsession with race: their Great Compromise to count slaves as three fifths of free persons. And from the beginning, skeptics in and out of government doubted whether a complete count even of the unfractionated people was possible. In 1791, as 16 United States marshals and their 650 assistants were completing the first official count that found 3,929,326 Americans, Thomas Jefferson confided to George Washington on a cover sheet: "I enclose you also a copy of our census, written in black ink so far as we have actual returns, and supplied by conjecture in red ink, where we have no returns, but the conjectures are known to be very near the truth. Making very small allowance for omissions (which we know to have been very great), we are certainly above four millions."

Two centuries later, blacks are still being undercounted, though not as a matter of law. And while the returns are still flawed by omissions, statisticians are better armed today to conjecture about whom the official count actually reflects. The census takes the measure of America like an imprecise scale: Dieters may never know their exact poundage, but by weighing themselves periodically they get a pretty good idea of their losses and gains over time. Viewed not as a single snapshot but as a frame in a moving image of America, the census captures an animated vision of a nation in flux. The trends and shifts in where and with whom we live, where we work, what we earn and what we learn provide a unique self-portrait of Who We Are. Like all self-portraits, its individual parts are vulnerable to artistic license; its whole suggests a unique, but recognizable, persona.

What do we count for? It's the law, to make democracy more representative and responsive. The census determines how political power and how tens of billions of dollars in federal funds will be apportioned among the states. It guides business decisions, such as when Maybelline would introduce its Shades of You cosmetics line and tap a growing market of nonwhite women, or whether an orthodontist will leave New York and identify, as he hoped to from census figures, a dream community within ten miles of the beach in a city between Los Angeles and San Diego with a large concentration of teenagers in high-income households. Perhaps the census' greatest potential contribution is to provide context for the mind-boggling number of problematic decisions with which we must cope at an increasingly numbing pace. Journalists, like their readers and viewers, tend too often to view events in isolation. In fact, those events are usually flanked by a beginning that has already been recorded and by an end that can only be guessed. General Creighton Abrams' version of why America floundered in Vietnam is a metaphor for our continuing failure to place seemingly unprecedented events and evolutionary developments in perspective. The problem, Abrams said, was not that we had ten years of experience, but one year of experience ten times.

While the science of statistics originated in Germany, the word *census* is derived from the French verb for "to assess." The practice is rooted in the Roman head count and property evaluation that was computed every five years. In the United States, the census began solely as a political tool to guarantee that as the country grew, the original states and those yet to be carved out of uncharted territory to the west and south would be proportionately represented in Congress. Rhode Island was admitted in time to be included in the first count. Vermont wasn't. Once the question of whom to ask was settled, what to ask was next. If the threatening image of Big Brother loomed 150 years ahead, harsh recollections of King George's intrusiveness were painfully fresh. Suggestions for a detailed census questionnaire were scrapped after one congressman warned that prying by government agents would cause alarm. "Their purposes," he cautioned, "can not be supposed the same as the historian's or philosopher's — they are statesmen, and all their measures are suspected of policy." Finally, only six questions were posed: to distinguish free persons, their sex and color, and the number of free males age 16 and over (a category designed to assess the nation's military and industrial potential).

The first census, which cost one cent per person in 1990 dollars to conduct, found 3.9 million people. Among them, 694,280 were slaves and 59,557 were described as "free Negroes" — meaning that fully one in five persons was black. Indians, except the relatively few who were taxed, were not tallied at all. In 1790, families were made up of an average of six people. Among whites whose nationality could be determined, more than eight in ten traced their origins — many, quite recent — to England. There were fewer than ten people per square mile, although population density varied enormously, from sixty-three people per square mile in Rhode Island to fewer than one in Tennessee. Asking how people got to work would have been superfluous. For those who worked away from home, transportation alternatives were largely limited to boat or horseback — or, for those lucky enough to live near a post road, to emerging stagecoach companies. Only the year before the first census, it took a full week to convey to George Washington in Virginia news of his election on April 7, 1789, in Philadelphia.

By the census's centennial in 1890, the nation's population had grown tenfold. The census questionnaire had grown even more. The government did not share the sentiments of Emily Dickinson's mid-century paean to anonymity:

> I'm Nobody! Who are you?
> Are you — Nobody — too?

Punch cards — the first major installation in the world of an electrical tabulating system, inspiration for the stern admonition and metaphor, "do not fold, spindle or mutilate" — were used for the first time to calculate answers to 233 separate schedules that covered 22 subjects and produced a possible 13,161 questions (including whether the respondent was white, black, mulatto, quadroon, octoroon, Chinese, Japanese or, since 1860, American

Indian). Census takers were advised to, among other things: "Distinguish carefully between housekeepers, or women who receive a stated wage or salary for their services, and housewifes, or women who keep house for their own families or for themselves, without any gainful occupation." Also, the instructions cautioned census takers to record physical and mental defects and advised that in listing the occupation of Indians, "special attention is to be directed to reporting 'Medicine-man,' as it is the only occupation among Indians resembling a profession in civilization." And the instructions defined the head of a family as "a husband, father, widow or unmarried person of either sex." The census form was subsequently pared to delete objectionable questions (religion among them) — also because other government agencies began collecting some of the same data themselves.

An introduction to the 1890 census results touted unequaled progress and achievement; the accompanying figures confirmed spectacular growth. The number of Americans had soared to 63 million (about the current population of California, Texas and Florida combined), which also had raised the cost of counting them to eighteen cents a person. Average family size had declined to five; the median age had jumped from about 16 to 22. And the number of people per square mile had increased nearly fourfold. Only a decade earlier, in 1880, the census had gauged that, for the first time, more Americans were living beyond the nation's original boundaries than within them. The 1890 count suggested that Americans would continue to be lured by the prospects of a better life in the West. But bigger wasn't necessarily better. Already, three states west of the Mississippi (Iowa, Missouri and Texas) had elbowed their way into the top ten in population. Chicago surpassed Philadelphia as the nation's second most populous city. Remarking on the flow, a census official concluded in 1891 that "there can hardly be said to be a frontier line." And before the decade ended, Frederick Jackson Turner concurred that, indeed, the West had been won.

But in the twentieth century, the West would do the winning. First, in 1920, the census found that what Jefferson feared most had finally happened: More Americans were living in urban places than in rural ones. In 1970, what cosmopolites dreaded most had occurred: The population of the suburbs surpassed that of the central cities. In 1980, the population of the Northeast and Midwest was overtaken by that of the West and the South. And by 1990 the West finally edged out the Northeast.

The actual head count was still being conducted by human beings. But the tabulations had largely been taken over by computers, although they could be programmed to conform to political agendas and preconceptions and were still subject to mathematical manipulation. Confounded by the information they were being fed, census computers decided that nobody could be more than 112 years old—a chronologically correct point, perhaps, in the machines' favor. But programmers also overruled gay and lesbian couples who demanded to be recognized as more than roommates: When two people of the same sex living in the same household identified themselves as spouses, the computer unilaterally corrected them. (For the first time, though, the census form offered a dicey alternative self-identification—unmarried partners—but did not necessarily conclude that, even if they are the same sex, they are gay.) Write-in entries such as "Don't know" or "NA" were not accepted. Instead, demographers impudently resorted to a process called imputation, which creates fictional individuals with a complete set of social characteristics and which the census rationalized this way: "When there was an indication that a housing unit was occupied, but the questionnaire contained no information for the people within the household, or the occupants were not listed on the questionnaire, a previously accepted household was selected as a substitute, and the full set of characteristics for the substitute was duplicated." Even age and sex were imputed when, for whatever reason, the question-

naire was left incomplete. The Census Bureau frankly acknowledged that the process of imputation had a potentially unwelcome
side effect: transforming an incomplete picture into a distorted
one. In releasing more detailed profiles from individual questionnaires, to protect privacy the Census Bureau has resorted to an
even more bizarre method of obfuscation called suppression.

Since people tend to round their age up if they are close to
having a birthday (the 1990 questionnaire no longer asked age
by quarter year), chances are that, as the Census Bureau put it,
"approximately 10 percent of persons in most age groups are
actually 1 year younger," a revelation sure to please the most vain
respondents. This imprecision became especially acute among
the youngest group: "The problem is most pronounced at age 0
because persons lost to age 1 may not have been fully offset by
the inclusion of babies born after April 1, 1990, and because there
may have been more rounding up to age 1 to avoid reporting age
as 0 years."

Indians presented a special problem. Too many respondents identified themselves as Cherokees in places that were,
presumably, all but devoid of American Indians at all. In 1990,
8 percent of the 1.8 million people who identified themselves
as American Indians then said they belonged to these tribes:
Haitian, Polish, African-American, Hispanic, or Arab. Other
Indian groups may have been undercounted. In upstate New
York, census takers were booted off the Onondaga Reservation.
Nonetheless, they produced what they described as a reason-
able count, with one caveat: "A problem with the processing
of the incomplete records for the Onondaga Reservation, ob-
tained using our 1990 census 'last resort' procedures, resulted
in the misclassification of race. Most of the population on the
reservation should be classified as American Indian." A similar
oversight occurred on the Tuscarora Reservation. (For the first
time, in 1990 the census recognized still another geographic
category, tribal-designated statistical areas.)

Geography figured in another census question that became the province of the Federal Office of Management and Budget and of another government agency, the Federal Executive Committee on Metropolitan Areas (the acronym for which would be FECOMA, which is why it is known instead by its full name). To qualify, a metropolitan area must contain either a Census Bureau–defined urban area (one or more central places plus an urban fringe with 1,000 or more people per square mile for a total of at least 50,000) and a total metropolitan area population of 100,000 or more, except in New England, where the minimum must be 75,000. The full definition goes on for several paragraphs, distinguishing between central cities and the densely settled "urban fringe," identified in 1950, without ever mentioning in the index of its official glossary the area that has emerged as, perhaps, the most significant of all: the suburbs.

Census officials insisted that answering the fourteen questions on the short form, which was sent to five in six of the nation's 90 million households, would take all of fourteen minutes. The other households received the long form. That unabridged version, census officials estimated, could be completed in forty-three minutes (twice the mean travel time to work of American commuters in 1990), but only if you had already calculated and could readily remember, among other figures, the percentage of your household income spent on gross rent. For many sophisticates weaned on computer keyboards and cellular phones, the first impediment was finding the requisite "black lead pencil" that the instructions demanded. For ordinary Americans, some of the questions themselves might have proved nettlesome. "Usual residence" was defined as the place where you live and sleep "most of the time," but sons and daughters attending college elsewhere or serving in the armed forces and living somewhere else were not to be included among the occupants. Among married couples, whoever filled out the form was supposed to describe himself or herself as Person One—thus relegating the spouse to Person Two. Even so, this represented an improvement over previous questionnaires. Not so long ago, the census referred to "adult family members other than head and wife." The 1990 census removed the head altogether, opting instead for the gender-neutral coinage "householder," which some dictionaries still define as the "master" of the house but which the Census Bureau described as "the person, or one of the persons, in whose name the home is owned, being bought, or rented" and who, in the case of married couples, has a "spouse." When asked to list the number of bedrooms, Person One was invited to exaggerate the size of the family homestead when the insistent census form phrased the question another way: "How many bedrooms would you list if this house were on the market?"

For Americans who defy traditional compartmentalization, some questions were completely mystifying. How, performers with Ringling Brothers and Barnum & Bailey Circus wondered, should they explain that they usually live on a train? To describe themselves as people "with no usual place of residence" would be misleading since their residence goes wherever they do. Probably the most accurate, if ambiguous, response was "other." The circus, which bills itself as "The Greatest Show on Earth," was performing at Madison Square Garden on April 1, 1990. That still doesn't explain why the number of people in New York City who listed their residence as "other" in 1990 surpassed a mind-boggling 50,000.

Suffering from a surfeit of surveys, more than twice as many Americans as ever before (by one count) failed to return their census forms. None incurred the criminal penalty, census officials said—a $100 fine for failing to participate and a $500 fine for falsifying answers. A seventy-one-year-old man in Monticello, Mississippi, generally fed up with being pestered, was charged with shooting a census taker, though not fatally—thereby slowing but not skewing the count. The Census Bureau figured it had missed 5.6 percent of the population (or about 8 million Americans) in its 1940 survey and had overlooked a smaller and smaller proportion of people in every count since. But the stakes were too high for the losers to agree that good or getting better was good enough. They were less concerned with the total count than with who had been missed — mainly, their own constituents.

In 1990, the bureau commissioned a post-census survey to help locate the 5 million people, or roughly 2 percent of the total, who some demographers and a conglomeration of special interest groups insisted had gone unrecorded in ghetto tenements, in apartment buildings guarded by unobliging doormen, and in bountiful fields where migrant harvesters assiduously avoided anybody from the government. "It's auditable," was how Michael R. Darby, the undersecretary of commerce, described the tally when asked whether it represented reality. There was no shortage of challengers. More than 6,000 of the nation's 40,000 localities, including all 51 of the largest cities, contested the results as shortchanging population or civic pride. Only one jurisdiction in the country formally complained that it had been overcounted, though. Tavistock, New Jersey, encompasses 180 acres in Camden County — all but 2 of which are occupied by a country club. According to preliminary figures, the borough had grown by 288 percent, or more than any other town in New Jersey. Tavistock preferred to retain bragging rights to another title: the state's smallest town. Its population had, in fact, skyrocketed, Mayor George J. Buff III, who is related to fully one fourth of the residents, conceded, but from nine to thirteen — not to thirty-five, as the Census Bureau maintained. After invoking the "count question resolution process," the bureau acknowledged that, indeed, it had overcounted. Tavistock's title was restored. On July 29, 1992, Tavistock's population was officially recorded as twelve.

That modest overstatement was more in keeping with the

national count in 1980, when the census found 5.1 million more people than it had expected. In 1990, though, about that same number seemed to be missing from the original calculations. But by the time it forwarded the final tally to the president, the Census Bureau claimed to have located 3.8 million of them. Fifteen months after the official count, Commerce Secretary Robert A. Mosbacher overruled the bureau's director and top staff and decided not to adjust the total — and to "impute" them proportionately to tracts across the country — to reflect the number of Americans that census takers conceded they had probably missed. (The Census Bureau later cut its estimate of the undercount from 2.1 percent to 1.6 percent; Congress's General Accounting Office estimated that the bureau had misstated not only the total number of Americans but also the undercount, by about half.) The sloppiest counting jobs appeared to have been done in California, Florida, Georgia, New Mexico, North Carolina, South Carolina, Virginia and West Virginia. Because formulas for reconciliation were less reliable for smaller localities, Mosbacher said, "The paradox is that in attempting to make the actual count more accurate by an adjustment, we might be making the shares less accurate." No one was satisfied. "At this point," said Representative Thomas C. Sawyer, the Ohio Democrat who headed a House census subcommittee, "it's fair to say that the real question is not whether we've counted everyone. We know that the nation has never counted everybody. The real question is, how close has the Census Bureau come to the truth and can they come closer?"

In New York City, which, the census revealed, had lost 38,000 people since 1980, local officials insisted that another 500,000 people had gone uncounted. City officials justified their claim with evidence ranging from testimony by the managers of Starrett City, a mammoth housing development in Brooklyn, that they had 20,000 tenants, not 16,000 as the census had said. Ingenious population estimates, which at various stages incorporated everything from how many times a day all of the city's toilets were flushed to aerial reconnaissance photographs, suggested that there were 254,534 houses or apartments that the census had overlooked. In the South Bronx, census taker Ada Gonzalez said that as she was introducing herself to one of two families with children that appeared to be tenants in a single-family house, the owner emerged from a separate door to announce that only one family, his, lived there. The Census Bureau finally revised the New York City count upward by 289,385 people, not units — an adjustment that also reversed what would have been a statistical net population loss over the decade. In Detroit, desperate officials scoured the city for lost souls after the census decided that the population had fallen below the 1 million mark. Prestige was the least concern. Federal funds and state laws that empowered Detroit to levy special taxes because of its size were also jeopardized. The recount turned up just enough people to nudge the population to 1,028,000.

Census officials themselves were not sanguine. Even they acknowledged that millions of Americans had been missed. And what skewed the results disproportionately was that the 1,392 categories into which the census placed the American people had surely not been miscounted uniformly (5.4 percent of black men and 5.8 percent of Hispanic men may have been missed, compared to .6 percent of non-black women and 2.1 percent of the total population). But the Census Bureau and other relevant federal agencies were in a quandary. "We have all the symptoms of an undercount," said Peter Bounpane, an assistant census director, "but we have to make sure that the cure is not worse than the ailment." While many cities would have won more representation in Congress and in their state legislatures, the big winners in an adjusted count probably would have been the same bruisers that had registered such stunning gains in the first place. California would have been awarded yet another congressional seat; so would Arizona. Wisconsin and Pennsylvania each would have lost another. Cities generally would have benefited at the expense of rural areas. "There is no perfect truth in a census or in an adjusted census," said Barbara Everitt Bryant, the former director of the census.

The proposed technical adjustment had been calculated mainly in response to an ongoing suit contesting the 1980 census — a suit that was tentatively settled only the year before the 1990 count was to start. "The message to the American people is the poor don't count," said Raymond Flynn, who was the Mayor of Boston and president of the United States Conference of Mayors. David N. Dinkins, New York City's first black mayor, recalled: "There was a time when folks who looked like me were counted as three fifths of a person. This is not far removed from that." (Actually, in one historical respect this represented an improvement: the southern states wanted Dinkins's forebears counted as three-fifths of a person; the North didn't want them counted at all.) New York, joined by an array of jurisdictions that included Inglewood, California — by census estimates, the most undercounted city in the country — promptly moved in federal court to reopen a suit against the 1990 census that was originally filed a full three years before the count was even begun. The legal challenge was not dealt a final rebuff until 1993 when officials were well on their way to conducting the twenty-second census — a count that may be conducted largely by mail, telephone and home computer, and after which, a federal judge suggested, a postcensus adjustment "is probably inevitable." Meanwhile, there were either 248.7 million people living in the United States on April 1, 1990, or 253.9 million — or, more likely, some elusive number in between. Whatever the exact figure, everyone agrees that there are still more Americans today and they neither look nor live the way the nation did two hundred, one hundred, fifty, or even ten years ago.

CHAPTER III

HOW
WE LIVE

M urphy Brown was no trendsetter. Candice Bergen's unconventional television character, whose out-of-wedlock birth provoked a public rebuke from Vice President Dan Quayle in 1992, was the quintessence of art imitating life. Or caricaturing it — just as *Ozzie and Harriet* had done for the typical white middle-class family nearly two generations before. If Murphy Brown's prime-time pregnancy defied traditional family values, her unwed motherhood nonetheless reflected a new reality that is redefining the American family — just as Rick Nelson's less celebrated but real-life experiences with teenage sex, drugs and divorce heralded the post–*Ozzie and Harriet* era.

What today is regarded longingly as traditional was always more idealized than real. Nor is it any longer even universally considered ideal. As the 1990s began, the nuclear family was reeling from several decades in an economic and social atom smasher. Spouses, siblings and generations were separated at dizzying speeds. Only one in four families is made up of a married couple with children — a category that has fallen to third most common among the nation's households, behind people living alone and also trailing married childless couples. In the new American family, working couples share the pants. For the first time, a majority of mothers with preschool children are in the labor force. Just one in four children lives in the prototypical two-parent family with one parent working. In Washington, D.C., only one in ten children do. Only three in one hundred households now conform to the classic family headed by a working husband with a dutiful wife and two children at home (the census does not enumerate dogs and station wagons). Just one in seven families in the United States in composed of a married couple with two children under age 18 living at home.

The second half of the twentieth century has witnessed epochal changes in the American family. Some are not uniquely American, but mirror evolving patterns in other developed nations. More women are unmarried. More children are living with one parent. Fewer young adults are forming their own families. Woody Allen notwithstanding, a man who leaves his crosstown lover to woo her twenty-one-year-old adopted daughter is not yet the norm. Murphy Brown, the white, well-paid, sitcom character, isn't either. But if her single-motherhood is still unconventional it shouldn't have been shocking. A fourth of the children born in the 1980s and 1990s are being reared by a single parent. The Atari and Nintendo generation born in the 1960s and 1970s has hung around its parents' house in a prolonged adolescence. And, in a potential bonanza for singles bars, manufacturers of single-portion prepared dinners, and makers of the appliances that every household has to have, many children of the 1950s are living alone.

The 1980s marked the rise and fall of yuppies and the ascendancy of Dinks — double income, no kids. Sociologists discovered clusters of the elderly in NORCs — an unfortunate acronym that evokes the military junta in Myanmar but which stands for naturally occurring retirement community. Later marriage and parenthood may add years to the definition of "generation." What James W. Hughes, a New Jersey demographer, has dubbed the "3 D's" — delayed marriage, deferred childbirth, and divorced couples — has given typical American togetherness a whole new dimension. The Census Bureau can barely keep pace with the terminology, much less the psychology, of changes wrought by liberalized no-fault divorce laws, feminism, the sexual revolution, the influx of women into the work force, the legalization of abortion, the availability of contraceptives, artificial insemination and the gay and lesbian rights movement. Those changes are transforming already complex debates over a partner's rights to medical coverage, child custody and inheritance of everything from death benefits to shared rent-controlled apartments. The AIDS epidemic demanded a new nomenclature for survivors listed at the end of news obituaries: "longtime companion." But the 1990 census prudishly recorded only those cohabiting couples constituted by two unrelated adults of the opposite sex — a category that was further skewed because it could miss couples in households with more than two adults and also might inadvertently create a couple by pairing a householder with a live-in boarder or employee (or, in the case of Seward Johnson, the pharmaceutical heir, not inadvertently).

The derivation of the word *family* is hardly familiar or traditional in the modern sense. It comes from the Latin *famulus*, or "servant," among whom were a man's wife, children and other household helpers. A century ago, the government's official questionnaire specified: "The word family, for the purposes of the census, includes persons living alone, as previously described, equally with families in the ordinary sense of that term, and also all larger aggregations of people having only the tie of a common roof and table." Not until 1950 did the census distinguish between a household and a family, described as two or more people related by blood, marriage or adoption. When the Massachusetts Mutual Life Insurance Company challenged Americans to define *family* in a 1990 survey, three fourths of the respondents rejected a narrow legal interpretation. Instead, they chose this expansive alternative: "A group of people who love and care for each other." That definition might exclude some traditional families, but allows for a lot of other lifestyles."A family is not an association of independent people; it is a human commitment designed to make possible the rearing of moral and healthy children," Professor James Q. Wilson argues. "Governments care — or ought to care — about families for this reason, and scarcely for any other."

Blaming the 1992 Los Angeles riots on family disintegration, Vice President Quayle distinguished between poor, unwed black mothers and Murphy Brown, who, he said, belittled "the importance of fathers by bearing a child alone and calling it just another 'lifestyle choice.' " (Interestingly, Donald Trump's second fatherhood, with Marla Maples, his girlfriend, did not provoke the same public rebuke.) Republicans tried to appropriate family values exclusively as their campaign theme, but the message sometimes sounded exclusionary, hollow and even hypocritical: no more legal abortion for black teens *or* births to black single mothers. "When Mario Cuomo stressed the words *family* and *values* in his speech to the 1984 Democratic convention, he used them in a warmly positive sense," the columnist William Safire wrote in 1992. "But this year, packaged in a single phrase, the terms are an assertion of moral traditionalism that carries an implicit charge: the other side seeks to undermine the institution of the family by taking a permissive line on (*a*) abortion rights, (*b*) homosexual rights and (*c*) the 'character issue,' code words for marital infidelity. Sometimes pot smoking is included, but sex is most often the common denominator."

But the traditionalism on which that assertion of morality is based is suspect. Premarital sex may have been less frequent, but abstinence and chastity were rarely the norm. Sex was simply swept under the bed. And pregnancies were "righted" by marriage. The stereotypical nuclear family — the breadwinner-homemaker couple — was often a model to be emulated, but it hardly has been the historic or universal norm. Early in the nineteenth century, public schools were promoted for the urban poor to instill moral values that, reformers feared, would never be taught by dysfunctional families. Before the Industrial Revolution, most couples worked together at or near home. By 1890, 18.9 percent of American women were in the work force (though the vast majority then were single, often working six or seven years before marrying; today, a slim majority of working women are married). "*Leave It to Beaver* was not a documentary," Stephanie Coontz reminds us in *The Way We Never Were: American Families and the Nostalgia Trap*. Less than a half century ago, wife battering wasn't even considered a crime and incest was described as a "one-in-a-million occurrence." In the glorified 1950s, one in four Americans was poor. Meanwhile, GI benefits, housing loans, highway construction and other federal programs, Coontz writes, left the typical suburban family "far more dependent on government handouts than any so-called 'underclass' in recent U.S. history." But the stick figures who populated Beaver's middle-class utopia were the paradigm of the happy (or repressed) family. Everyone knew his or her place. His mom was not a single mother, a working spouse or even a homemaker. She was, unapologetically, a housewife, and Betty Friedan notwithstanding, she rarely chafed at a role that helped perpetuate a stereotype that was already becoming less compatible with social and economic imperatives and with demands for sexual equality.

"Happy families are all alike," Tolstoy wrote. "Every unhappy family is unhappy in its own way." Increasingly, though, the way to unhappiness has become familiar: More and more

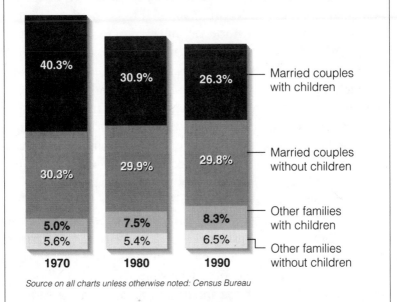

"TRADITIONAL" FAMILIES ARE FADING

Percentage of households in each category. Not shown are single people living alone and nonrelated people living together. "Children" are a family's own children under age 18 living at home.

1970	1980	1990	
40.3%	30.9%	26.3%	Married couples with children
30.3%	29.9%	29.8%	Married couples without children
5.0%	7.5%	8.3%	Other families with children
5.6%	5.4%	6.5%	Other families without children

Source on all charts unless otherwise noted: Census Bureau

Americans are growing up in a society reshaped by the geometric rise in mothers who are working, raising children without the financial or moral support of a spouse, or both. In 1960, two in ten mothers with children under the age of 6 were in the labor force, though not necessarily working. Three decades later (after a particularly sharp rise in the 1970s), the proportion had tripled to nearly six in ten. A single parent presides over three in ten American families. Nearly two thirds of black households are headed by a single parent. Between 1970 and 1990, the proportion of children growing up in single-parent families more than doubled, to over one in four — driven by the greater numbers

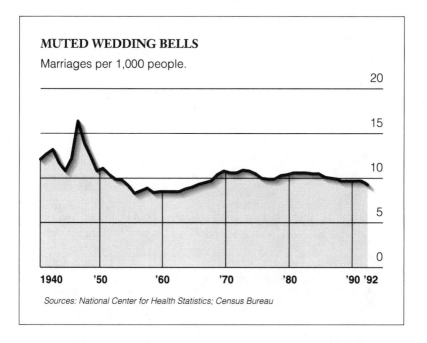

MUTED WEDDING BELLS

Marriages per 1,000 people.

Sources: National Center for Health Statistics; Census Bureau

among blacks but the steeper increase among white women (the black-white statistical ratio has remained constant since 1950). Fully fifty-five of every hundred black children live with one parent, compared to about thirty of every hundred Hispanic children and nineteen of every hundred whites.

But some measures of white family structure today are alarmingly similar to the structural flaws in black families that Daniel P. Moynihan detected a quarter of a century earlier when he was assailed as racist for even broaching the subject. Today, the percentage of never-married whites is the same — one in five — as it was among blacks in 1970. In 1965, David Popenoe, cochairman of the Council on Families in America, recalls, 51 percent of black teenage mothers were single and 26 percent of black babies were born to single mothers. In 1990, 55 percent of white teenage mothers were single and 19 percent of white babies were

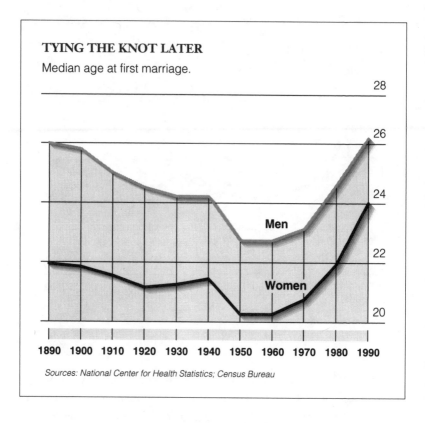

TYING THE KNOT LATER

Median age at first marriage.

Men

Women

1890 1900 1910 1920 1930 1940 1950 1960 1970 1980 1990

Sources: National Center for Health Statistics; Census Bureau

born to single mothers. Behind those figures lies another troubling development: why the women were single. The trend lines of single mothers who are separated, divorced or widowed and of those who never married have been veering toward each other since the late 1960s. Among blacks, the lines actually intersected in the 1980s. For the first time, the number of black single mothers whose marriages ended in separation, divorce or death now is smaller than the number who had never married at all.

"The ones who were married, as a group, have higher family incomes, are older, better educated, more likely to hold full-time jobs, less likely to go on welfare," said Douglas J. Besharov, who

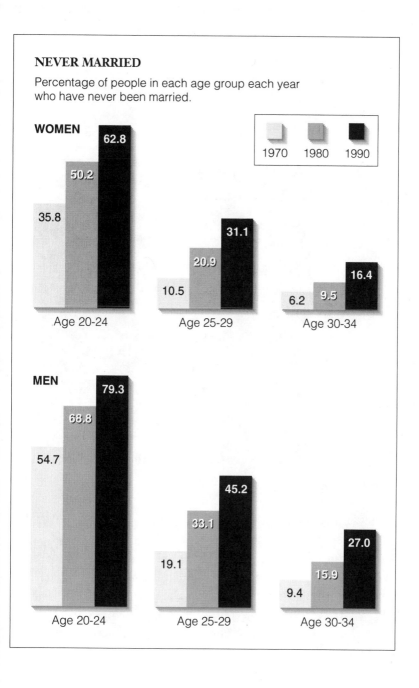

NEVER MARRIED

Percentage of people in each age group each year
who have never been married.

1970 1980 1990

WOMEN

Age 20-24: 35.8 / 50.2 / 62.8
Age 25-29: 10.5 / 20.9 / 31.1
Age 30-34: 6.2 / 9.5 / 16.4

MEN

Age 20-24: 54.7 / 68.8 / 79.3
Age 25-29: 19.1 / 33.1 / 45.2
Age 30-34: 9.4 / 15.9 / 27.0

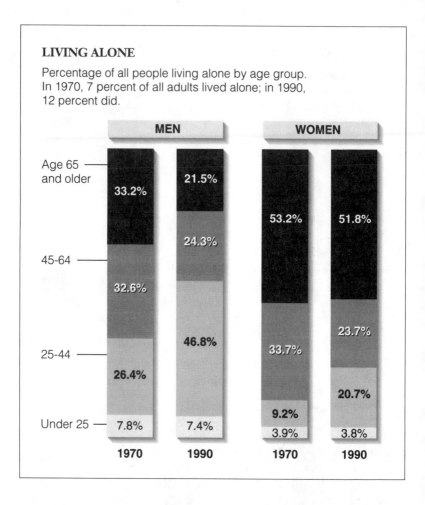

LIVING ALONE

Percentage of all people living alone by age group.
In 1970, 7 percent of all adults lived alone; in 1990,
12 percent did.

	MEN		WOMEN	

Age 65 and older — 33.2% (1970 Men), 21.5% (1990 Men), 53.2% (1970 Women), 51.8% (1990 Women)

45-64 — 32.6% (1970 Men), 24.3% (1990 Men)

25-44 — 26.4% (1970 Men), 46.8% (1990 Men), 33.7% (1970 Women), 23.7% (1990 Women)

Under 25 — 7.8% (1970 Men), 7.4% (1990 Men), 9.2% / 3.9% (1970 Women), 20.7% / 3.8% (1990 Women)

| 1970 | 1990 | 1970 | 1990 |

studies family policy at the American Enterprise Institute. "When we talk about single parents as a social problem, we're really talking about the young unmarried mothers, 40 percent of whom end up as long-term welfare recipients, compared to only 14 percent of the divorced mothers. The worrying thing is that never-married mothers account for most of the children now entering single-parent households." And teen fathers *want* to make babies, too.

MOTHERS AND JOBS

Percentage of women with children under 6 years old
in March 1991. "Unemployed" women were those seeking jobs.

ALL MOTHERS

Working part-time 16.2% — Unemployed 5.3%

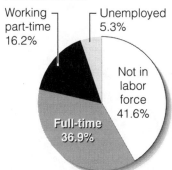

Not in labor force 41.6%

Full-time 36.9%

MOTHERS WITH HUSBANDS

Working part-time 18.1% — Unemployed 4.0%

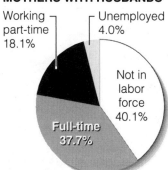

Not in labor force 40.1%

Full-time 37.7%

DIVORCED, SEPARATED AND WIDOWED

Working part-time 10.2% — Unemployed 7.6%

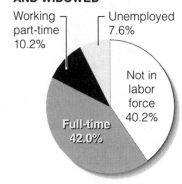

Not in labor force 40.2%

Full-time 42.0%

NEVER-MARRIED MOTHERS

Working part-time 10.6% — Unemployed 10.7%

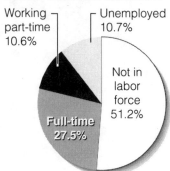

Not in labor force 51.2%

Full-time 27.5%

Sources: Bureau of Labor Statistics; Census Bureau

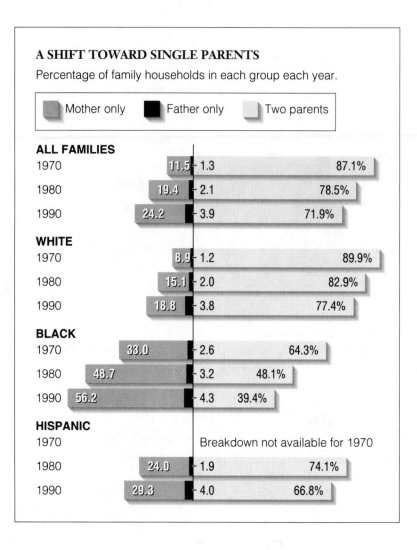

A SHIFT TOWARD SINGLE PARENTS

Percentage of family households in each group each year.

Mother only   Father only   Two parents

ALL FAMILIES

	Mother only	Father only	Two parents
1970	11.5	1.3	87.1%
1980	19.4	2.1	78.5%
1990	24.2	3.9	71.9%

WHITE

	Mother only	Father only	Two parents
1970	8.9	1.2	89.9%
1980	15.1	2.0	82.9%
1990	18.8	3.8	77.4%

BLACK

	Mother only	Father only	Two parents
1970	33.0	2.6	64.3%
1980	48.7	3.2	48.1%
1990	56.2	4.3	39.4%

HISPANIC

	Mother only	Father only	Two parents
1970	Breakdown not available for 1970		
1980	24.0	1.9	74.1%
1990	29.3	4.0	66.8%

If a father's inability to provide for his family has taken a psychological toll on men, the brunt of changing roles is being borne by conflicted women like Toni Rumsey, a thirty-four-year-old mother of two who inspects Gerber's baby food at a factory in Michigan from seven A.M. to three P.M., or Jan Flint, who works nights and whose husband works days in a Welch's juice and jam plant so one parent can always be home. "I never feel like I'm a full mom," Toni Rumsey said. "I make the cookies, the homemade costumes for Halloween. I volunteer for everything to make up to them for not being here. When I do all that, I make myself so tired that they lose a happy cheerful mom, and then I'm cheating them again. It's hard when you were raised with Donna Reed and the Beav's mom." But it would have been even harder, she figured, if her family were forced to give up its home and move into a trailer. Jan Flint returned to work in the mid-1980s when family expenses exceeded her husband's salary. "That's what God meant for me — to stay home, cook and sew, and I can't do that," she said. "I used to have a clean house all the time. I always enjoyed being involved in my older two's education. Last night was open house and my children wanted me to go. I bribed them — 'I'll let you bring friends over if I don't go.' That's what's happening to the American family. Nobody's there, and the children don't have full-time guidance."

Government cannot be a surrogate parent. Nor can caring teachers, settlement house social workers or baby-sitters systematically suffice as substitutes. "I remember once attending a lecture by an eminent child psychologist, who said, 'Every child needs some person who's crazy about that kid,' " Diane Ravitch, a historian and former assistant secretary of education, recalled. "I don't know of any institution or governmental program that can take the place of that caring human being." Full-time guidance from one parent or even part-time parenting by two parents is neither always possible nor, necessarily, always desirable. Plenty of well-adjusted children have been raised by one parent.

Examples abound of dysfunctional children reared by two parents who were ill-equipped, poor role models, or who chose self-gratification over self-sacrifice. A Rand Corporation study, citing a correlation but not necessarily a causality between female-headed households and poverty, cautions that "marital discord has a stronger relationship with delinquency and aggression than parental absence." Traditionalism, necessity and morality aside, though, is one form of family preferable to the other? "Sure, nontraditional families can be successful, and they deserve our sympathy and support," says David Popenoe, who is also associate dean for social and behavioral science at Rutgers University. "But here is what social scientists call a confirmed empirical generalization: these families are not as successful as conventional two-parent families. Want further confirmation? Ask any child which kind of family he or she prefers."

A century ago, the median age at which men got married was 26.1. For women, it was 22. Over the next six decades, the median marrying age declined. By 1956, it had dropped to 22.5 years for men and 20.1 for women. But then a reversal began. During the 1980s, the median actually returned to the 1890 level for men — 26.1 by 1990. For women, the median marrying age rose to 23.9 — breaking a century-old barrier. As recently as 1975, 63 percent of women 20 to 24 years old had married. By 1990, the percentage had plunged to about 38 percent.

Why is marriage being delayed or denied? The women's liberation movement and the social acceptance of cohabitation have all but erased the pejorative *spinster* from politically correct dictionaries and relegated *old maid* to the name of a card game. For women, in particular, other options became available — among them, educational and professional opportunities in fields that were solely the province of men not so long ago and salaries that are trailing men's but growing faster. Marriage may still be an institution, but, as the joke goes, who wants to live in an institution? More and more Americans are making other choices or having alternatives forced on them.

In 1990, of all Americans 18 and over, 22 percent, or more than 40 million, had never married. Between 1970 and 1990, the proportion of 20- to 24-year-olds who had never married soared from 55 percent to 79 percent for men and even more dramatically, from 36 percent to a startling 63 percent for women. Among 25- to 29-year-olds, the proportion more than doubled for men, from 19 percent to more than 45 percent, and nearly tripled for women, from 11 percent to 31 percent. Life in the thirties was nearly as noncommittal. Among 30- to 34-year-olds, the proportion who had never married leaped from 9 percent in 1970 to 27 percent for men and from 6 percent to 16 percent for women. For people 35 to 39 years old, the still-single share doubled, from 7 percent to 15 percent for men and from 5 percent to 10 percent for women.

Young adults are doing other things. More are remaining in or returning to their parents' nest, tethered by an elongated umbilical cord that promises financial and emotional nourishment. Housing and higher education costs, combined with declining wages, have feathered the empty nest. Between 1960 and 1990, the proportion of unmarried 18- to 24-year-olds living in their parents' home increased from 43 percent to 53 percent. Meanwhile, the proportion forming their own families was pared by half, from 42 percent to 22 percent. The share of those living alone or with a roommate rose from a mere 2 percent to 9 percent. The nation's 25- to 34-year-olds followed suit, although the changes over three decades were less severe and, after age 30, most unmarried adults have their own homes. The proportion forming their own families fell from 83 percent to 65 percent—

or, collectively, fewer than half the nation's adults younger than 35. And the proportion living alone or sharing a house or apartment quadrupled, from 3 percent to 13 percent.

Census Bureau demographers suggest that the number of single people still living at home is the highest ever. Among those 18 to 24, 77 percent had not married and two thirds of those were still living with their parents. Among the 38 percent of 25- to 29-year-olds who had never married, a third were living with their parents. More are Peter Pans than Wendys. Among 25- to 34-year-olds, 32 percent of single men and 20 percent of single women were living with their parents, suggesting, perhaps, that the men may need more pampering but that their parents intrude less than they would in their daughters' affairs. That means one third of those single men return to their parents' home after a date. That more mothers are divorced and not remarried and might welcome a man at home may be another incentive. Most young adults living with their parents had never been married, although 3 percent of the youngest young adults and 20 percent of the 25- to 34-year-olds had been. The proportion who moved into their parents' house with children of their own varied inversely with age: Four percent of the 18- to 24-year-olds (or 1 percent more than the proportion who were married) and 13 percent of the 25- to 34-year-olds transformed their parents' household into a three-generation family.

Compared to 1890, though, more Americans are willing to give marriage a try. The sheer number of marriages recorded during the last decade — more than 2 million a year — constituted a record. In 1890, 44 percent of all the men 14 and older and 34 percent of the women were still single; 55 percent of Americans 14 and older were married (so, according to another fading tradition, were .2 percent of the 14-year-old girls). By 1940, the overall proportion of married Americans had increased to 60 percent. From 72 percent in 1970, it began to decline again, to 61 percent by 1991. In 1990, 26 percent of all men 18 and older and 19 percent of the women had never married, but only 6 percent of men and 5 percent of women 40 and older had never married. The marriage ratio that peaked at 16.4 per thousand in the 1946 post–Second World War frenzy and sank to 8.4 in 1958 has never even approached the high again. The ratio has hovered instead between 9 and 11 per thousand for the last two decades.

Married couples accounted for 83 percent of white family households in 1990, but only 48 percent among blacks. And during the last half century, the proportion of blacks who marry declined faster. Less than half of black adults were married in 1990 – only 44 percent, compared to 64 percent only two decades before (and compared to 64 percent of white and 60 percent of Hispanic adults). Fewer than 75 percent of black women expect to ever marry, compared to about 90 percent of white women. Both sets of expectations are below the historical 95 percent marriage rate. (The number of interracial marriages doubled, from under 1 percent of all married couples in 1970 to a still minuscule nearly 2 percent in 1990.) Among Hispanic people, the proportion currently married also declined, but to 61 percent from 72 percent, about the same decrease as for all whites. But to say that so many people never married no longer implies that they are living alone. During the 1980s, the number of unmarried couples living together – of the opposite sex and unrelated – soared by 80 percent, to 2.9 million. Most were under age 35 and had never been married, although people who had been married and divorced, many with children, comprised a third of the more than 5.7 million unmarried partners. The good news, for traditionalists and for bridal gown manufacturers, is that almost everybody gets married eventually, even if they don't stay married. By the time they turned 44, only 9 percent of Americans had still never married. For those 45 and older, the proportion dipped to 5 percent. Marriage rates in the United States actually are among the world's highest. But so are divorce and remarriage rates.

Only 8 percent of the adult population tried marriage once and failed — about the same proportion who were widowed. But by the mid-1980s, almost one in four people who had ever been married had also been divorced. Among Americans who were divorced and had not remarried, men outnumbered women, as they consistently do at the age when most people wed. The annual divorce rate per thousand people has seesawed in a half century. It was 2 in 1940 and 5.2 in 1980. The rate seemed to decline slightly during the 1980s when anxiety over AIDS and the costs of setting up another household made breaking up harder to do. (In fact, fewer divorces may have been recorded because people marry later; and break-ups among cohabiting couples are not recorded in divorce rates.) But the ratio of divorced Americans to those still married and living with their spouses soared to a record high. That ratio doubled between 1970 and 1980, from 47 per thousand to 100. It then rose by another 50 percent in the 1980s. By 1990, there were 142 divorced persons for every thousand married ones. Black and Hispanic couples fared even worse. The ratio of divorced to married people mushroomed between 1970 and 1990, from 83 to 282 per thousand among blacks and from 61 to 129 among Hispanic people. So much for "till death do us part." A Census Bureau survey covering two-year periods in the 1980s found a startling symmetry in what demographers ambiguously call "household discontinuation rates" between elderly couples — whose households are more often than not discontinued when one partner dies — and younger couples — which are more likely to be dissolved by divorce. For married-couple households in which the husband was 65 and older and for those with husbands under the age of 30, the rate was the same — 14 percent. Whether children are the glue in a marriage or a solvent is arguable. When the father was younger than 65, the discontinuation rate was virtually the same whether or not the couple had children. Census demographers found that women who married younger and had conceived or given birth to a child before marriage are more likely to divorce. So are women between the ages of 30 and 44 — fully four in ten. And scratch the seven-year itch from the lexicon of marriage counselors: The median duration of first marriages that end in divorce is only about 6.3 years (although that may follow several years of living together).

In 1990, 2.4 million marriages were performed — typically, between a woman and a man who was slightly older than she was; 1.2 million divorces were filed. While the divorce rate appears to have plateaued during the 1980s, the number of divorces and the rate itself doubled since the 1960s — higher than in most other developed countries but rising at comparable rates. Only the elderly, out of habit, resignation, or having placed a higher premium on marriage, were defying the trend. The Population Reference Bureau calculated that nearly 30 percent of couples married in 1952 were divorced before their twenty-fifth wedding anniversary. Silver anniversaries were even more elusive in subsequent generations. It took only twenty years for 30 percent of the couples married in 1957 to get divorced, fifteen years for those married in 1962, and ten years for couples married in 1967.

A century ago, only .4 percent of people 14 and older were divorced; a half century ago, the proportion had tripled, but only to 1.2 percent. Since then, the bonds have been loosened by no-fault divorce laws. The proliferation of women in the work force modestly reduced some of their risks of financial independence. Surging divorce rates in recent decades suggest a casual lack of commitment. Also, perhaps, a less threatening phenomenon that earlier generations contemplated wistfully but eschewed because of social and economic taboos: Fewer couples are willing to remain locked in unsuccessful marriages.

Had there been any doubt, the Census Bureau's Donald J. Hernandez irrefutably linked the separation rate to the dynamics of a family's financial condition. Among whites, the rate was lowest when the father worked, regardless of whether his wife did — suggesting, Hernandez said, "that the stresses associated with economic insecurity or need when the father did not work may have contributed to marital separation." Among black couples, the rate was lowest only when both parents worked — in part, because the median income of married black men who worked full-time in 1990 lagged 23 percent behind the income of married white men (a smaller gap than for single men, though). Overall, though, the discontinuation rate was consistently higher when both the husband and wife worked full-time than when the husband worked full-time and the wife worked only part-time — a reflection of economic stress, of the pressures on both partners of raising children, and of the fact that having a higher income may have made separating easier. Black two-parent families were half again more likely than white ones to break up because of separation or death within two years. Half the black single mothers and one third of the white single mothers who were not poor while they were married were likely to be living in poverty within a year (though white single mothers were much more likely to get married). Fully one fourth of all divorced women entitled to child support received no payments whatsoever; only half received the amount they were due.

Most divorced people don't remain single, although women are less likely to remarry than men. Half the people who do remarry do so within 2.5 years. Overall, there are 95 men for every 100 women in the United States. The ratio of single men to women is higher, though, among young people. The census doesn't say how many of those men are eligible — the number who haven't soured on marriage, are gay, or are engaged or otherwise committed. Among the 36 million men and 43 million women who never married or were widowed or divorced, there were 111 men for every 100 women under the age of 25, 127 for every 100 women ages 25 to 29, and 125 men for every 100 women ages 30 to 34. Then the tables turn. Fewer men are available because they have either remarried or died. There are only 60 men for every 100 women between the ages of 45 and 64, and just 29 for every 100 women 65 and over.

In 1890, 11 percent of the population 14 and over was widowed. But a half century later, the decline in death rates became more pronounced for men than for women. As a result, the number of men began to grow faster than the number of women for the first time since the twentieth century began. Still, for fifty years, since 1940, women have outnumbered men in the United States. That's because while more boys are born than girls, women live longer. The numerical edge is not universal. A half century ago, women predominated in the suburbs, their numbers boosted by maids and other domestic servants. Today, women outnumber men in the central cities, although they don't necessarily enjoy their edge. In California, higher birth rates, immigration from abroad (though, except for Koreans, men usually outnumber women among adult immigrants), and the influx from other states gave men a majority for the first time since 1950 — a boon for Valley Girls in the southern Van Nuys–northern Sherman Oaks area, where, remarkably, never-married men outnumber never-married women by almost 50 percent. For every 100 women in the United States, the ratio ranges from 78 men in South Boston City, Virginia, to 212 men in West Feliciana Parish, Louisiana — site of an all-male state penitentiary.

In fifty years, family lifestyles have changed radically. In 1940, less than 10 percent of all households were headed by a single mother. Under 8 percent were people living alone. Only a quarter century ago, 74 percent of white households and what the Census Bureau described as "only" 57 percent of black households were maintained by a married man whose wife was living with him — a proportion that social workers would crave to replicate today. As recently as 1970, one in ten family groups were headed by one parent. Today, about three in ten are — including

23 percent of all-white, 61 percent of black, and 33 percent of Hispanic family groups.

Children are growing up in another world. In a growing share of families, there aren't any children at all. During the last decade, the total number of children under age 18 declined slightly to 63.6 million. Their proportion of the population dipped to 26 percent. In thirty-three states, the total number of children shrank (while in all of those thirty-three, except in Iowa and West Virginia, the adult population grew). New York State lost 428,300 children, or 9 percent. In West Virginia, the population under 18 plunged by 21 percent. Chicago, alone, had 130,200 fewer children at the end of the decade than when the 1980s began — even with the "explosion" of inner-city out-of-wedlock births. Most of the decline was among teenagers.

Singles, newlyweds and retirees depress the proportion of typical nuclear families. Immigrants raise the ratio. In California, which registered a 21 percent gain in the number of children statewide, the child population of Fresno exploded by 85 percent. Among major cities, El Paso, Texas, had the highest share, with one in three residents under age 18. Ranked last was San Francisco, where only one in six residents was a child. Of the five counties with the highest proportion of childless couples, four are in Florida — topped by Charlotte County, with nearly 50 percent.

For the first time, the proportion of married couples without children exceeds the proportion of married couples with children — 42 percent to 37 percent. Married couples with children accounted for nearly half the families in 1970 but barely more than one third by 1990, and only about one fourth of all households. That ratio may move more into equilibrium as younger Baby Boomers check their biological alarm clocks and discover time is running out. Potentially, more may be prekid parents than postkid. In the Baby Boom generation, only a majority of 25- to 29-year-olds, the youngest group, are childless, which may explain why BMW began promoting itself as the car for "quality carpooling." Counties with the highest percentage of married couples with children include those with suburbs, military bases, large Hispanic families, small towns that are synonymous with family values, and Utah, with its majority of Mormons. The median age of the householder in all married-couple families ranged from 31.2 for families with children less than 1 year old to 37.9 for those with children up to age 18.

Many children are being raised by younger parents and by older ones than prevailing social custom and medical convention have dictated. About one in three infants is being born to women 30 and older. More young teenagers are also giving birth — below the 1970 rate, but reversing a decline. While the rate for black teenagers remains higher than for whites, white teenagers are having two thirds of the babies. Among developed nations, the United States has nearly double the teenage birth rate of second-ranked Great Britain. It's higher even among white Americans than among all British women.

Psychologists may not have detected any cumulative decrease in sibling rivalry, but there are fewer siblings nowadays with whom to fight. Only one in five families with children now has three or more — about 7.2 percent of all households — compared to two in five as recently as 1970. The average number of children per family is a figure only a demographer could love: 1.83, or 183 per 100 families. And, for the first time, the average number of children under the age of 18 slipped below 1 during the 1980s — falling to .96 percent from a high of 1.44 in 1965.

When the first census was taken, American women typically bore half a dozen or more children with the expectation that high rates of infant mortality and childhood diseases would claim many of them. By the centennial census in 1890, a typical American mother would bear half that many. The fertility rate continued to decline until the Baby Boom. It rose to 3.7 in the 1950s, only to fall two decades later to match the Depression low of 2.1 —

raising a jingoistic alarm that there were too few births to replace the current population and that the nation would be mongrelized by immigrants and increasingly outnumbered in the global village. By 1990, boosted by the surge in out-of-wedlock births, the level returned to what demographers consider a replacement rate of about 2.2. More babies were born then — 4,179,000, or 71 for every 1,000 women 15–44 years old — than in any year since 1961 (more on Tuesdays and in August than any other day or month). The boomlet nearly broke the nation's record high of 4.3 million in 1957. The baby bubble astounded demographers, but they quickly recovered. With benefit of hindsight, they attributed it to the surge in immigration during the 1980s and to the delayed parenthood of graying Baby Boomers, many of whom were past the peak childbearing age. The experts also figured the bubble would deflate again in the 1990s.

No single family group grew faster than single parents. They account for 9 percent of all American households and 26 percent of households that contain children — down from 31 percent in 1980. The proportion of children under age 18 living with two parents declined from 88 percent in 1960 to 73 percent in 1990, or fewer than three in four. Even those children may not be living with their biological parents. As a result of remarriages and of premarital births, the census estimates that about 15 percent of children living with two parents are stepchildren, which would mean that just over half the children in the United States today are being reared by both their biological parents. Fully one in three black children being raised by two parents is living with the biological mother and a stepfather.

Among the ten counties with the highest proportion of single-mother families, nine were in the South, in rural equivalents of big city ghettoes. The lone exception was the Bronx, which ranked third with 20 percent, behind Holmes and Bolivar counties in Mississippi, with 22 and 21 percent, respectively. (In

Orem, Utah, though, only one in ten families is headed by a single mother.) The proportion of children living with only one parent has nearly tripled since 1960 and doubled since 1970, to 25 percent. In other words, about one family in four has either no father or no mother at home. Whites account for six in ten single-parent families, but the number is increasing faster among blacks, Hispanic people and Asian-Americans.

For the first time, perhaps, since slavery, more than half of the black children living in America today are being raised by one parent. That proportion more than doubled since 1960, from 22 percent to 55 percent. During the same three decades, though, the proportion of white children living with one parent tripled — to 19 percent. And, while blacks constitute a growing share of children being raised by a single parent, the sheer number of white children in that category is substantially higher. Among Hispanic children, 30 percent are living with one parent, an increase of nearly half since 1980 alone.

The vast majority of children growing up with one parent — 87 percent — live with their mother. But an emerging group is being raised by their fathers, a consequence of men's evolving equity partnership in parenting, the blurring roles between breadwinners and homemakers, and the proliferation of joint custody agreements. That proportion rose from 9 percent to 13 percent in the 1980s. Given the number of divorces, remarriages and single mothers, children of some single fathers may see more of their dads than most children do — despite the warm and fuzzy images of what *Population Today* described as "the thirtysomething baby boomer, domesticated but never dull, a conscientious caregiver, pushing a stroller."

Most single parents — 39 percent — are divorced. The proportion of children whose parents divorced has doubled, from one in four earlier in the twentieth century to as many as half as the century closes. But another group is gaining fast. Between 1960 and 1990, the proportion of children living with a parent who had never married ballooned, from 4 percent to 31 percent (a striking increase that the Census Bureau attributes, in part, to improved counting procedures but which may also be a consequence of more honesty by the women. In the past, many unwed mothers would say they were "separated," resulting in the anomaly of many more "separated" women than men). In 1970, about one in ten births was out of wedlock. By 1990, according to the National Center for Health Statistics, nearly one in four women who gave birth wasn't married — 17 percent of the white women, 23 percent of the Hispanic women and 57 percent of the black women. Among teenagers, the proportion soared to two in three. Among black teenagers, nine in ten were unmarried when they had a child. Nearly four in ten first births to women 15 to 34 years old in the late 1980s were to mothers who were not married when the baby was conceived, born, or both (one in five first births for white women, seven in ten for blacks and four in ten for Hispanic women). The rate for whites is accelerating much faster. The growth is staggering, although, particularly among blacks, it may reflect less a sharp increase in teenage pregnancy than a decline in two other categories: the marriage rate among black teenagers and the number of children born to married couples. Only a half century ago, while out-of-wedlock births were also higher among blacks than whites, fully five in six black families were headed by two parents. One figure cries out: Among all black women, in no age group do women living with a spouse constitute a majority.

In the last half of the 1980s, for the first time, more than half of all births to 18- and 19-year-olds were to unmarried mothers. The proportion among that group swelled to 59 percent, from 37 percent in the late 1970s and 20 percent in the late 1960s. Why? The government didn't ask. But demographers offer several explanations: less stigma (those children are no longer "illegitimate" but are simply born out of wedlock); more day care; delayed marriages because of education or career; a growing recognition that marriage, too, comes with no guarantees; but not, most agree, merely to get more from welfare — a theoretical agenda with less appeal to sociologists than to politicians in New Jersey, which denied additional benefits to women on welfare who bore more children. "There is a common belief that unmarried women are choosing to have babies in order to draw welfare, but the evidence just does not support that," said Larry L. Bumpass, a sociology professor at the University of Wisconsin. "The increase in births to unwed women is not a consequence of their deciding to have babies while they are married. Rather, it is a consequence of accidental pregnancy and a decision not to get married. Over two thirds of all unwed births are not planned." Still, availability of welfare encourages some women who are pregnant to bear and rear babies. Many births may not have been planned but are left to choice. And how many unwed pregnant women have a proposing suitor to turn down?

Yet while more and more teenage mothers are single and fewer of them get married before their baby is born (one fourth in the late 1980s among women 15 to 34 who were pregnant with their first child, compared to one half a quarter century earlier), the greatest increase in unwed mothers has been among women 20 and older. Compared to other developed nations, the United States has a disproportionate number of teenage births. But the percentage of births to unmarried women is about the same as in Canada, France and Great Britain. In Sweden, fully half the births are to unmarried women, although the father is usually in residence.

By most statistical measures, children being raised by two parents are better off: Generally, at least one parent is a college graduate (college graduates, though, are the one group the census found in which the percentage of whites who are single parents is greater than the percentage of blacks who are). At least one parent is likely to have a job, own a home, and make more than a single parent. Hence, the Quayle assertion that "marriage is probably the best antipoverty program of all" — an assertion that, if valid, depends largely on whether at least one partner in the couple works. The federal government estimates the average cost of raising a child to age 18 at well over $100,000, so parents' earning power is a vital ingredient in growing up. Among the 15.9 million children living with one parent, just 9 percent had a parent who had attended college for four or more years (compared with 27 percent of the children in two-parent families), 58 percent had a parent who was employed (compared to 87 percent), 11 percent had a family income of $40,000 or more (compared to 49 percent), and 35 percent lived in a home owned by their parent (compared to 73 percent). Less than a third of American households headed by married parents, often including a disabled father, earned what the Census Bureau defines as a low income. Nearly half of single-parent households did. Fully 55 percent of black and Hispanic one-parent households had low income. One in five married-couple households receives public assistance in the form of either welfare or Supplemental Security Income — an astonishingly high proportion in itself, but lower than the more than one in three one-parent households that do.

Between 1970 and 1990, the proportion of married couples with only one wage earner dropped from 21 percent of households to 8 percent. The proportion of married working women with children under 6 nearly doubled to almost 60 percent. Among those with older children, between the ages of 6 and 17, the proportion increased by about half to nearly 75 percent. During the 1980s alone, the proportion of women 18 to 44 working outside the home and with infants under 1 year old increased from 38 percent to 53 percent — the first time they constituted a majority. Among women college graduates, the rate increased strikingly, from 44 percent to 68 percent. Both spouses were employed in seven of ten married couples with children. In just one in five, the husband worked full-time while his wife had no other job. More than six in ten of the children who live with both parents have to share both parents with their jobs. So do seven in ten children who live with one parent.

Feminism helped free women from housework — or home-making, as it is now known — as demanding a job as any outside the home. The perpetuation of traditional family values may have suffered as a result. But the shift was driven by another value: the need for a second wage earner as salaries trail inflation. The phenomenon is more Middle American than cosmopolitan, more Middle West than Manhattan West Side. Iowa, Minnesota, Nebraska, New Hampshire and South Dakota recorded the highest proportion of working mothers. In Colorado, a higher percentage of mothers with children under age 6 leave their homes in the affluent suburbs to work than the proportion who do in Denver. In California's San Diego County, in six of ten families the single parent or both parents are working. In South Florida, the number of working mothers with children under 6 in 1990 nearly equaled the total of all mothers with children under 6 a decade earlier. And in Rock County, Minnesota, 84 percent of the women with children under 6 say they work outside the home.

In 1990, 5 percent of American children lived in "sub-families" in their grandparents' home, but 30 percent of those were still largely two-generation families: Neither of the child's parents were present. If the extended family is making a come-back, it may be more out of necessity than tradition. Just 2 percent of married couples with children live doubled up in another house-hold; 21 percent of single parents do. The Census Bureau found that the number of single parents who do not head the households in which they live about doubled during the 1980s, from 859,000 to 2.1 million. Among black children, 12 percent were living in the home of their grandparents. Fully 38 percent were being raised by their grandparents because neither parent was present.

For some grandparents, that may be preferable to living alone, which is what a growing proportion of Americans are doing. In 1990, more than one in nine people 15 and over lived alone — 12 percent, compared to 7 percent in 1970. The loners accounted for 9 percent of all people living in households but fully one fourth of all households. Most were women. In Fort Myers–Cape Coral, Florida, of the 2,679 elderly people living alone, 2,038 were women. But the number of men in this category is multiplying more rapidly. Since 1970, there was a 91 percent increase in the number of women living alone, but a 156 percent increase among men. More of the women are elderly and widowed. Among them, 52 percent were 65 or more, but only 22 percent of the men were. Put another way, more than half the women and one in five men age 75 and over live alone. Nearly half of the men living alone had never been married and 54 percent overall were younger than 45.

The average size of American families was 3.17 (down from 3.67 in 1960). Households shrank slightly in the 1980s to a record low of 2.6 people — down from 2.7 in 1980 and 3.01 in 1973, the last time it topped 3 people. Both extremes were in the West; the region had the smallest number of persons per household, 2.53 among blacks, and the highest, 3.62 among Hispanic households. The average is below 2 people in only two counties: Hawaii's Kalawao, which contains 62 households and a leper colony, and New York's Manhattan, which had 716,422 households whose average size was 1.99 people. More were young than elderly.

The median age of Americans living by themselves is steadily declining.

In 1990, 21 percent of them were 75 and older. But 31 percent were between the ages of 25 and 44. Since 1970, the proportion of that younger group living alone doubled for women and nearly doubled for men. College towns and resort communities are meccas for single people under the age of 65. But no county tops Manhattan, where 36 percent of nonelderly house-holders live alone. Of all those living alone in Manhattan, only about one in four is elderly. San Francisco ranked seventh, with 28 percent. Boston and surrounding Suffolk County were ninth, with 24 percent. Single adulthood is no longer considered a transient state and single people are no longer as stigmatized by the rest of society. They are ranked by Dr. Lawrence Hatterer, a Manhattan psychoanalyst, in this descending status: single, at-tractive, heterosexual men; widowers; widows; divorced men and women; never-married women; and homosexuals. Status is in the eye of the beholder, though.

Still, there must be something to be said for togetherness. Households have been getting smaller since the first census, from an average of nearly 6 people in every dwelling in 1790 to about 5 in 1890, to 3.67 in 1940, to 2.76 in 1980, the first census that recorded fewer than 3 people per household. During the 1980s, though, the decline all but halted. Hard times kept more young adults doubled up in their parents' home. Baby Boomers gave birth to more babies themselves. And immigrants arrived to rear their children in a better world.

CHAPTER IV

OUR CHANGING COMPLEXION

M elting pot was largely a metallurgical term until Israel Zangwill, a Jewish playwright living in London, transformed it into an icon of American mythology. Inspired by his marriage to a non-Jew, Zangwill depicted the United States at the start of the twentieth century as a crucible in which exotic and antiquated immigrant traditions would be melded into a homogenized whole. His play *The Melting Pot* was produced in New York City in 1908, just one year after a record 1.7 million legal immigrants entered the nation. The record still stands. The melting pot metaphor, engraved in an earlier version of diversity subsumed on the back of every penny as E Pluribus Unum, is no longer universally celebrated either as a means or as an end.

If the United States was the world's first truly multicultural society, the first universal nation, the country has never been as diverse as it is today — even if that diversity is unevenly divided. One in ten white Americans lives in California, where also nearly one in four residents is foreign-born. In Mississippi, less than one in a hundred was born overseas. While the majority of the nation's population lives in nine states, the majority of blacks is concentrated in eight states, the majority of Asians in three states, and the majority of Hispanic people in just two states. In 186 counties, blacks, Hispanic people, Asians and American Indians make up more than half the population. But in 24 states, those groups do not constitute a majority in a single county.

Only the degree of diversity is new, though, not its consequences. More than 150 years ago, one of three celebrations organized by the incoming president, William Henry Harrison, was presciently called a Native American Inaugural Ball to salute America's first former majority group. Today most Americans are white, but every American is a member of some minority. And, after a decade of unparalleled immigration from the Caribbean, Latin and South America, and the Far East, the sheer volume of newcomers may demand that if assimilation remains a goal it will require more give and less take by the nation's nonimmigrants than has been customary. Managing diversity may be the greatest challenge facing America as it begins the twenty-first century.

The American Century witnessed a profound shift in its pluribus. In 1900, nine in ten residents of the United States were non-Hispanic whites, mostly of western European ancestry. As the twentieth century ends, their proportion has shrunk to fewer than three in four. Census figures, typically conservative in counting immigrants, reveal that the nation has achieved a startling historic milestone: For the first time since the first official count was taken two hundred years ago, more Americans can trace their roots to the forty-eight million who emigrated to the United States since 1790 than to the English, Dutch, Spanish, Indians, and Polynesians who lived within the nation's boundaries before then. Perhaps by the end of this decade, blacks, Latinos, and Asians may constitute nearly a majority of the nation's children. America's changing hue has produced wrenching political, social, and economic ramifications that are even more fundamental than the consequences of previous foreign influxes.

The ramifications run the gamut of American culture and government. Crayola had already discontinued its standard light pink "flesh"-colored crayons (they were renamed "peach"). President Clinton crafted a cabinet that he said would mirror the nation's ethnic and racial diversity. New York City granted the ultimate imprimatur to its Moslem minority by suspending alternate-side parking rules on six Islamic holy days (prompting demands from an Irish group for a similar dispensation on St. Patrick's Day). Nearly 15 percent of the city's public school children are not proficient in English and speak a different native language — including 90,000 who speak primarily Spanish, 13,000 who speak Chinese, 7,000 who speak Haitian Creole, 5,000 who speak Russian, and 500 who speak Farsi. Of the 230 million Americans over the age of 5, more than one in eight, or nearly 32 million, speaks a language other than English at home, a 38 percent increase over 1980. About 2 in 10 of those say they don't speak English very well or at all. In California, 5,478,712 said they speak Spanish at home. In New York, 400,218 speak Italian; in North Dakota, 106 do. Another 117,323 New Yorkers speak mostly Yiddish; so do 12 residents of Alaska. In Massachusetts, 133,373 still speak Portuguese. Nationwide, more than 17 million people speak Spanish at home. Recording people in 380 language categories, the census found 1.4 million Spanish-speakers, 696 Hebrew-speakers, 20 Ute-speakers, and 5 Welsh-speakers who don't speak English at all.

The euphemism "changing neighborhood" can be applied to the nation. And while the change may be threatening and even wrenching at times, history suggests that things will not necessarily be worse — just different, as they have been after every earlier ethnic and racial evolution and succession. "Make it like it was," an elderly woman once pleaded with Mayor Edward I. Koch of New York. While seeking to reassure the woman, Koch later acknowledged that even he didn't have the heart to tell her that the city probably never was the way she remembered it.

Among the 249 million Americans recorded by the 1990 census, about one in twelve, or 21 million, was foreign-born. Almost 9 million of them entered the United States since 1980. The foreign-born total was a record high, nearly five times the number counted in 1970. The ratio was well below the 16.6 percent a century ago, but nearly broke the record set in 1910, which was the last census to record an increase in the foreign-born proportion of the population until 1980.

The statistics translate into stories of remarkable resilience and of protracted pain: of struggling newsstand concessionaires from India and Pakistan, of Koreans who have raised the median income in whole neighborhoods but at the cost of keeping their family working fifteen or more hours a day, of Central Americans hired by resourceful Korean immigrants to do their grunt work, of migrant workers to whom rows of ripening tomatoes define their field of dreams, of cabdrivers from the former Soviet Union, of Chinese who return from long shifts in garment sweatshops to the crowded basement cubicles in some of the same tenements that nineteenth-century immigrants called home, of a profusion of bias-related violence, of xenophobic and well-motivated English-only movements, and of nineteen-year-old Manny Ramirez, the high school outfielder and son of a cabbie and a seamstress, who, six years after he and his family moved from the Dominican Republic to Manhattan's Washington Heights, was drafted by the Cleveland Indians and signed to a $250,000 contract.

More than 6 million legal immigrants came into the country during the 1980s, nearly double the number who arrived during the 1960s. The number of new arrivals has grown every five years, from 1.5 million between 1960 and 1964 to the peak of 5.6 million between 1985 and 1990. Millions more slipped into the United States illegally, evading border patrols along gullies of the Rio Grande, overstaying their visas, braving the Caribbean or the South China Sea in flimsy boats, or methodically making their way up the island chain to San Juan, where, posing as Puerto Ricans, they boarded the air bridge to Miami or New York. The census does not distinguish between legal and illegal immigrants. But, reconciling 100 million records over 11 years, a 1993 analysis by the Immigration and Naturalization Service conjured up about 3.5 million illegal residents in the United States — most of them in California, New York, Florida, Texas and Illinois. Nearly 300,000 were Salvadorans; about 100,000 each also came from Canada, Poland, the Philippines and Haiti. New York state was home to twice as many illegal immigrants from Italy as from China; not surprising, said Joseph J. Salvo, a City Planning Department demographer, "since the legal pathways for them have pretty much dried up." Political and economic refugees flooded the United States, beginning the decade with a boatlift from Cuba and ending, again in Cuba, where American officials tried to contain an exodus of Haitians seeking asylum. Unless Congress closes the Golden Door, the 1980s probably signaled the beginning of a new age of immigration, not its culmination. Relaxed regulations that, among other categories, grant 10,000 visas to entrepreneurs and capitalists who agree to invest $1 million or more in a venture that creates ten or more jobs, are likely to swell the already flooded immigrant ranks.

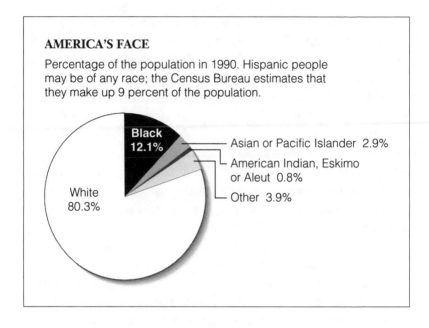

AMERICA'S FACE

Percentage of the population in 1990. Hispanic people may be of any race; the Census Bureau estimates that they make up 9 percent of the population.

White
80.3%

Black
12.1%

Asian or Pacific Islander 2.9%

American Indian, Eskimo
or Aleut 0.8%

Other 3.9%

"There are suppos'd to be now upwards of One Million English Souls in North-America, (tho' 'tis thought scarce 80,000 have been brought over Sea)," Benjamin Franklin wrote four decades before the first census. "This Million doubling, suppose but once in 25 Years, will in another Century be more than the People of England, and the greatest Number of Englishmen will be on this Side of the Water." Franklin was right. Except that they would no longer consider themselves Englishmen, and they, too, were destined to be surpassed by the descendants of subsequent immigrant waves. Ironically, in the western United States today, non-Hispanic whites — whose origins range from Ireland to Israel and Italy — are routinely lumped together under a single name: Anglos.

Drawing on historical records and earlier research, Campbell Gibson, a Census Bureau demographer, found that when Columbus arrived in the Americas, about 96 percent of the people

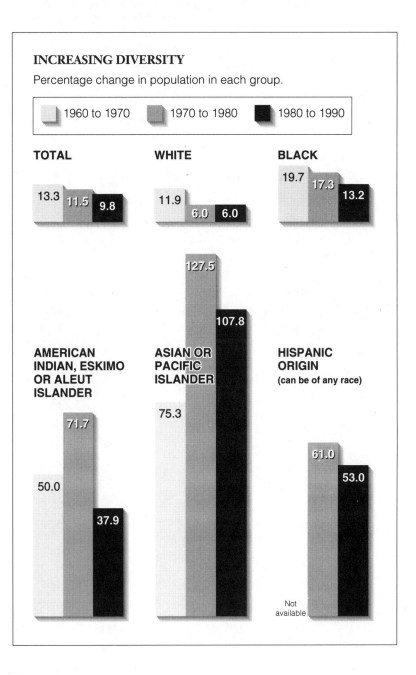

67

THE LEAST WHITE AREAS

Percentage of the population in each metropolitan statistical area that was white in 1990.

AREA	WHITE POPULATION (non-Hispanic)
Laredo, Tex.	5.6%
McAllen/Edinburg/Mission, Tex.	14.2
Brownsville/Harlingen, Tex.	17.4
El Paso, Tex.	25.6
Honolulu	29.9
Las Cruces, N.M.	40.7%
Corpus Christi, Tex.	43.3
San Antonio, Tex.	44.3
Miami/Fort Lauderdale, Fla.	47.8
Los Angeles/Anaheim/Riverside, Calif.	49.8
Fresno, Calif.	50.7%
Salinas/Seaside/Monterey, Calif.	52.3
Santa Fe, N.M.	52.9
Albany, Ga.	52.9
Merced, Calif.	54.2
Yuma, Ariz.	54.4%
Visalia/Tulare/Porterville, Calif.	54.6
Albuquerque, N.M.	55.8
Pine Bluff, Ariz.	55.8
Jackson, Miss.	56.6
Memphis, Tenn.	57.7%
Houston/Galveston/Brazoria, Tex.	57.9
Columbus, Ga.	58.1
Stockton, Calif.	58.8
Victoria, Tex.	58.9

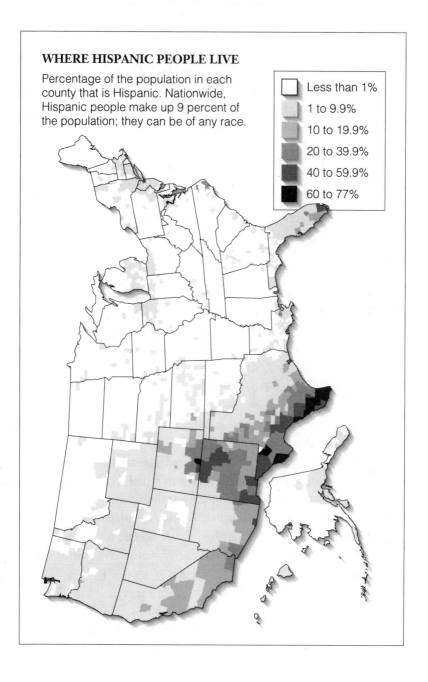

WHERE HISPANIC PEOPLE LIVE

Percentage of the population in each county that is Hispanic. Nationwide, Hispanic people make up 9 percent of the population; they can be of any race.

Less than 1%
1 to 9.9%
10 to 19.9%
20 to 39.9%
40 to 59.9%
60 to 77%

living in what is now the entire United States were Indian and the rest were of Polynesian descent. By 1790, when the first official count was conducted, the comparable population is estimated to have been about 64 percent white, 16 percent Indian, 11 percent black, and 4 percent Polynesian. Among the whites, nearly half — according to a study of their surnames — were of English heritage. Nearly a century later nearly all the whites in the United States were still of northwestern European ancestry.

The census counted blacks from the beginning. Indians and Chinese were added as categories in 1860 shortly before the nation became more selective about who would be allowed to immigrate. Before 1875, immigration was virtually unrestricted except for convicts and prostitutes. But then what became known as the New Immigration began. Despite its nonjudgmental name, it distinguished between the western and northern Europeans who had dominated the population and the surging tide from eastern and southern Europe. Thinly veiled racism and overt concerns over potential competition for jobs inspired the Chinese Exclusion Act in 1882. After 1890, the Chinese population declined for six successive decades. Fearing that the swarm of Italians and Jews was further diluting the nation's ethnic purity, in 1921 Congress imposed the National Origins Quota Act, which was intended to freeze the racial and ethnic profile at its 1910 composition. (Clarifying eligibility for citizenship, the Supreme Court defined Armenians and Syrians as white, but not Japanese and immigrants from the Indian subcontinent; by the end of the century, though, being identified legally as nonwhite could be both fashionable and remunerative, qualifying an individual for government and private sector compensation and preference.) Three years later, a successor law reverted to the 1890 profile as the nation's racial and ethnic model. During the Second World War, when the Chinese were America's allies against Japan, the Chinese Exclusion Laws were finally abandoned. The quotas, which had been circumvented anyway by postwar legislation, were relaxed marginally in 1952 and repealed altogether in 1965. In their place, Congress limited visas to 170,000 a year for the Eastern Hemisphere and 120,000 for the Western. In 1986, illegal immigrants who had lived in the United States continuously since 1982 were granted eligibility for citizenship; others would be subjected to severe penalties, including imprisonment and deportation. (Some of their employers were fined; another, Connecticut lawyer Zoe Baird, was forced to withdraw as President Clinton's nominee for attorney general after she acknowledged that two illegal aliens from Peru had worked for her at home.) In 1990, the annual number of U.S. visas available worldwide was lifted to at least 675,000, or about the number of immigrants who had entered the country legally each year in the 1980s. Spouses and unmarried children of resident aliens were granted preference.

The final decades of the American Century are transforming the nation into the least "American" it has ever been by the conventional definition — or the *most* American, if Central and South America count as American, too. The transformation is typical of a half-dozen evolutionary periods that preceded this one, most of them prompted by events abroad. Well before the English landed in Jamestown, the Spanish established a foothold in what is now New Mexico as America's first minority — motivated first by a vain search for gold and then to convert the native population to Catholicism in a melding of religious zeal and political expediency to achieve numerical superiority over England. The common denominator during ensuing phases of the nation's transformation was that whether or not the streets were paved with gold, they were, at least, paved, and the prospects for employment and for advancement seemed greater than they would have been at home. For many, those goals proved elusive. But one trend that continues to differentiate the United States from most other nations is that immigration has, with the possible exception of the 1930's, consistently exceeded emigration. And, at their own pace and with varying degrees of pain, immigrants are absorbed, if not always assimilated, into a country that historically has been hypocritical about Emma Lazarus's unselfish greeting to immigrants (though her own characterization of the struggling masses as "wretched" and "teeming" human "refuse" might have reflected popular sentiment more accurately). In the nineteenth century, Protestants of English origin were aghast at the Irish tide of immigration that followed periodic potato famines. "Dreadful riots between the Irish and the Americans have again disturbed the public peace," Philip Hone, a diarist and former mayor of New York, wrote in 1834. German Jews feared their own precarious stature would be jeopardized by the arrival of their less cosmopolitan co-religionists from eastern Europe. Italians were relegated to peasant status and stereotypes. And the more recent newcomers from the Caribbean and from Central and South America escaped the cellar, in part, by speaking Spanish so they would not be mistaken for the one group that everybody seemed to look down on: American-born blacks. National quotas for admission into the country were eased and finally abolished, but informal though no less insurmountable barriers barred more than a token number of Jews from prestigious colleges and prevented Italians, including a St. John's University graduate named Mario Cuomo, from being interviewed by white-shoe Wall Street law firms that have only now begun to recruit Hispanic and black associates and still have disproportionately few partners who are not white men. Only the players change, not the plot.

In 1940, the number of Italian nationals entering the United States surpassed the number of Germans for the first time. In 1960, the number of West Indians arriving exceeded the number of Italians. In 1970, Japanese arrivals overtook Scandinavians who were born abroad. People of German origin still constitute the largest group of Americans who give their ancestry — nearly one in four. But the proportion of German natives among all foreign-

born people in the United States has plummeted to only about one in twenty as older immigrants die and are succeeded by newcomers from Central America and Asia. Among foreign-born Americans, Europe has fallen to third place among continents of departure. In the 1980s, half as many people emigrated from Europe to the United States as in the 1960s; more than five times as many came from Asia; twice as many from Mexico, the Caribbean and Central America; and nearly four times as many from Africa — including as many from Nigeria as from Greece. As the 1990s began, more than one in five foreign-born Americans was from Mexico. No other nation accounts for even 5 percent of the foreign-born residents of the United States. The Philippines ranked second as the most common country of origin, followed by Canada, Cuba and Germany, which dropped from second in 1980 to fifth in 1990 (those five, and the United Kingdom, Italy, South Korea, Vietnam, and China, were each the source of 500,000 or more foreign-born residents of the United States). One in four immigrants is from Central America, another one in four is from Asia, about one in five is from Europe and one in ten is from the Caribbean (where, in Jamaica, fully one in ten residents immigrated to the United States during the 1980s). One in twenty is from Africa, a proportion that represented more than 400,000 immigrants — perhaps more than at any time since the slave trade was abolished. In 1990, five countries of origin made their debut on the list of the twenty-five largest foreign-born groups: El Salvador, Taiwan, Guatemala, Haiti and Laos.

The Census Bureau, which, except for Puerto Ricans in some states, did not even include a category for Hispanic people in the decennial count until 1970, now segments the population into 197 ancestry groups. The English, now ranked third, are, with the Germans and Irish, the only nationalities to register in double digits. Proportions vary widely across the country, though, and, despite the commercial and cultural homogenizing of America, are manifested in distinct ways ranging from bizarre ethnic stews (Mexican-Chinese restaurants) to obscure state holidays. People of Italian, Polish and Russian origin are concentrated in New York, Slovaks in Pennsylvania, French Canadians in Massachusetts, and Norwegians in Minnesota. People of Hispanic heritage are clustered according to which country they came from. Nearly nine in ten Dominicans and two thirds of the Puerto Ricans live in the Northeast (half the Puerto Ricans in the mainland United States live in New York and New Jersey alone). About seven in ten Cubans live in the South. More than six in ten Salvadorans and Guatemalans live in the West. In Rhode Island, nearly one in four people is of Portuguese heritage, including black Cape Verdeans. In Iowa, half claim German ancestry. Most Americans still identify with a single ancestry — twice the proportion that listed multiple places of origin on the census questionnaire. Some people may have been offended by the question, others confused, since, after several generations, their roots are too entangled to differentiate. Given four choices of race — white, black, American Indian/Alaskan Native, and Asian/Pacific Islander — 10 million Americans (most of whom, as it turned out, were Hispanic) chose "other." Far down on the list of responses was an ancestry reported by only 5 percent of Americans: "American." Even lower, just three tenths of one percent of the population listed their ancestry group as "United States."

America has always grown more because births exceeded deaths than it did because of immigration. Net immigration — the number of people coming minus the number leaving — as a percentage of the nation's population at the beginning of each decade has been rising steadily since 1940, though. But the last decade was one of only four — including the 1850s, the 1880s and 1900 to 1910 — in which immigration constituted 30 percent or more of the nation's population growth. What distinguished the latest wave was not merely the degree of the flow — the number of Asians in the United States more than doubled and the number of Hispanic people grew by 50 percent—but its source and its destinations. As recently as the 1970s, nearly four in ten immigrants were from Europe. By the 1980s, that share, fed by an influx from what was the Soviet Union, had shrunk to one in four. Moreover, the Hispanic and Asian newcomers themselves hailed from a wide variety of countries. During the last decade, the Asian population grew by 108 percent, the Hispanic by 53 percent, the black by 13 percent, and the white by only 6 percent.

Hawaii is still the only state in which whites constitute a minority. But, barring an influx of retirees from the Midwest and Northeast, the Hispanic population could emerge as a majority in New Mexico; it outnumbers all other groups combined in forty-five counties in Texas, New Mexico, Arizona, Colorado and California; and already dominates in a number of cities. In Laredo, Texas, less than 6 percent of the residents are whites. In ten other metropolitan areas, including El Paso, San Antonio, Miami and Los Angeles, whites now represent a minority. When the decade of unprecedented change had ended, Asians outnumbered blacks in Arlington and Fairfax counties in Virginia. The Fresno telephone book listed as many Vangs—Hmong refugees from Laos, some via Vietnam—as Joneses. Asians, more mobile than blacks, emerged as the largest minority in the village of Schaumburg, outside Chicago. The Asian and Hispanic proportions of the population in metropolitan Seattle doubled (more Asians now live in the city's Beacon Hill than in its International District). In Minnesota, the number of Asians tripled, to a not inconsiderable 77,000. In Boston, immigrants have made only negligible inroads in the Irish bastion of South Boston, but Vietnamese noodle parlors and Spanish fast-food storefronts sprouted in Dorchester, Jamaica Plain, and even compete with pizzerias in predominantly Italian East Boston.

No state was reshaped more dramatically by immigration in the 1980s than California, where a demographic upheaval reverberated far beyond its barrios and traditional Chinatowns. One in four of the Asians in the United States lives in California, where Asians constitute one in ten residents. Nearly three in ten residents of San Francisco County are Asian, but Asians accounted for less than 1 percent of the population in seven of eight counties nationwide. More than one in three of the nation's Hispanic people live in California, where they represent one fourth of the population. The state's Hispanic population grew 70 percent to 7.7 million, which is more than the total population of all but eight states. Anglos — non-Hispanic whites — comprised 76 percent of the state's population in 1980. By 1990, their share had plunged to barely 57 percent. Among the nine counties in the San Francisco Bay Area, more than one third of the population is Asian or Hispanic — double the proportion only a decade earlier. Two in three residents of Daly City are Asian or Hispanic. In Santa Clara and San Mateo counties, El Camino Real is flanked by so many Chinese, Indian and Korean stores that the thoroughfare's very name seems anachronistic. Around Los Angeles, more people in the suburbs than in the central city don't speak English at home. Anglo and Hispanic Angelenos have almost equal shares of the population. In Maywood, a city in southeast Los Angeles County, more than nine of every ten residents are Hispanic. With too many students who speak only Spanish and not enough teachers who do, some California and New York communities imported instructors from Spain.

Among all the foreigners lured to the United States in the 1980s, one in every two settled in either California or New York. People born abroad constitute nearly half the population of Dade County, Florida, and more than one third in New York City's Queens County. Miami; Huntington Park, California; and Union City, New Jersey, are among the cities where foreigners actually outnumber American-born residents. In Santa Ana, California, 50.9 percent of the population is foreign-born — and nearly two thirds of those foreigners arrived in the 1980s. In Hialeah City,

Florida, 70 percent of the residents are foreign-born. New York City has the highest number of immigrants — more than 2 million. But, proportionately, they accounted for only about half the nearly 40 percent of Los Angelenos who were born abroad. "Not only is New York the nation's melting pot," its former mayor John V. Lindsay once said, "it is also the casserole, the chafing dish and the charcoal grill." (Decades earlier when life supposedly was more serene, New York Governor Thomas E. Dewey suggested another metaphor that reverberates today: "New York City is not a melting pot, it's a boiling pot.") New York Telephone announced that it would begin offering repair service to customers in 140 languages, including Fiji, French, Russian, Sioux, Swahili, Twi and Yiddish — with interpreters provided, naturally, by a California company.

In New York City, immigrants revived whole neighborhoods and infused the city that Mayor David N. Dinkins hailed as a "gorgeous mosaic" with a vitality that helped it survive hard times. Without them, the city would have lost population during the decade. Instead, greengroceries sprouted in every community, cultivated by Korean immigrants whose entrepreneurship compensated for their lack of knowledge of fresh produce (which had enabled Italians to succeed in the grocery business when the century began). The elevated Flushing Line of the city's subway system was dubbed the Orient Express. Clattering past communities of Greeks and Colombians, it also pointed the way for Asians to thrive outside the traditional confines of Chinatown in lower Manhattan — just as, earlier in the century, the newly laid subway tracks opened Brooklyn, Queens, and Bronx neighborhoods to Italian and Jewish immigrants graduating from the Lower East Side ghettos. By 1990, four in ten New Yorkers over the age of 5 spoke a foreign language at home. Nearly half of those didn't speak English very well — among them, a member of a community school board in Brooklyn who spoke only Spanish, echoing the circumstances of parents at the turn of the century whose primary language was Yiddish but who joined parents' associations to lobby on behalf of their children anyway. At City College of the City University of New York, which had educated the sons and daughters of Irish, Italian and Jewish immigrants, half the student body was born abroad. And only in New York could the United Nations representative of the Palestine Liberation Organization live as just another anonymous neighbor in a Manhattan apartment building in which the landlord and the majority of tenants were Jewish.

Also like their predecessors, the newcomers paved the way for their fellow countrymen who gravitated toward neighborhoods and to employment that seemed less foreign. A county by county analysis of the 1980's found that Hispanic people often settled in centers of migratory agriculture and blacks congregated at sites of universities, military bases and, in some cases, unfortunately, prisons. Cubans fleeing Fidel Castro's revolution established a beachhead in Union City, New Jersey. Three decades later, Hispanic people now outnumber blacks and non-Hispanic whites in Union City, Passaic, Paterson and West New York. Storefronts along Bergenline Avenue that once beckoned customers with signs that said "We Speak Spanish" now welcome the new minorities with reassuring placards that proclaim "We Speak English." In 1981, Allied Maintenance in New York City hired one Cambodian refugee for its office-cleaning staff. Within a few years, the company had recruited hundreds more Cambodians who were referred by family and friends and who, as cleaning people, often displaced blacks. Antonio Valencia, a live-in housekeeper from Mexico who was hired by a suburban New Rochelle couple in 1954, pioneered a migration that in the 1980s alone nearly doubled the Westchester County community's Mexican population to 7,200. Albanians created an enclave in the Bedford Park section of the Bronx, Dominicans coalesced in the Washington Heights section of Manhattan, and Soviet Jews settled in Brighton Beach, Brooklyn — transforming a needy neighborhood bordering Coney Island into a vibrant Little Odessa. Haitians were drawn to the West Indian concentration in Brooklyn's Flatbush, where they were largely unnoticed by other New Yorkers until, galvanized by a summons from their own local radio station, tens of thousands marched across the Brooklyn Bridge to protest American policies toward their homeland. And in lower Manhattan, Chinatown — whose insularity preserved an identity appealing to immigrants and tourists alike — bulged northward to encroach on another ethnic enclave, Little Italy, which, having outlived its original rationale, was shrinking into an urban ethnic theme park of restaurants, trattorias and salumerias. Queens, where more than one third of the residents were born outside the United States, recorded recent arrivals from 112 countries. Once symbolized by the parochialism of Archie Bunker, an anti-Catholic Protestant, Queens is now considered the most diverse county in the nation — with almost equal proportions of blacks, Hispanic people, non-Hispanic whites, and other races. San Francisco, Los Angeles, Brooklyn, and Alameda, California, follow.

New York was the destination for the majority of legal immigrants from Guyana, the Dominican Republic and Barbados. Each fall, Brooklyn's West Indian Day parade draws as many as 3 million participants and spectators. Because of their location or a critical mass of earlier arrivals, other cities also became kaleidoscopes in which different colors predominated. In Boston and San Francisco, the most newcomers came from China; in Washington, D.C., from Korea; in Chicago and Los Angeles, from Mexico; in Miami, from Cuba; in San Jose, from Vietnam.

No group grew more than Hispanics, who had been, after all, the first Europeans to colonize what became the United States. Spanish explorers founded St. Augustine, Florida, and Sante Fe, New Mexico, years before the first permanent English settlement was established in Jamestown, Virginia, in 1607. Nearly four centuries later, their numbers are increasing at five times the pace of the non-Hispanic population.

But while 22 million Americans claim Hispanic origin, they still account for less than 1 percent of the population in eleven states. Immigration contributed to about half the growth and today there are nearly as many nationalities represented as Goya makes beans (the New Jersey–based company, the nation's largest privately held Hispanic enterprise, actually sells about 750 varieties of beans, spices, rice, flour and frozen food to a market with a growth potential that Campbell's and IPC International have begun to tap). Among all people who identified themselves as of Hispanic origin, 61 percent were Mexican, 12 percent were Puerto Rican and about 5 percent were Cuban — percentages that mask smaller but still significant numbers of other Hispanic people, including 565,000 Salvadorans, 520,000 Dominicans and 378,000 Colombians.

The West is home to the highest concentration of Hispanic people, about one in five of all residents. The Midwest has the smallest share, fewer than one in thirty. Only two states — California and Texas — account for a majority of the Hispanic population. Two thirds of the nation's Hispanics live in California, Texas and New York. Eight percent live in Florida, 4 percent each in Illinois and Arizona, and 3 percent each in New Jersey and New Mexico. Among the four states with a Hispanic population of 1 million or more, the Hispanic growth rate in the 1980s was highest in Florida (83 percent), followed by California (69 percent), Texas (45 percent) and New York (33 percent). New York, Florida, Nevada and New Jersey were the only states outside the Southwest that had a higher proportion of Hispanic people than the national average. In San Antonio, El Paso, Miami, Santa Ana, Corpus Christi and Hialeah, Hispanic people are the majority. In Brownsville and Laredo, Texas, Hispanic people account for more than 90 percent of the population. Nearly twice as many Hispanics live in Miami (where nearly three fourths of the people speak a language other than English at home) as blacks and non-Hispanic whites combined. And in Los Angeles, Hispanic people now constitute a slim majority.

No group of immigrants grew at a faster rate than Asian-Americans — more than doubling nationally and exploding by more than 40 percent in every state except Hawaii, which had the highest proportion of Asians and Pacific Islanders, as the category is called officially, at both ends of the decade. By 1990, though, the Asian population in Hawaii was surpassed by New York's. In five of the seven states that had 100,000 or more Asians when the decade began, the Asian population more than doubled. A majority of Asian-Americans lives in just three states: California, New York and Hawaii. They are becoming less isolated geographically, though. In 1980, Asian-Americans accounted for less than 1 percent of the population in thirty-seven states; by 1990, they accounted for less than 1 percent of the population in only twenty-two states.

Few immigrant groups have been received so unevenly. Cheap Chinese labor was imported to build the nation's railroads in the nineteenth century, nativist fears of a "yellow peril" prompted Congress to shut off Asian immigration in 1924, and Japanese-Americans were interned in prison camps during the Second World War. The 1960 census found 891,000 Asian-Americans. By 1970, after immigration restrictions had been eased, their numbers had grown to 1.4 million. Between 1980 and 1990, they more than doubled again, from 3.5 million to 7.3 million — a total equal to about half the number of Hispanic people who lived in the United States ten years earlier. Half the growth resulted from immigration. In 1980, the number of Japanese-Americans was surpassed by the Chinese, who now account for almost 23 percent of all Asian-Americans. Filipinos rank second, with 19 percent, and those of Japanese heritage are a distant third, with 11.7 percent. Koreans are gaining. During the 1980s, the largest number of Asian immigrants came from China, including Hong Kong and Taiwan. But Vietnamese, Asian Indians and Koreans recorded the greatest percentage increase among the major Asian groups (Hmong tribesmen, mostly from

Laos, logged the highest percentage increase of all, 1,631 percent, or from 5,204 in 1980 to 90,082 a decade later).

More than half the nation's Asian-Americans live in the West, where their share of the population — 7.7 percent — is now higher than the percentage of blacks. Among the major groups, the only ones of whom a majority live in other regions of the nation are Asian Indians, Koreans, Thais, Malayans, Pakistanis and Sri Lankans. Bangladeshis are the only group that constitutes a majority of Asians in another region, the Northeast. After California, Massachusetts was favored by Hmongs, Texas by Vietnamese and New York by Chinese, Asian Indians and Koreans.

The staggering numbers of immigrants suggest only one aspect of their arrival. Their geographic, economic and social diversity is another. By 1990, Birmingham, Alabama, could boast of sixty Chinese restaurants — about ten times as many as a decade before. Asians manned the assembly plants of Silicon Valley. Filipino nurses were recruited by understaffed hospitals. Asians were compared, largely favorably, to Jews who had arrived a century before and who suffered, similarly, as victims of stereotypes and even of quotas. U.C.L.A.'s freshman classes now have more Asians than whites. Generally, Asian-Americans have the highest median income and academic credentials of any racial or ethnic group, but their success came with a price: Poorer Vietnamese or illiterate Hmong tribesmen, as well as simply average Chinese, Japanese and Koreans, had to carry the burden of high expectations. If restaurants gave most Americans the first taste of Asian influence, the flood of imported cars, electronics equipment and highly visible investment in American corporations and prime real estate left a bitter aftertaste. It fueled resentment that was manifested in renewed calls for quotas on immigration and trade.

The only other major group distinguished by the census is that of American Indians, Eskimos and Aleuts, whom the 1990 complete count identified by tribe for the first time. A majority lives in six states. They comprise the highest percentage in Alaska (15.6), but Oklahoma, California, Arizona and New Mexico have more people who identified themselves as American Indians. The first foreigners, Native Americans — or First Americans, as some also preferred to be called — posted an implausible 38 percent population increase during the decade, a consequence, perhaps, of ethnic pride and faddishness embellished by greater precision by the Census Bureau and exaggerated by ambiguous questionnaires. Growth among other groups was so much greater, though, that American Indians still constituted more than 1 percent of residents in only a handful of metropolitan areas (including Phoenix, Sacramento, Seattle, and Rapid City, South Dakota — where they accounted for 7.2 percent). In 1890, the census counted 248,253 American Indians, presumably an undercount. In 1990, 1,878,285 people identified themselves as American Indians — more than seven times the number recorded (in fewer states, though) a century before and, quite possibly, an overcount. More than one in five live on reservations.

Most other Americans are less isolated. Diversity has been marketed as a virtue by the advertising industry — even if two of the most prominent promotions (Nissan's cars engineered "for the human race" and Benetton's "united colors") were mounted by foreign firms. But the melting pot metaphor is, in some respects, even more farfetched today than it was when the century started. The ethnic stew has more ingredients, but some remain in colloidal suspension. "A salad bowl," was how Suzanne Ramos, a lawyer for the Mexican-American Legal Defense Fund, described it. But which dressing?

Inevitably, newcomers jostled for jobs and for living space. They competed politically, just as their predecessors had done for generations. "Multilingualism is great," said U.S. English, which wants to keep English the official language of government, "but let one of those languages be English." In Brooklyn, Hasidic refugees from Eastern Europe scrapped with Hispanic immigrants from Latin America and with Caribbean blacks over scarce federal housing funds and city services. Urban migrant workers, many of whom entered the country illegally, gathered at prearranged big-city street corners every morning, often distinguished only by their nationalities, in al fresco hiring halls for day laborers who are open to exploitation. A Korean man was killed in Detroit by an unemployed auto worker who mistook him for a Japanese. A non-English-speaking Japanese youth was shot to death in Louisiana when he approached the wrong house for a Halloween party. In Los Angeles, the proliferation of unlicensed street peddlers competing with taxpaying store owners for customers became emblematic of an episodic American ambivalence toward foreigners. Pomona required Chinese and Korean shopkeepers to place English signs on their storefronts (a requirement that was later rejected by a federal judge of Japanese ancestry). Filipino nurses there fought for the right to speak to each other at work in Tagalog. A nationwide drive was begun for a constitutional amendment that would deny citizenship to the American-born children of illegal immigrants. In Jackson Heights, Queens, earlier newcomers protested when Indian merchants, as prideful as, if more presumptuous than, their predecessors, asked city officials to formally designate their enclave as Little India. "This used to be an American marketplace," one resident, Joseph Gallo, groused. "These merchants have taken over our neighborhood. They have invaded us. And they are just standing there not understanding why we're complaining."

In south-central Los Angeles, many accounts of the 1992 riots took for granted that not much had changed since Watts erupted a quarter century earlier. In fact, the neighborhood — those who lived and worked there — had been dramatically transformed by immigration. Among more than 6,000 people counted in the Florence-Normandie census tract where the rioting erupted in 1992, fewer than one in ten residents were of Hispanic origin in 1980. By 1990, nearly three in ten were, and the proportion of blacks had declined from nearly nine in ten to slightly more than seven in ten. On one block that resembled the set of *Blade Runner*, rioters looted a flea market owned by Korean immigrants, a discount store belonging to Iranians, and a tropical fish emporium owned by Taiwanese. The disorder that ensued following the initial acquittal of four police officers charged with beating a black man was, in one sense, emblematic of change: It was a multiracial riot. The children and grandchildren who had inherited the legacy of 1965 Watts were joined by disillusioned Latin American immigrants. Their rage, justified or not, was a consequence of isolation, of political impotence, and of the unfettered freedom of nothing left to lose except their potential to prosper in a place that, for some recent immigrants, too, had degenerated from a dream to an illusion. Immigration agents, ostensibly searching for looters and their booty, corralled about a thousand illegal aliens, mostly from Mexico, and promptly deported them. Simmering frustration boiled over into violence in other cities, too, including the nation's capital, where a curfew was imposed to contain rioting largely by Hispanic-Americans.

However disenfranchised blacks remain, the Hispanic population is still several steps behind: Perhaps a third are not even citizens, which means they are ineligible to register, much less to vote. A census survey of the 1990 elections found that 47 percent of the white adults and 39 percent of the blacks but only 21 percent of Hispanic people voted. About half the Hispanic people who didn't vote said they were not United States citizens. "You can already hear people saying that this is an isolated instance, that things are different in other cities, that we should leave things to local officials and everything will be fine," Margarita Roque, executive director of the Congressional Hispanic Caucus, said after the disturbances in the nation's capital. "But in cities across the country, our people feel like they do in Washington — no access, no elected officials, no recourse."

Despite their enduring underrepresentation, racial and ethnic minorities made enormous political strides in the 1980s — though sometimes at each other's expense. L. Douglas Wilder was elected the nation's first black governor in Virginia, where blacks account for fewer than one in five residents of voting age. Bob Martinez was elected the nation's first Hispanic governor in Florida, where the voting-age population is only 11 percent Hispanic. Black candidates won for the first time in mayoral elections in New York, Seattle, Denver, Kansas City and New Haven — cities where blacks constitute far less than a majority. Still, they were largely the exceptions to a political rule that has rarely been broken: Whites rarely vote for black candidates when there is a white alternative. When the final decade of the century began, there were no black or Hispanic United States senators and none had been elected in more than a decade, since Edward Brooke, a Massachusetts Republican, resigned in 1979. The 1990 census helped change that. A black woman was elected to the Senate from Illinois in 1992. So was an American Indian man. In the House, reapportionment, which bunched blacks or Hispanics into tortuous districts, helped boost the number of blacks from twenty-five to thirty-nine and the number of Hispanic representatives from eleven to nineteen.

Nearly six in ten foreign-born residents counted in 1990 were not United States citizens — including about three in ten Germans but more than eight in ten Salvadorans and Guatemalans. Nonetheless, voting rights advocates have succeeded in empowering traditionally disenfranchised constituencies and harnessing the political potential of newcomers as never before. "Immigrants' rights are the civil rights of the 1990s," said Jamin Raskin, an American University law professor who is the intellectual spirit behind an emerging campaign in Los Angeles, New York, Washington and other cities to grant legal immigrants who are not citizens the right to vote in local elections — a right they enjoyed at one time or another in nearly half the states until it was revoked in the nationalist fervor of the First World War. In 1991, voters in Takoma Park, Maryland, a suburb of 17,000 with about 2,000 noncitizen immigrants from Guatemala and El Salvador, narrowly extended the franchise to fellow parents and taxpayers who had either declined to renounce their foreign citizenship or were not yet eligible to become full-fledged Americans. In New York City, noncitizens already are allowed to vote in elections for community school boards.

Another device to encourage voting by minority groups is the bilingual ballot — a right that Congress extended from the 175 counties covered by the 1965 Voting Rights Act to 38 more counties in which 5 percent of the voting-age residents or 10,000 residents, whichever figure is lower, primarily speak the same foreign language and are not proficient in English. In metropolitan New York alone, the law required that Spanish language ballots be offered in Westchester, Suffolk, Essex, Middlesex, Union and Queens counties. In Queens, ballots also have to be printed in Chinese.

Creative redistricting to reflect the 1990 census was expected to produce a surge in black and Hispanic legislators by the end of the decade. Ostensibly, the goal of the Voting Rights Act was to protect the power of an ethnic or racial minority to elect a representative of its choice — not necessarily someone who happens to look the same as most of his or her constituents. The number of congressional districts in which blacks constituted a majority of the population nearly doubled, from eighteen after the 1980 census, to thirty-two. Three were created in Florida alone. The Hispanic-majority districts did double from nine to eighteen, including five in California. Reapportionment, cheerfully supported by Republican legislators, produced two other consequences: the political isolation of black and Hispanic voters from whites and from white elected officials; and competition between blacks and Hispanics for the fruits of redistricting. "In today's reality," said State Representative Ron Wilson, a black from Houston, "if you are black or brown, the numbers game is the only game in town."

Houston's amicable accommodation between black and Hispanic politicians produced agreement on a reconfigured City Council that protected black incumbents but encouraged Hispanic newcomers in other districts. In San Antonio, where Hispanic citizens were a majority of the population but not of the electorate, ethnic coalitions helped elect Henry Cisneros mayor in the 1980s. Blacks and Hispanic people were pursuing what seemed like a perpetual challenge to City Council districts in Dallas, where blacks, who constitute 30 percent of the population, held only two of the eleven council seats and Hispanic residents, with 21 percent of the population, had no representatives at all. In Florida, the legislature's stalemate sent the question to the courts in what was viewed as a harbinger of Hispanic claims to the voting rights that had only belatedly and often begrudgingly been granted to blacks. Hispanic and black Floridians each account for between 12 and 14 percent of the state's population, but are culturally and ideologically divided, as is the Hispanic community itself—disagreeing even over a collective name for the fragmented population. ("Hispanic" is favored in Florida and Texas and by Cubans; "Latino" is preferred in California. The Census Bureau, according to one account, switched from "Latino" to "Hispanic" at the eleventh hour to avoid confusion with Ladino, an ancient language now spoken only by a small number of Spanish Jews.) In Miami, some black politicians maintained that their Hispanic counterparts don't even deserve protection under the Voting Rights Act because they no longer constitute an endangered minority. In Los Angeles, the 1993 mayoral race to succeed Tom Bradley drew more than fifty candidates who reflected the city's diversity. But while two thirds of the population is Mexican-American, black and Asian-American, two thirds of the voters in Los Angeles are non-Hispanic whites. A white, Richard Riordan, won. A state assembly race in California's polyglot 46th District generated fifteen candidates — representing virtually every constituency, including Filipinos, Japanese, Jews, Koreans and Latinos. In neighborhoods of transplanted villages from Asia and Latin America, whites accounted for 15 percent of the district's 360,000 residents but more than 60 percent of the electorate in 1991. Their share is shrinking, though. "My district," said Michael Roos, the incumbent whose resignation sparked the special election, "is what all of California is going to look like by the year 2025."

Even in New York City, where multiculturalism was elevated to political orthodoxy, no black or Hispanic congressman had been elected from a predominantly white district since 1970. In 1991, the City Council was expanded and remapped to conform to court rulings and to fulfill the revised City Charter's mandate for diversity. A districting commission whose members were supposed to personify precisely the city's changing ethnic and racial mosaic — a legally required quota that a court later overturned — drew bizarrely shaped districts to overcome the handicaps of assimilation by encompassing as many Hispanic and Asian residents as possible. The ascension of the first councilman from the Dominican Republic, the first woman from the West Indies, and two self-proclaimed gay candidates cloaked deep ethnic and racial divisions in self-congratulation. Dr. Gabor Nagy, the visiting chairman of the city council committee on minorities in Budapest (where the predominant minority group is Gypsies, who make up less than 10 percent of the population), was ambivalent about the sort of fragmentation that he had witnessed in the Balkans and that was about to further fracture Yugoslavia. It was symptomatic of the "Where's mine?" mentality that had been suggested jocularly more than once as the unofficial motto for the city of Chicago, but that seemed to be embraced with fervor by every faction from Moslem fundamentalists to white Staten

Islanders bent on seceding from a city where they, too, had become a minority. "Each group in this city is a minority, but this is not just a city of ethnic concerns," Nagy observed, echoing Tocqueville (whose subjects were largely Anglo-Americans riven by politics rather than ethnicity). "It's a city that requires taxation and services. This guy will represent the gays, and that one the African-Americans and this one Hispanic people and that one the Asians. But who will represent the majority?"

CHAPTER V

OUR NATIONAL OBSESSION

B lacks are America's indelible immigrants. They are the nation's largest racial minority, as they have been for two hundred years since the first census, when they accounted for nearly one in five counted Americans. With higher fertility rates and a growing share of young people, blacks made up a greater proportion of the population in 1990 than they had for more than a century. Yet, with social advancement often dependent on residential mobility, they are, as W. E. B. Du Bois said, "a part of the larger whole and yet apart from it." In Chicago, which has been described as the nation's most segregated city, integration was once cynically defined by an alderman as the brief hiatus between the arrival of the first black in a neighborhood and the departure of the last white.

Hispanic people are gaining on blacks — numerically, politically and, in many places, economically. Black progress toward equity with white society, with newer immigrants of other races and even with foreign-born blacks, has been slow by every socioeconomic measure. Even in New York City's *Village Voice*, a weekly bible of the cultural and political avant-garde where people advertising jobs and apartments to rent are forbidden to discriminate (the film *Single White Female* notwithstanding), suggestive personal ads unabashedly invite responses not merely according to sexual preference but invariably by race.

In his memoirs, Jefferson forecast this chromatic divide nearly two centuries ago: "Nothing is more clearly written in the book of destiny than the emancipation of the blacks; and it is equally certain that the two races will never live in a state of equal freedom under the same government, so insurmountable are the barriers which nature, habit and opinion have established between them." More than 150 years ago, Tocqueville presciently described what had already become an American obsession: "These two races are fastened to each other without intermingling; and they are unable to separate entirely or to combine," Tocqueville wrote. "Although the law may abolish slavery, God alone can obliterate the traces of its existence. You may set the Negro free, but you cannot make him otherwise than an alien to those of European origin." In the middle of the twentieth century, Gunnar Myrdal succinctly dubbed that legacy "the American dilemma." And as the century closes, Andrew Hacker, the Queens College urban anthropologist, calls lingering racial disparities, both real and perceived, "the American tragedy."

Staggering numbers only begin to suggest the lines that corrosive racism and its consequences have etched in American society. Black infants are twice as likely to die as white ones.

While the infant mortality rate has fallen substantially, the ratio between the rate among blacks and the rate among whites has actually increased in the last fifty years. Black children are three times more likely to live in poverty. They can expect to live about six years less than white children born at the same time. They are half as likely as whites to go to college. If they graduate, black men with college degrees earn an average of three quarters of what white college graduates do. The percentage of blacks whose household income is over $100,000 has nearly tripled in twenty years, but the percentage of poor blacks is still forty times greater. The death rate for black men from murder is seven times higher than for whites; from AIDS, three times higher. Among black men between the ages of 20 and 29, nearly one in four is in prison or on probation or parole. The number of black adults who have never been married now exceeds the number who are married. And as many black households are now headed by single women as by married couples.

Abstract stereotypes, often rooted in concrete statistics, inflict a painful if intangible toll. Anna Deavere Smith, a black writer and actress, recalls that every black remembers a seminal childhood awakening that defined him or her by race. "Usually they have this experience before they're two years old," she said, "and usually it's unpleasant." Smith's *Fires in the Mirror: Crown Heights, Brooklyn, and Other Identities* was a compilation of conversations in a neighborhood where blacks and whites live side by side but not together. "There's a girl in my show who starts out by talking about how she found out she was black," Smith said. "She looked in a mirror, she said, or she looked at her parents. When she goes to Manhattan she knows she's black. Because she goes into stores and, compared to Crown Heights, it's all white people and it really frightens her. And when I spoke to her, I thought, that really hasn't changed that much since my own youth."

In Chicago, only two miles of 111th Street separate the

black Roseland section from white Mount Greenwood, but they might as well be in separate hemispheres. For the first blacks, Roseland represented an integrated sanctuary from the ghetto. For many whites, Mount Greenwood was a refuge from the changing Roseland. "It's fine for them to live in their neighborhoods and us to live in ours," said Peggy O'Connor, a waitress who lives in Mount Greenwood with her police officer husband. "I guess that's the way it's supposed to be." "The time, energy and money spent on creating enclaves safe from black people," said Robert T. Carter, a psychology professor at Columbia University Teachers College, takes an enervating psychic toll on whites. The toll on blacks is more tangible. In 1990, Roseland households made $2,700 less, adjusted for inflation, than they had a decade earlier. Households in Mount Greenwood made $5,097 more. Race, which manifests itself as a series of daily obstacles for blacks, is often a mere abstraction for whites. "They can't even imagine," said Myshawn Davis, a Roseland hairdresser, "what it's like to be black."

After New York City's first black police commissioner, Benjamin Ward, publicly acknowledged the black community's "dirty secret" — that vicious young black men are virtually committing genocide — Carlos Russell, a Brooklyn College professor, agreed: "No white person comes into Bedford-Stuyvesant to rape a grandmother." When a *New York Times*/WCBS-TV News team polled black subway riders, four in ten said they would feel unsafe if they were seated in a subway car and several loud, white teenaged boys entered. Five in ten acknowledged that they would feel unsafe if the boys were black. Representative Charles B. Rangel of Harlem, dean of the city's congressional delegation, once cautioned a group of black prosecutors that while they epitomized law and order, "don't take off your shirt and tie and put on a pair of sneakers because you and I could get shot running for a bus."

Few white politicians risk such frankness. One, Senator Bill Bradley of New Jersey, suggested that Americans will never rec-

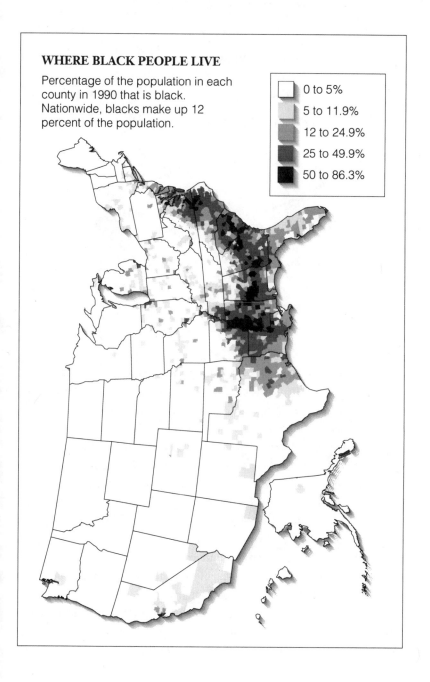

WHERE BLACK PEOPLE LIVE

Percentage of the population in each county in 1990 that is black. Nationwide, blacks make up 12 percent of the population.

0 to 5%
5 to 11.9%
12 to 24.9%
25 to 49.9%
50 to 86.3%

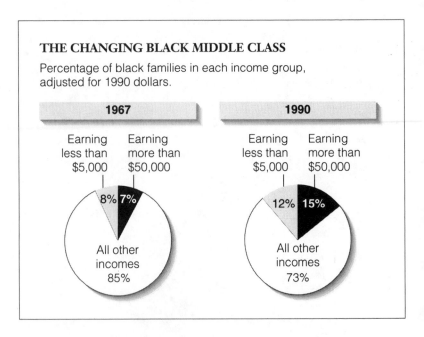

THE CHANGING BLACK MIDDLE CLASS

Percentage of black families in each income group, adjusted for 1990 dollars.

1967	1990

1967

Earning less than $5,000 — 8%
Earning more than $50,000 — 7%
All other incomes — 85%

1990

Earning less than $5,000 — 12%
Earning more than $50,000 — 15%
All other incomes — 73%

oncile racial differences unless they are first acknowledged. "In a kind of ironic flip of fate," Bradley said, going beyond merely echoing his constituents, "the fear of brutal white repression felt for decades in the black community and the seething anger it generated now appear to be mirrored in the fear whites have of random attack from blacks and the growing anger it fuels. . . . Today, many whites responding to a more violent reality, heightened by sensational news stories, see young black men traveling in groups, cruising the city, looking for trouble, and they are frightened. . . . The divide among races in our cities deepens, with white Americans more and more unwilling to spend the money necessary to ameliorate the conditions or to see why the absence of meaning in the lives of many urban children threatens the future of their own children." At the same time, Bradley said, "to say to kids who have no connection to religion, no family outside a gang, no sense of place outside the territory, no imagi-

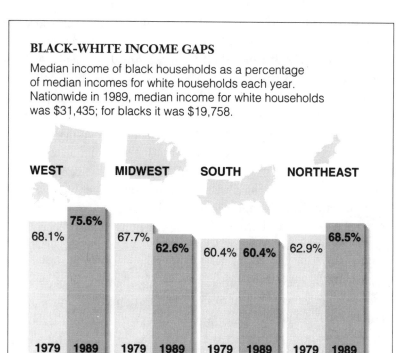

BLACK-WHITE INCOME GAPS

Median income of black households as a percentage of median incomes for white households each year. Nationwide in 1989, median income for white households was $31,435; for blacks it was $19,758.

WEST   MIDWEST   SOUTH   NORTHEAST

	WEST		MIDWEST		SOUTH		NORTHEAST	
	68.1%	75.6%	67.7%	62.6%	60.4%	60.4%	62.9%	68.5%
	1979	1989	1979	1989	1979	1989	1979	1989

nation beyond the cadence of rap or the violence of TV, that government is on their side rings hollow."

The Census Bureau debated how to plumb America's obsession with race without perpetuating it. Indeed, why ask about race at all? Continuity aside, the figures on race generated by the census provide invaluable grounds for the Justice Department's review of congressional redistricting, evaluation of affirmative action and other guidelines for employment, mortgage lending and desegregation. Anecdotal or impressionistic evidence might have been insufficient to win epochal racial discrimination cases. But it's arguable whether routinely comparing groups of people by race serves any valid purpose, as if race uniquely distinguished them politically, socially or economically. News that the racial balance of a neighborhood or of a city has "tipped" in favor of blacks has largely been greeted by other groups as a more profound harbinger of other changes than similar ethnic successions have been. Less than two decades ago, when the New York *Daily News* had more readers than any other newspaper in America, a crime involving a black person might reflexively evoke a single dismissive response from veteran editors: cheap. Morality and the market have driven most editors to be more inclusive whether weighing the news value of a crime or of a wedding announcement. But even considering all of the other variables — location included — it was still no surprise that as the 1980s ended, the rape and beating of an upper-class white woman jogger in Manhattan's Central Park grabbed more attention than the brutal rape of a poor black woman on a Brooklyn rooftop at about the same time. More than 130 years after slavery was abolished in America, race remains largely synonymous with class. I once asked David N. Dinkins, New York City's first black mayor, whether he believed that non-black New Yorkers were biased against him because he is black — a bias that, to some people, may have been manifested in earlier derision of his passion for tennis. "If I had gone to a basketball game, it would be all right," the mayor replied brittlely. "I've said very clearly, my language was, people aren't biased against me because I like tennis. I said they're biased against tennis."

Like Tocqueville, the 1990 census used the word *black* interchangeably with *Negro*. The census form usage was one of the last vestiges of a word that had fallen out of favor — so much so that some blacks skipped both categories altogether and, further distorting the results, wrote in "African-American" under "Other." Not until 1910 had the census's white enumerators stopped differentiating between Negroes and mulattoes, a simplification that also, intentionally or not, removed ambiguity in distinguishing between black and white in what the government views as largely a process of self-identification. (Of course, few blacks born in America are any more black than the chocolate half of a black-and-white cookie, or, for that matter, than most Caucasians are as pale as the vanilla half.)

Blacks accounted for 19.6 percent of the people counted in the first census, a peak from which their proportion declined for more than a century, from the 1810 census — two years after the importation of slaves was prohibited — to 1930. Fifty years ago, though, the proportion began inching up again. So did blacks themselves. When the twentieth century started, 90 percent of them lived in the South. The combination of tough times there and the hiatus in immigration from Europe during the First World War sparked a migration that, in each of three decades beginning with 1940, sent a million or more blacks northward. In the 1950s, a machine — the John Deere company's mechanized cotton picker — freed more blacks from the land than any judge or politician could have unshackled for nearly a century.

A half century ago, New York was the only state outside the South among the ten with the largest black populations. By 1990, among the sixteen states with 1 million or more black people, seven were outside the South (New York, California, Illinois, Michigan, Ohio, Pennsylvania and New Jersey). Among those states, the growth rate during the 1980s ranged widely, from 31 percent in Florida to 1 percent in Illinois. The black population increased more than 65 percent in Sacramento, 52 percent in San Diego, 50 percent in Miami–Fort Lauderdale and 35 percent in the Boston-Lawrence-Salem metropolitan area. Now, four of the ten states with the highest percentage of blacks are in the Northeast, Midwest or West, but there is evidence that more northern blacks are going south, either to retire or to find jobs in the Sun Belt. Rebutting allegations that new immigrants were driving out blacks, Elizabeth Bogen, director of New York City's

Office of Immigrant Affairs, found that more than half the people, mostly blacks, who moved from New York to Alabama and South Carolina were returning, presumably voluntarily, to the states in which they were born.

During the 1980s, the nation's black population grew at double the rate logged by whites. Immigration accounted for about 15 percent of the black increase — including a continuation of what may be the first major influx from Africa since the slave trade. The number of blacks declined slightly in metropolitan Chicago and Pittsburgh, but their share in America's central cities increased. Los Angeles and New York became truly multicultural — neither whites nor any other group constitutes a majority any longer (3.7 million whites lived in New York in 1980, 421,716 more than in 1990; the number of blacks also declined but by a much smaller proportion, 60,128 of 1.7 million). But the black population grew to 76 percent in Detroit, 67 percent in Atlanta, 63 percent in Birmingham and 62 percent in New Orleans as a result of higher birth rates among a younger black population and of continuing middle-class white flight. Blacks now outnumber whites in Chicago, too. In East St. Louis, the 1990 census found 40,061 blacks and 641 whites.

Not far from East St. Louis, in rural and small-town Illinois, the ratio of blacks to whites was virtually the reverse. Half the whites but only one fourth of the nation's blacks live in the suburbs, an increase, nonetheless, since 1970, when only about one in six did. "Residential mobility is a major avenue of social mobility," Douglas Massey of the University of Chicago's Population Center maintains, though most people move to a better neighborhood with the proceeds from a higher-paying job. To William Simpson, this was no abstract notion. After a federal judge ordered Vidor, Texas, to desegregate an all-white public housing project, Simpson and another black man became the city's first black residents in 70 years. They had been lured by a modest goal: to live safely. But after six months of racial harassment, Simpson gave up in 1993 and moved to nearby Beaumont. Hours later, he was shot dead by four blacks who accosted him on the street and demanded money.

No group has been more immobilized by segregation in America than blacks. A study by two Census Bureau demographers, Roderick J. Harrison and Daniel H. Weinberg, affirmed that the nation's most segregated large city is Chicago. Detroit, Cleveland, Milwaukee, New York, Newark, St. Louis and Philadelphia followed. The most segregated cities are in the Northeast and Midwest, the least segregated in the South, except for Honolulu, where blacks are only 3 percent of the population. The study found that among the major metropolitan areas, Hispanics were most segregated in New York, Hartford, Newark, Philadelphia, Chicago and Los Angeles. But there was no disputing which group is most isolated: "Blacks are most segregated of the four groups using 18 of the 19 measures," the demographers found. They suggested, though, that divining motivation was another matter entirely: "In the post–civil rights era, American society has perhaps reached virtual consensus that segregated residential patterns are inherently and by definition problematic to the extent that they reflect conscious and deliberate policies of racial discrimination and exclusion, past or present. There is no similar consensus on whether residential segregation is inherently problematic if and when it might instead reflect the reasonably free and unconstrained decisions and choices of people — especially of minorities — to reside among people of similar heritage and culture."

Blacks are still the largest minority in every region except the West. They constitute a majority in eighty-nine of the nation's counties — all of them in the South — and represent between 40 percent and 50 percent of the population in two counties: Essex, New Jersey, and Wayne, Michigan. In nearly half the nation's counties, though, less than 1 percent of the population is black. And in more than a hundred counties, the census found no blacks whatsoever. In Montana, blacks are outnumbered by whites four hundred to one. But while prejudice knows no political boundaries, rural America often erects fewer racial barriers because the threat is too small to herald social or political upheaval. The gap between black and white median income is narrowest in overwhelmingly white, rural states. "Where there is prejudice here, it's based on ignorance, not hate," said Gwen Kircher, a black United Parcel Service worker from Warden, a town of three hundred people near Billings. Elsewhere, though, prejudice is often based on condescension and fear fed by predispositions of people who prefer to rely on stereotypes rather than to risk personal contact.

Westat, Inc., a consulting firm commissioned by the federal government, examined those census block groups in the United States in which blacks made up less than 10 percent of the population. From 1980 to 1990, the proportion of all blacks living in those virtually non-black neighborhoods barely increased, from just below 10 percent when the decade began to 12 percent when it ended. Residential segregation is self-perpetuating. Where people live generally determines where their children go to school. Which school they attend usually influences lifelong friendships and perceptions. In nineteen states where blacks are a minority, a majority of black children attend segregated schools, which are by definition separate and unequal. Sometimes they are unequal because, in part, blacks are more likely to be poor, and poorer districts typically spend disproportionately less per pupil on education than wealthier ones. The schools are often separate because voluntary or court-imposed integration goes only so far — rarely any farther than the city gates, which means that in a growing number of central cities there are too few white students left to apportion. In Connecticut, where Hartford parents sued to correct the racial and budget imbalance between the city and its suburbs, Governor Lowell P. Weicker, Jr., proposed a bold solution: splitting the state into six regional school districts whose boundaries disregarded archaic county lines that have been an invisible but insurmountable barrier to integration. David Rusk, the former mayor of Albuquerque, warned that what he called "modern American urban apartheid" and the poverty it perpetuates can only be overcome "by bringing down the walls between cities and suburbs."

Even more insurmountable than those political barriers is an apartheid of the spirit. In Yonkers, which borders the Bronx, blacks began integrating insular all-white neighborhoods only after a federal judge ordered the city to scatter clusters of low-income apartments beyond a west side ghetto of public housing. But a court cannot order camaraderie. For months after twenty-four low-income families moved into Colonial-style town houses on the former site of a parking lot, they and their white neighbors on the opposite side of Clark Street had not exchanged a single word. "It shouldn't be like this," said Erwin Dixon, a thirty-three-year-old printer who moved to one of the town houses with his wife and three children, "but it's like we all have to stay on our own side of the street."

In New York City, despite huge population shifts in the 1980s, blacks and whites — regardless of their incomes — remained as segregated as they had been when the decade began. A study by Dr. Andrew A. Beveridge, a Queens College sociologist, found that more than half the city's blacks lived in block groups in which they constituted 75 percent or more of the population. Despite gains in income by blacks, integration of the city's private and public housing had proceeded glacially, if at all. To achieve complete integration of all blacks and whites in the city, more than eight in ten blacks would have had to move from one census block group to another — almost precisely the proportion that existed in 1980. Moreover, the survey found that for blacks, in particular, race was a far greater gauge of segregation than class.

It's difficult, as the Census Bureau demographers noncommittally concluded, to gauge the degree to which segregation results from private decisions of people to live with fellow members of a racial or ethnic group. Also, it is presumptuous, at best, to assume that blacks reflexively want to live with whites — except that many associate more responsive public services with neighborhoods that are middle-class and, therefore, more likely to be mostly white or about evenly mixed. Whites have a choice. Blacks usually don't. From real estate advertisements that feature white models only to outright racial steering and firebombings, a pattern of discrimination creates obstacles that few whites have ever had to confront. Donovan Martin, a black police officer from Brooklyn, was shocked when he and his wife, Sandra, a registered nurse, were denied an apartment in the borough's Midwood section. The apartment was subsequently rented to a white couple working as testers for the Open Housing Center, an advocacy group. "It's not by accident that certain parts of the city stay the way they are," Officer Martin said. Some segregation has even been perpetuated by public policy, however benign. A strategy to prevent what the Board of Education blandly called "tipping" in New York City's high schools propelled two goals into conflict: encouraging integration and ending discrimination. The policy collapsed of its own weight when there simply were not enough whites left to go around, but not before provoking a largely academic debate over whether race or class is more divisive. "Socioeconomic status is probably more important than race," said Joseph Elias, who directed the Board of Education's integration office, "but in New York City there is practically a one-to-one correlation between being a member of a minority group and being poor."

Nonpoor blacks are fine if there are not too many of them. Just how many is too many became the crux of protracted litigation involving the mammoth Starrett City housing development in Brooklyn. Fair-housing advocates and managers of the development had agreed to a formula that would provide apartments for blacks but also keep the population of the 20,000-person complex from tipping to a black majority. While there is nothing intrinsically wrong with a project whose population changes from predominantly white to black, Starrett City's managers suggested, the metamorphosis typically accelerates middle-class flight — by whites *and* blacks. "Historically what happens is that the upwardly mobile black and Hispanic people also move out," said Starrett's Robert C. Rosenberg. "They move out before the whites because they have already escaped the ghetto once. Then the only ones moving in are the ones with the most severe economic and social problems." But the Justice Department objected to the policy altogether and the agreement was largely voided by the United States Supreme Court in 1989. Three years later, New York City's own Housing Authority renounced a similar policy that steered black and Hispanic applicants away from public housing projects in predominantly white neighborhoods. "White fears over tipping seem to be the most ominous factor and biggest deterrent to integration," Dr. Kenneth B. Clark, the sociologist, argued in defense of Starrett City's quota. Enduring integration, he said, could not be left to shortsighted purists or to chance. "In order to get beyond racism, we must first take account of race," he wrote, echoing the Supreme Court in the Bakke "reverse discrimination" case. "To be color-blind in a color-conscious society is to perpetuate rather than eradicate discrimination and segregation."

If blacks left behind in the ghetto have become even more isolated, desperate optimists may regard that in itself as a measure of progress: at least there is a growing black middle class with the mobility to flee and to leave behind the social pathologies associated with poverty and with race. In 1960, one census tract on the border of Los Angeles and suburban Inglewood was 98 percent white. By 1990, it was 84 percent black. But, defying the stereotype, the racial transformation there actually improved the neighborhood by some objective benchmarks.

Home ownership rose from 62 percent in 1960 to 70 percent in 1990. And the proportion of people with high school diplomas increased from two thirds to nearly nine in ten over the same period. Still, whites typically flee even from stable, homeowning blacks.

In Chicago, the number of blacks in the city fell by 113,000 during the 1980s; in Chicago's suburbs, the number of blacks increased by 103,000. Washington lost black population but suburban Prince Georges County, Maryland, gained. George Wallace carried Prince Georges in the 1968 presidential election a generation ago when the county was a bastion of anti-busing sentiment. It now has a black majority, although, in many enclaves, the familiar grid of segregation was merely transplanted from Washington: More than half the census tracts are either 70 percent black or 70 percent white. In Shaker Heights, a Cleveland suburb — which, like Oak Park and University Park, Illinois, Montclair and Teaneck, New Jersey, Columbia, Maryland, and Reston, Virginia, had gone out of its way to encourage integration as a matter of enlightened self-interest — the population in three of the nine neighborhoods remains 50 percent or more black although the suburb's overall population is 30 percent black. Shaker Heights actually bribed homebuyers with mortgage assistance if they moved into neighborhoods where their race is underrepresented — a variation on Oak Park's social engineering strategy of equity assurance, or guaranteeing that integration will not reduce the value of any home. "It's working," said Dr. Winston Richie, a retired dentist who was one of the first black residents of Shaker Heights, "but compared to what?"

Anticipating the 1996 summer Olympics, former president Jimmy Carter, who had managed to bring together Arabs and Jews, was trying to do the same for blacks and whites with the Atlanta Project to revitalize the city's urban core. But in *The Closing Door: Conservative Policy and Black Opportunity*, Gary Orfield and Carol Ashkinaze warned that Atlanta, like other cities, needs "leaders willing to raise large, uncomfortable issues about the need for basic racial change."

Segregation is only one manifestation of a separation that can cause and perpetuate persistent inequality. The Savannah in which Supreme Court Justice Clarence Thomas was raised is vastly different from the city that exists today except that black unemployment in 1990 was just where it was in 1960 — twice the rate for whites. Nationwide, the 1980 census estimated that a black household typically brought in sixty-two cents for every dollar that went to a white household. Ten years later, the black household income had risen to sixty-three cents for every dollar brought in by a white household (or $19,758 compared to $31,435). The Census Bureau found that 33 percent of black men were employed as operators, fabricators and laborers, compared to 19 percent among white men. White men were more likely to be working in managerial and professional specialty jobs — 27 percent did, compared to 13 percent of black men. Overall, the median earnings of employed black men are less than 70 percent of what white men earned. Black salesmen made $14,380, compared to $23,930 for white salesmen. Blacks working in service jobs and as handlers, equipment cleaners, helpers and laborers, though, reported median earnings equal to or even above the earnings of white men in those jobs. Among women, the earnings differential had generally shrunk more dramatically. Black women surpassed the median pay of their white counterparts in clerical and private household jobs (although these white maids may be mainly Hispanic).

Blacks account for about 10 percent of the work force, but are woefully underrepresented in some occupations. They have no trouble being hired as hospital orderlies, cabbies, mail clerks, hotel maids and bus drivers. But only 3 percent of the nation's doctors and lawyers and less than 1 percent of the architects are black. So are only 2.5 percent of dental hygienists. A community college in the Bronx canceled its program in dental hygiene because too many graduates couldn't get jobs, a consequence, Andrew Hacker suggested, of whether white society will put its oratory about harmony where its mouth is. "While white patients seem willing to be cared for by black nurses," he wrote, "they apparently draw the line at having black fingers in their mouths."

The marginal narrowing of the income gap was measured before a recession that hit blacks disproportionately, particularly in the slumping steel and automobile manufacturing heartland of the Midwest. In Indiana, median income for whites eroded by 1 percent; for blacks it plunged by 16 percent. Comparable declines were recorded in Ohio, West Virginia, Indiana, Michigan, Wisconsin, Missouri and Minnesota. Of the ten states where the disparity in household income increased most, seven were in the Midwest.

But in California, Connecticut, Maryland, New Jersey, New York and Washington, gains in black household income actually outpaced those for whites. And in Queens, a mecca for New York City's middle class for a century, blacks like Winston St. Kitts, a thirty-eight-year-old subway car maintenance man who had emigrated from Guyana, found the American Dream. St. Kitts and families like the Grimsleys — a schoolteacher, an auditor, and their two children — and the Cooks — a retired nurse, a computer operator, and their three children — personified a startling statistic: The median income for black households in the borough had virtually matched that of white households. The statistical gains were tempered by caveats, of course. The growing population of Hispanic people tended to depress the income gains among all whites. Some wealthier whites had moved away during the decade. Many white households are composed of elderly people living alone. Also, black gains may have been a greater reflection of emigration from the Caribbean than of progress by American-born blacks. And those gains were achieved, in part, because in black households more people typically worked than in white ones. But all the caveats do not diminish the basic benchmark:

The median income of black households in Queens, adjusted for inflation, rose in a decade by 31 percent, compared to an increase of 19 percent for white households. Even more impressive than the rate was the result. In 1980, the census found that the black household median income was 9.5 percent less than it was for whites. By 1990, the disparity had shrunk to a statistically insignificant .2 percent.

Enormous political gains were recorded by blacks during the 1980s, generated, in part, by voter registration drives conducted in concert with the Reverend Jesse L. Jackson's two presidential campaigns and by congressional and legislative districts contrived to concentrate members of minority groups. Blacks had grown accustomed to voting for white candidates; the reverse has rarely been true. Los Angeles Mayor Tom Bradley was the most notable exception. But during the 1980s, voters in more and more places defied that tradition. Black candidates won the mayoralty of Seattle, Denver, Roanoke, New York, Tallahassee and Charlotte — all cities in which blacks constituted a third or less of the population. Waterbury, Connecticut, where fewer than one in twenty residents is black, sent a black Republican to Congress. And Virginia voters (including a minority of the whites) elevated L. Douglas Wilder to a national political presence as the nation's first black governor since Reconstruction and, briefly, as a presidential candidate whose race seemed largely incidental.

Spike Lee's film *Jungle Fever* may have made the rare interracial relationship only marginally more socially acceptable — it still "has not passed the 'no blink' test," according to Tom W. Smith, a University of Chicago researcher. But in the two decades since the Supreme Court overturned miscegenation laws in sixteen states, the number of marriages between blacks and whites tripled, to 211,000 in 1990. And, with the focus on Clarence Thomas's premarital erotic overtures, almost nobody blinked at the Supreme Court nominee's white wife.

Minority, wrote Gayle Pemberton, associate director of African-American Studies at Princeton, "is a word for statisticians, not a self-identification of victims." Whites are still so far ahead economically, socially and politically, though, that even when they become members of a minority, they rarely invoke the word *victim* to identify themselves. When was the last time a black bombed the office of a real estate agent who showed a house in a black neighborhood to a white? Nathan Glazer, who co-authored *Beyond the Melting Pot* with Daniel P. Moynihan, acknowledged years later that he had been laboring under a "New York illusion" when he wrote that blacks would escape the ghetto just as other ethnic and racial groups had. "Ethnic identity," Glazer concluded, "is pretty thin gruel compared to race."

William Julius Wilson has written that the standard designation "lower class" cannot capture "underclass" isolation from the mainstream. That isolation, some of it self-imposed, was manifested in Brooklyn when an altercation provoked a prolonged boycott by blacks of a greengrocery owned by Korean immigrants. Not far from the grocery, a video store was promoting the film *Do the Right Thing*, in which Spike Lee's screenplay had presciently captured the resentment behind the boycott.

"I bet you they haven't been off the boat a year before they open up their own place," says Coconut, one of the film's three black sidewalk philosophers who survey a Korean-owned market from beach chairs across the street. "They already have got a place in our neighborhood — a good business occupying a building that had been boarded up for longer than I care to remember." Must be, Coconut suggests, either because Koreans are geniuses or his black brethren aren't.

"It's got to be because we are black," says another character, M.L. "There ain't no other explanation."

To which Sweet Dick Willie replies: "Tired of hearing that old excuse."

A half century after the colonies declared their independence, Tocqueville drew a distinction between the legacy of slavery in ancient times, when master and slave could rarely be distinguished by physical characteristics, and the American version:

> There is a natural prejudice that prompts men to despise whoever has been their inferior long after he has become their equal; and the real inequality that is produced by fortune or by law is always succeeded by an imaginary inequality that is implanted in the manners of people. But among the ancients this secondary consequence of slavery had a natural limit; for the freedman bore so entire a resemblance to those born free that it soon became impossible to distinguish him from them.
>
> The greatest difficulty in antiquity was that of altering the law; among the moderns it is that of altering the customs, and as far as we are concerned, the real obstacles begin where those of the ancients left off . . . This arises from the circumstance that among the moderns the abstract and transient fact of slavery is fatally united with the physical and permanent fact of color.

Today, almost wherever Americans live, the physical and permanent fact of color seems chronically united with the concrete and intransigent fact of poverty.

CHAPTER VI

WHERE
WE LIVE

When Faith Whitaker and her husband built a weekend house nine miles southeast of Steelville, Missouri, in 1963, they were seeking a refuge from the bustle of suburban St. Louis. In 1991, their bucolic Ozarks retreat was transformed into a historical footnote: The Census Bureau declared that their densely wooded tract within the Mark Twain National Forest marked the nation's hypothetical center of population. It's the closest the point has ever been to the geographic center of the forty-eight contiguous states, near Lebanon, Kansas, and epitomizes a nation that is becoming as dispersed as it is diverse.

"My husband would've thought this was the neatest thing," said Mrs. Whitaker, a widow, who said she planned to plant a tree in his memory at the precise site.

The nation's official center of population is a device only a statistician could contrive: It marks the pivot at which a perfectly level map of the United States would balance if each resident weighed exactly the same. The mythical fulcrum is a mobile manifestation of mathematical constants that have defined the nation's internal migration since the first census two centuries ago. It is the temporary landfall of a nation in flux, a nation in which emerging regional agendas have rendered original political boundaries anachronistic. America is being transformed into a twenty-first-century Metropolis — not the city on the edge associated with Superman, but interdependent edge cities in adjacent suburbs where people not only live but work and on whose fringes new bedroom communities are sprouting. The 1970s' back-to-the-land rural spurt sputtered in the 1980s. More than half the population now lives in metropolitan areas with 1 million or more people. Within a few decades, half the population may live in the nation's metropolitan suburbs. The West overtook the Northeast in population. More than one in three Americans now lives in the South. One in five lives in the Northeast. As the 1990s began, though, America was on the cusp of what demographers call migration equilibrium. The West and South were attracting fewer people and exporting more; the Northeast and Midwest had cut their population losses.

If the Census Bureau's designation generated largely unwanted publicity and intrusive visits from strangers for Mrs. Whitaker, it produced a bonanza for Steelville, a fourth-class city, by Missouri standards, of 1,465 persons and the Crawford County seat. Steelville, ninety-five miles southwest of St. Louis, was named after a person, not a product. It had grown up around a gristmill early in the nineteenth century and thrived until the railroad to Little Rock and then Interstate 44 bypassed it. The 1990 census literally put Steelville back on the map. Several hundred people, including census officials and Miss Missouri State Fair, turned out on September 29, 1991, for the dedication of a brass surveyor's marker. Refreshments, courtesy of local banks, were served under a tent loaned by a local funeral home.

"We've been taking advantage of it," acknowledged Dennis Bell, a thirty-three-year-old machine shop operator and part-time mayor who lives by himself in the city in which he was born and raised. Steelville boosters ordered coffee cups that heralded the city's sudden fame. A half-dozen new businesses opened — mostly gift and craft shops that catered to tourists who rediscovered the virtues of canoeing and rafting on the Meramec River — and existing storefronts were remodeled to evoke the 1920s, when they were first built.

For most of America, the infatuation with Steelville was fleeting. But its designation by the Census Bureau signaled the inexorable shift of America's population and its state of mind westward and, just as relentlessly if less sharply, southward. Census enumerators placed the nation's population center in 1790 at Chestertown, Maryland, 23 miles east of Baltimore and not far from the nation's capital-to-be. As the population was tallied every decade, the center edged an average of 40 miles westward and three miles southward with the manifest inevitability of a tectonic plate. In 1980, two decades after the National League expansion made baseball bicoastal, the imaginary pivot breached the nation's historic continental divide of population, the Mississippi River — leaping from a soybean field near Mascoutah, Illinois, to the tiny city of De Soto in Jefferson County, Missouri, just south of St. Louis. The shift to Steelville took it another 39.5 miles southwest to a point more than 818 miles from where the center of population had first been plotted in 1790.

At the beginning of every decade for about a century, Census Bureau demographers have meticulously plotted the center of population (the decennial landfalls dating back to 1790 were charted retroactively) with increasingly sophisticated precision for a formula that presupposes each American weighs precisely the same. Generally, the population is grouped in "square degrees," the mass between consecutive parallels and meridians. Within those squares, demographers identify the "centroid," or the densest point. Once the individual centroids are plotted, the longitude and latitude of the nation's center is derived from a complex mathematical formula. In 1990, the Census Bureau computed the mean point at latitude 37 degrees, 52 minutes, and 20 seconds North and longitude 91 degrees, 12 minutes, and 55 seconds West. Then the bureau enlisted a sister agency, the National Geodetic Survey, which coupled the technology of its satellite mapping system with the scutwork of navigating a heavily rutted truck trail to within 20 yards of the precise spot on Mrs. Whitaker's property. Barring an unforeseen population explosion elsewhere in the country, the center is likely to remain in Missouri at least through the twenty-second census as it inches toward Arkansas or Oklahoma.

Human gravity concentrated in the growing metropolitan areas of the West and the South are exerting a formidable grip on the nation's population point and its politics. Tiny Steelville affirms the direction, but not the density. Gregarious Americans coagulated in clusters. That in 1990, for the first time, half the nation's population lived in the thirty-nine metropolises of 1 million or more persons is an even more staggering figure considering that the term *megalopolis* had been coined only three decades earlier and that as recently as 1950 million-plus metro areas contained only 30 percent of the population. Then, the only metropolitan areas with five million or more people were New York and Chicago, which together accounted for 12.2 percent of the nation's population. By 1990, the 5 million club had been joined by Los Angeles, San Francisco–Oakland–San Jose, and Philadelphia. Nearly one in four Americans now lives in one of those five giant metropolises. By 1993, three more qualified: Washington-Baltimore, Boston, and Detroit. Also, for the first time, three of every four Americans live in urban places, which make up only 2.5 percent of the nation's land mass. Those figures

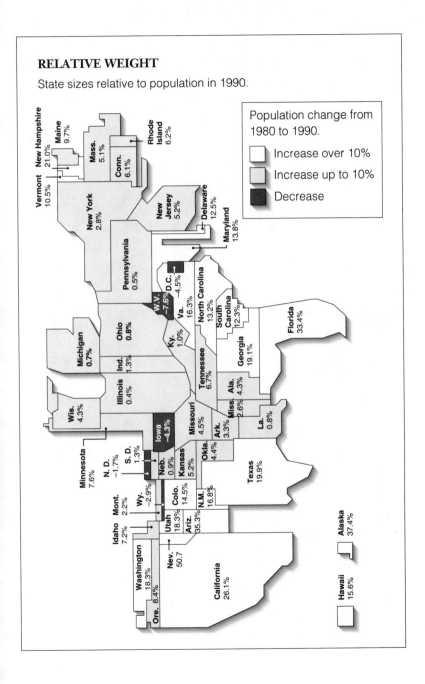

RELATIVE WEIGHT

State sizes relative to population in 1990.

Population change from 1980 to 1990.

☐ Increase over 10%
▨ Increase up to 10%
■ Decrease

New Hampshire 21.0%
Maine 9.7%
Vermont 10.5%
Mass. 5.1%
Conn. 6.1%
Rhode Island 6.2%
New York 2.8%
New Jersey 5.2%
Delaware 12.5%
Maryland 13.8%
Pennsylvania 0.5%
W.V. -7.6%
D.C. -4.5%
Va. 16.3%
North Carolina 13.2%
South Carolina 12.3%
Florida 33.4%
Michigan 0.7%
Ohio 0.8%
Ind. 1.3%
Ky. 1.0%
Tennessee 6.7%
Georgia 19.1%
Ala. 4.3%
Miss. 2.6%
La. 0.8%
Wis. 4.3%
Illinois 0.4%
Missouri 4.5%
Ark. 3.3%
Minnesota 7.6%
N.D. -1.7%
S.D. 1.3%
Iowa -4.3%
Neb. 0.9%
Kansas 5.2%
Okla. 4.4%
Texas 19.9%
Mont. 2.2%
Wy. -2.9%
Colo. 14.5%
N.M. 16.8%
Idaho 7.2%
Utah 18.3%
Ariz. 35.3%
Washington 18.3%
Nev. 50.7
California 26.1%
Ore. 8.4%
Alaska 37.4%
Hawaii 15.6%

NET MIGRATION'S WINNERS AND LOSERS

Percentage gain or loss in net migration
from 1980 to 1989.

Nevada	29.1%	Missouri	0.0%
Florida	26.2	Connecticut	−0.4
Arizona	19.5	Oklahoma	−0.5
New Hampshire	13.2	Minnesota	−0.6
California	12.4	Kansas	−0.6
Georgia	9.6%	Massachusetts	−1.0%
Alaska	8.9	Pennsylvania	−1.5
Texas	7.6	Utah	−1.9
Virginia	7.1	New York	−2.4
Washington	7.1	Wisconsin	−2.7
Delaware	6.6%	Idaho	−2.9%
North Carolina	6.0	Kentucky	−3.2
South Carolina	5.0	Mississippi	−3.3
New Mexico	4.8	Nebraska	−3.8
Vermont	4.7	Indiana	−3.8
Maryland	4.5%	South Dakota	−4.0%
Maine	4.0	Illinois	−4.4
Colorado	4.0	Ohio	−4.4
Hawaii	2.8	Louisiana	−5.4
Tennessee	2.7	Montana	−5.4
Rhode Island	1.8%	Michigan	−5.9%
Oregon	1.1	Iowa	−7.1
New Jersey	0.7	North Dakota	−7.3
Arkansas	0.5	West Virginia	−7.4
Alabama	0.2	District of Columbia	−9.4
		Wyoming	−11.0%

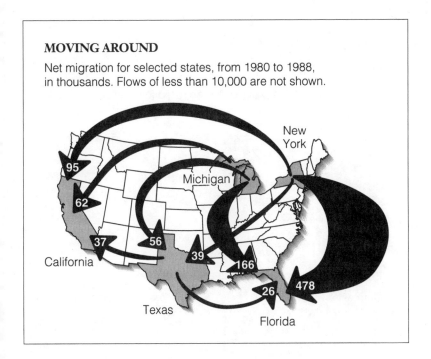

MOVING AROUND

Net migration for selected states, from 1980 to 1988, in thousands. Flows of less than 10,000 are not shown.

suggest an epochal change in the nation's culture. They have forced demographers to invent a new glossary of places that defy conventional categories and boundaries: exurbia, sub-suburbs, suburban cities, edge cities and strip cities. Apart from its commercial and cultural consequences, the change has potentially profound political implications. In 1990, more than half the population in fourteen states — including New Jersey, Maryland, Florida, Pennsylvania, Connecticut, California and Massachusetts — lived in the suburbs. The 1992 presidential election was the first in which voters in suburbia — putatively the province of wide lawns and narrow minds — constituted just about a majority of the electorate.

The first seismic migration of the twentieth century was from South to North. That exodus, coupled with the flood of

BAROMETERS OF CHANGE

Gain or loss between the 1980 census and the 1990 census.

MEDIAN HOUSEHOLD INCOME Adjusted for inflation

Greatest increases		Greatest decreases	
N.H.	+27.4%	Wyo.	−19.1%
Mass.	+25.5	W. Va.	−14.8
Conn.	+24.0	La.	−14.0
N.J.	+23.3	Wis.	−13.8
Me.	+20.3	Mont.	−11.1

POVERTY Percentage point change in rate

Greatest increases		Greatest decreases	
La.	+5.0%	Del.	−3.2%
W. Va.	+4.7	Vt.	−2.2
Wyo.	+4.0	Me.	−2.2
Mont.	+3.8	N.H.	−2.1
Tex.	+3.4	Ga.	−1.9

IMMIGRATION Population that came from another country

Largest influxes		Smallest influxes	
Calif.	+10.9%	Ky.	+0.4%
N.Y.	+6.6	S.D.	+0.4
Hawaii	+6.0	Miss.	+0.3
Fla.	+5.1	W. Va.	+0.2
N.J.	+5.0	Me.	+0.1

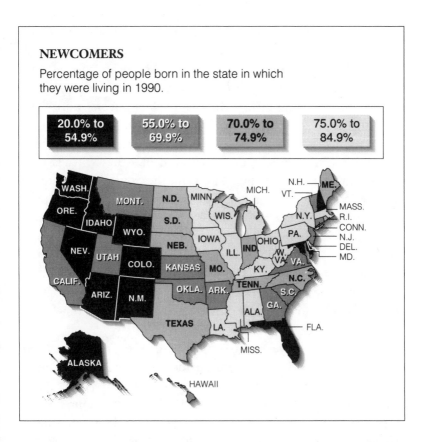

NEWCOMERS

Percentage of people born in the state in which they were living in 1990.

| 20.0% to 54.9% | 55.0% to 69.9% | 70.0% to 74.9% | 75.0% to 84.9% |

European immigrants to New York and other northern cities, was of such great proportions that the decennial congressional redistricting scheduled for 1920 was scrapped in an unprecedented power play by southern politicians (who managed, through the seniority system, to maintain their grip on Congress for decades until the South rose in population again). The shift from the South also heralded a rural decline that, except for the brief spurt in the 1970s, was reflected during every subsequent decade (although many rural counties gained again or stanched their losses as the 1990s began). Next, the most mobile city dwellers split for the suburbs, a phenomenon that accelerated in the 1980s. Meanwhile, the nation's population incessantly ranged West, which was home to one in twenty Americans in 1890 and more than one in five a century later. During the same period, the proportion living in the Midwest declined, from more than one-third to one-fourth; in the Northeast from more than one-fourth to one-fifth. During the second half of the twentieth century, the United States grew by 64 percent – the Northeast by 29 percent, the Midwest by 34 percent, the South by 81 percent and the West by 170 percent. The upheaval transformed a proportional map of the nation drawn on the basis of population into a mutated, bottom-heavy caricature anchored by California and Florida. The nation's earliest settlements were along the Atlantic coast, and nearly 1 in 4 Americans still lives in counties that border the Atlantic Ocean. Since 1960, though, counties on the Pacific Ocean and Gulf of Mexico have grown faster. In all, 54 percent of Americans live in coastal counties.

Two hundred years ago, only 5 percent of Americans lived in urban places, which the census defined as having 2,500 or more people. There were just twenty-four of them in 1790, led by New York City with a population of 49,401. That definition endured until 1950, when the Census Bureau, acknowledging the suburban explosion after the Second World War, classified urban areas as cities and their contiguous fringes within which at least 1,000 persons live per square mile. The conglomerated city and suburbs need at least 50,000 people to qualify as an urban area. The total urban population lives in densely populated areas and places of 2,500 or more people outside urbanized areas.

When the twentieth century started, metropolitan areas accounted for one fourth of the nation's population, with 19.7 percent in the cities themselves. Rural residents became a minority of the population in 1920 and the nation has grown even more urban with every census. By 1990, urban Americans accounted for more than twice the share of the nation's population than they had in 1890 (and only 7 percent of the rural households live on farms). The cities' share peaked at 32.8 percent in 1950 — swollen by an influx of blacks from the South. But the megalopolises grew. In 1950, five cities had 1 million or more people. By 1990 the eight-city 1 million club included two new members — Dallas, which grew 11.3 percent during the decade, and San Diego, whose population soared by 26.8 percent. The suburban proportion expanded during every decade, beginning at 5.8 percent in 1900, quadrupling to 23.3 percent by 1950 and doubling to 46.2 percent by 1990. Since 1940, the suburbs have accounted for more population growth than the central cities. Between 1989 and 1990 alone, net migration to the nation's metropolitan areas totaled 1.5 million, but only because while the central cities lost 2 million residents, the suburbs gained more than 3.5 million. Nearly four in five Americans live in metro areas.

During the 1970s, the urban population registered the smallest percentage gain in the nation's history (the change was smaller only once, when it declined to 7.2 percent in the 1810s). In the 1980s the proportion rose from 73.7 percent to 75.2 percent — boosted by gains in North Carolina and North Dakota where, for the first time, urbanites became a majority. The West has emerged as the nation's most urbanized region, followed by the Northeast, the Midwest and the South. In California, New Jersey and Rhode Island, nine in ten residents lived in an urban place in 1990. (New York is now tied with Massachusetts for tenth place, after California, New Jersey, Rhode Island, Hawaii, Utah, Arizona, Nevada, Illinois and Florida.) Vermont remains the most rural state, with nearly seven in ten residents still living in rural areas. But it, too, is no longer pristine. In 1980, Burlington became the first place in Vermont to qualify as a metropolitan area, a mixed blessing as the decade unfolded and growth was accompanied by a taste of drugs and violence. "It's been a loss of innocence for the community," Mayor Peter Clavelle said after a drug-related murder in 1992.

Other places lost more than innocence in the 1980s. More than 45 percent of the nation's 3,141 counties or equivalent jurisdictions (e.g., parishes in Louisiana, boroughs in Alaska) lost population, most of them in the Midwest. In New York's Erie County, a Great Lakes notch in the Rust Belt that is more Midwest than Northeast, the population declined by only 4.6 percent, but it was the only county in the country to be bounced from the 1 million club during the decade. Nine other counties lost fully 25 percent or more of their population — nearly all in states dependent on mining and energy. Two counties, Platte in Wyoming and Lake in Colorado, lost nearly one third of their residents. Meanwhile, eight counties more than doubled in population, including three each in Florida and Georgia. Flagler, north of Daytona Beach, exploded by 163 percent to 29,000. Douglas, a Denver suburb, ballooned by 140 percent to 60,000. The number of counties with 1 million people or more expanded by six during the decade — five of them in California or Texas.

The greatest population surge occurred in metropolitan areas. During the 1980s, metropolitan areas accounted for fully 90 percent of the nation's growth and even that figure probably is understated. Their population soared by nearly 20 million, or 11.6 percent — outpacing the national increase of 9.8 percent and careening past nonmetropolitan areas, where the population rose by only 3.9 percent. The 1990 census found 39 metropolitan areas with 1 million or more people, four more (Charlotte, North Carolina; Salt Lake City, Utah; Orlando, Florida; and Rochester, New York) than in 1980 and nearly three times as many as in 1950. Punta Gorda, Florida, which nearly doubled in population during the decade, was one of nine Florida places among the nation's ten fastest growing metropolitan areas; fifth on the list was Las Vegas. Some cities, like Colorado Springs and Albuquerque, gobbled up their borderlands to become cities without suburbs. Other metropolitan areas, like Vallejo-Fairfield-Napa in California, developed largely without traditional central cities at all. In both those hybrids, argues David Rusk, a former mayor of Albuquerque, economic and racial segregation is significantly lower than in older metropolitan areas where the central city implodes as wealth migrates to the suburbs.

"To suggest that growth in metropolitan areas means urban growth is misleading," John Herbers, a former *New York Times* reporter, cautions. "Almost everywhere in the United States the story of population growth in the 1970s and '80s was one of deconcentration and the emergence of development that is not urban, rural or suburban in the sense most people understand those terms but in a combination of all three." He detected a new phenomenon, which he hailed as a politically amorphous "new heartland": from southern New Hampshire, where workers in new industries live in semirural settings around old town centers, to southern New Jersey retirement and recreation communities, to North Carolina, where the population has dispersed from urban concentrations, to the frontiers between big cities in Texas, Arizona and New Mexico.

New York's consolidated metropolitan area, easily the nation's largest, with more than 18 million people, sprawls almost 150 miles south from Danbury, Connecticut, nearly to Atlantic City, New Jersey, and 200 miles west from Montauk Point on Long Island to the Pennsylvania border — an unincorporated but interdependent mass about the size of Delaware. (The Census Bureau's proposed New York Primary Metropolitan Statistical Area encompassed counties in three states, not counting Connecticut.) Greater Los Angeles, swarming with 14.5 million people, ranges from Long Beach inland to San Bernardino. Metropolitan San Francisco lunges halfway across California. Within those metropolitan areas are satellite cities that defy the traditional view of what, for better or worse, a city is supposed to look like. Nor are vast reaches beyond the central city characteristically suburban. Of all the people whom the census identified as living in urban places, fewer than half live in central cities anymore (the suburbs having surpassed their central cities in population since 1970).

During the 1980s, fifteen states recorded a decline in the population of their central cities. And central cities grew faster than their suburbs in only four of the thirty-nine metropolitan areas with 1 million or more people: New York, which reclaimed its historic place as a mecca for immigrants; and Portland, Oregon; Columbus and Charlotte, which augmented growth not by an indigenous surge but by annexing booming suburbs. New York, too, was being sapped by its satellites, but the city stanched its population loss during the 1980s. Reversing a decade of decline, New York recorded a gain of more than a quarter million people — the first time since 1950 that the population of all five of the city's boroughs had registered an increase. Immigration and the growth of service industry jobs accounted for most of the gain — just as earlier waves of refugees and job seekers had been enticed to make their fortunes in the nation's big cities for nearly a century. Among the nation's older cities, though, New York and a few of its neighbors, like Elizabeth and Jersey City, were the exceptions. Bright lights were burning brighter in newer cities that were getting bigger. Six of the nation's ten largest now are west of the Mississippi. In the 1980s Dallas and San Diego recorded their one-millionth residents; San Antonio and Phoenix came close. Most of the twenty-nine cities that topped 100,000 residents for the first time during the last decade were in California, including Rancho Cucamonga, a Los Angeles suburb, which grew by nearly 84 percent to 101,409 people — the second highest growth rate of any city in the nation. Chicago, America's second city since it overtook Philadelphia in 1890, dropped below 3 million people for the first time since the 1930 census and fell to third-ranked behind the ascending Los Angeles, which had gained a half million residents. Houston nudged ahead of Philadelphia to become fourth. San Diego gained the same percentage, 26 percent, that Gary lost, and brashly swaggered into sixth place—ahead of Detroit, which, until a recount, was poised to become the first city in the country to have reached and then relinquished the million-person mark as earlier white flight was followed by the wholesale departure of the most mobile blacks. Detroit contested only the degree of the decline, not the direction. The once muscular city that became synonymous with America's automobile manufacturing might—and, ironically, with its mobility—was shrinking into a ghost town. Since 1950, Detroit has lost nearly half its population—a number equivalent to the entire population of Phoenix—while its suburbs thrived. In the 1980s alone, the population of Rochester Hills rose by half, Novi's by a third. Detroit's losses were the most dramatic— indeed, proportionately the highest of any of the top ten cities and nearly large enough to cost Detroit ninth place to San Antonio.

Except for New Orleans, which straddles the river, the most pronounced losses among America's cities were suffered east of the Mississippi. Even Atlanta's revival fell victim to suburban competition. ("Areas that in Houston are in the city limits," said Census Bureau demographer Richard Forstall, "in Atlanta are in the suburbs.") But the prognosis for central cities in the West was not much healthier. Phoenix, which grew 24 percent in the 1980s as a result of spillover from nearby Scottsdale and Tempe, was itself outpaced by its suburbs, which mushroomed by 40 percent. The fastest growing city in the United States during the 1980s was Mesa, Arizona, which ballooned by 89 percent to 288,091—reaping the reflected glory of neighboring Phoenix as Phoenix itself had done from its neighbors. Mesa's self-promotion as a haven with no property tax appeared destined to be short-lived if Mayor Peggy Rubach, a New York expatriate, progressed toward her seemingly incongruous goal: "We want to operate as a big city but have a small-town feel," she said. Despite a growth rate during the decade of 15 percent, Los Angeles' share of the regional population shrank from 18 percent to less than 12 percent because its suburbs were growing even faster.

"The suburbs," said geographer Peter Muller, "are no longer sub to the urb."

The word *suburb*, which originally referred to the less desirable land below a walled hilltop town, is rooted in Old English. In the fourteenth century, Chaucer invoked it to describe the outskirts of Canterbury. In the nineteenth century, Nathaniel Parker Willis complained: "There is a suburban look and character about all the villages on the Hudson which seem out of place among such scenery. They are suburbs; in fact, steam has destroyed the difference between them and the city." Amazingly, though, in 1990 the word *suburb* was not in the formal lexicon of the census questionnaire, or of its official glossary (even *sex* was, as a synonym for *gender*).

Nor was suburban America high on the Democratic party's agenda until the 1980s, when debilitating social and economic characteristics traditionally associated with cities began to intrude on suburban sanctuaries and political alignments blurred. In 1988, Michael S. Dukakis got more votes in the suburbs east of the Mississippi than in their cities, compared to Walter F. Mondale, the Democratic nominee four years earlier. Bill Clinton was the first Democrat in nearly three decades — since another southerner, Lyndon B. Johnson, ran in 1964 — to win a plurality among whites. Segregating black and Hispanic voters to comply with the Federal Voting Rights Act and population losses in white neighborhoods forced state legislatures to reconfigure outlying districts, a cartographical exercise that further eroded the political clout of the cities and of their effort to place urban problems on the national agenda. Big-city Democrats suddenly inherited suburban constituencies. Two of Philadelphia's three districts were stretched into the suburbs. In Ohio, after Representative Marcy Kaptur's Toledo district was recast to encompass the state's northwestern agricultural communities, she bowed to political reality by milking a cow in public for the first time. In California, the state's third most powerful official — Democratic

State Senator David A. Roberti — metamorphosed from an urban liberal to a suburban law-and-order moderate after Hollywood was excised from his district. Struggling for political survival, he rented a house in the San Fernando Valley and ran for a vacant senate seat on a platform that demonstrated his resiliency: He proposed legislation to contain street gangs that threatened from just over the hills in Los Angeles.

Single adults, even gay couples, may be finding the suburbs more hospitable, but one other group still largely has not. The percentage of blacks in northern Fulton County, adjoining Atlanta, more than doubled, but to a mere 5 percent. In Texas, nearly nine in ten students in Plano's public schools are white, while in Dallas, for the first time, a majority of the city's student population is now black or Hispanic. Suburban growth has further bifurcated Americans by race and by class — leaving the older cities, and some newer ones, increasingly as bedroom communities for poor blacks who lack the skills or the jobs to survive without government subsidies. They have defied the American tradition of workers following employment opportunities, which is just fine with many suburbanites who fear that even teenagers bused in by McDonald's to service suburban franchises will bring with them the cities' antisocial culture. "Throughout our history spatial mobility and economic mobility have gone hand in hand," said John Kasarda of the University of North Carolina. "Now for the first time that connection has been broken."

Suburbs that escaped annexation became home to edge cities, a phenomenon exemplified by Stamford, Connecticut, and Tysons Corner, Virginia, and scores of places like them, where first retailers and finally jobs followed the homes that were the vanguard of the evolving metropolis. Peachtree City, outside Atlanta, exploded from 800 people in 1970 to more than 19,000 two decades later as nearby Hartsfield-Atlanta International Airport emerged as a regional hub. Plano, Texas, ballooned from 17,900 in 1970 to 128,700 in 1990 as the boom in neighboring Dallas–Fort Worth began to cool.

Plano is headquarters for Frito-Lay, Electronic Data Systems, and J. C. Penney, which abandoned midtown Manhattan for an office campus in the Legacy Park development.

Just what the legacy of edge cities will be is arguable. They are hybrids, still evolving and searching for the synergy that fires their bigger progenitors and that seems contrived in a stark atrium. Electronic mail and videophones still are no substitute for the urban streetscape's vibrant forum. In an earlier incarnation, mutant urban embryos were described as "a hundred thousand shapes and substances of incompleteness, wildly mingled out of their places, upside down, burrowing in the earth, aspiring in the earth, moldering in the water, and unintelligible as in any dream." If that vision evokes the mall of some commercial complex, it was also Charles Dickens' description of London in 1848. It represents what Joel Garreau, who coined the term, describes as the single best definition of an edge city. "This is no longer sprawl," Donald A. Hicks, a political economist at the University of Texas, suggested in a more contemporary description. "These suburban clusters are even more tightly integrated and specialized economically than the core cities used to be, and in the 1980s they became the new salt licks for population growth."

Traditional cities were typified by a hub that extended its spokes into concentric rings of bedroom suburbs. They largely housed commuters. Contemporary megalopolises include core cities that grow runners along the ground. Like plants, they send out stolons that reproduce themselves in every direction and become decreasingly dependent on their original sources of sustenance. Today, many central cities, says John Kasarda, have become like the "hole in the doughnut" — an ambiguous simile that could imply either emptiness or a custard-filled core flanked by fluff.

Metropolitan New York is growing faster at its fringes than in the traditional bedroom suburbs that adjoin it. The pattern has alarmed planners. They capsulize their concern in two words: Los Angeles. In Goshen, the county seat of Orange in the Hudson Valley, the John Deere dealership that depended on sales of hay balers and other farm equipment a few years ago now sells mostly lawn mowers and snow blowers. In northern Fairfield County, Connecticut, Monroe, which grew by 20 percent in the 1980s to 16,896, was girding for the unofficial but authentic certification that a critical mass of population had been achieved: its first McDonald's franchise. Eighteen counties that were home to 80 percent of the New York region's population gained about 320,000 people, or 2 percent. Nassau and Bergen counties actually lost 54,000 people in the last decade. But thirteen counties that comprise metropolitan New York's outer fringe — from Sullivan in New York to Litchfield in northeastern Connecticut to Monmouth and Ocean in central New Jersey — grew by 332,434, or 13 percent. The number of passengers traveling through oversaturated Kennedy, La Guardia and Newark airports declined during the late 1980s, but more than doubled at exurban alternatives like Long Island's MacArthur Airport and the airport in Atlantic City. Similar gains were recorded in largely rural fringes like Worcester County, west of Boston; Riverside and San Bernardino counties, east of Los Angeles; and Snohomish County, north of Seattle. When the 1980s ended, though, only in the Northeast was the nonmetropolitan growth rate higher than the pace in the region's metropolises.

Population growth is only one measure of economic vitality — and not always a valid one. To preservationists (loosely defined as people whose living-room view would be blocked by development), growth conjures up images of a wart rather than a windfall. But even Seattle's fierce no-growth orthodoxy was challenged in 1992. The city's mayor proposed creation of a series of "urban villages" on vacant or abandoned parcels of land if the surrounding suburbs would agree to maintain a buffer of parks between Seattle and the adjoining metropolitan area, which expanded by 500,000 people to nearly 2 million during the 1980s. To Seattle, even San Francisco, a dream city to many Americans, is anathema; Seattle's idol is Vancouver, 120 miles north, which halted development in the agriculturally rich Fraser Valley and encouraged construction of new housing in the city center.

Unbridled growth has transformed some suburbs into vapid places or infused them with just the sort of vibrance that many suburbanites left the city to escape. Downtown White Plains in Westchester was, with Stamford, Connecticut, and New Brunswick, New Jersey, among the first satellite cities to redefine the familiar low-rise suburban silhouette. It bulldozed so much of its old downtown for office development that not a single movie theater was left to lure stragglers after five P.M. "What attracts people most is other people," William H. Whyte, the urban anthropologist, has written, and that premise is the tenuous rationale for the survival of traditional cities. He warned, though: "Even within the city, suburbia is winning. Now coming of age is a whole new generation of planners and architects for whom the formative experience of a center was the atrium of a suburban shopping mall." Invoking the agora of ancient Greece, he concluded: "The city has been losing those functions for which it is no longer competitive. Manufacturing has moved toward the periphery; the back offices are on the way. The computers are already there. But as the city has been losing functions it has been reasserting its most ancient one: a place where people come together, face-to-face."

Dallas–Fort Worth now includes five suburbs with 100,000 people or more. Among the ten major cities that recorded the greatest growth, eight are on the edge of an even bigger urban area, generally Los Angeles. The other two—Bakersfield and Fresno—absorbed the runoff from Los Angeles and San Francisco. Two of the cities that topped 100,000 during the decade had not even been incorporated in 1980: Moreno Valley and Santa Clarita, both in California. They exemplify an exurban phenomenon: City dwellers bypass the suburbs altogether and suburbanites fed up with congestion and higher taxes escape once again to a glady utopia. Their transitory utopia is either within commuting distance of the jobs that followed people from the cities to the suburbs or is far enough away from the central cities for older people to enjoy hassle-free retirement.

Strip cities are the newest urban life-form. Their name is not necessarily a reflection of declining morality. Rather, it distinguishes an elongated edge city, usually defined by a single road on which most of its economic lifeblood courses. Strip cities were initially a product of commercial spontaneous generation. Now, they are being elevated into recognized political subdivisions. "I can drive down I-85 with both car doors open and hit every person in the district," said Mickey Michaux, a former United States Attorney who was vying for the Democratic nomination for Congress in 1992 in North Carolina's new 12th District. The district snakes 160 miles along the interstate, creating a narrow corridor that, to comply with federal voting rights imperatives by creating a contrived black voting majority, connects portions of Durham, Greensboro and Winston-Salem with a chunk of Charlotte one hundred miles south to pump up the volume for an eclectic if potentially powerful urban voice. The ten-county belt also includes the headquarters of the state's major banks and insurance companies, six historically black colleges and part of the Research Triangle corporate complex—nearly conforming to one Census Bureau formula for growth: "You get one star if you have a state capital, two if you have a college or university and three if there's a major medical center there," said John Connally, an assistant director of the bureau. In 1992, the 12th District, and another new one, elected the first blacks to Congress from North Carolina in this century.

Castle Rock, Colorado, meets none of that formula's criteria but is burgeoning nonetheless. Demographers call it a nonmetropolitan adjacent community. But it is, for lack of a better name, a sub-suburb in Douglas County. Castle Rock's population jumped in the decade by 140 percent — second only to Flagler County in Florida. An hour from Denver by car, Castle Rock typifies another phenomenon of urban sprawl. "The concept of suburban is almost becoming outmoded," said Carl Haub, a demographer with the Population Reference Bureau, "since they have become such large employment centers and that has allowed people to push farther out into rural regions." In New York City, 92 percent of the adults work within the five boroughs, which also means that another 250,000 residents of New York City commute to work elsewhere. In adjacent Westchester, which is synonymous with suburbia, fully 65 percent of the adults now work in the county in which they live. In Long Island's Suffolk County, 72 percent do.

The four states that lost population during the 1980s shared a common denominator: They were either victims of the bust in energy production or had a high proportion of rural residents, or both. West Virginia suffered the largest loss (7.6 percent), followed by Iowa (4.3 percent), Wyoming (2.9 percent), and North Dakota (1.7 percent). Searing droughts drove farmers from the grain fields of Iowa and North Dakota; declining demand for coal cost Wyoming and the Appalachian region population.

Nevada, Alaska and Idaho logged the greatest proportional gains of any state, but there was no competition with the Big Enchilada. One in nine Americans now lives in California, which, with Florida and Texas, accounted for more than half the growth of the nation's population during the 1980s. California expanded by 5.6 million people, or nearly the entire population of Massachusetts. Its population is now bigger than Canada's. In sheer numbers, California, which accounted for only 2 percent of the nation's population a century ago, has achieved the political dominance that New York wielded beginning in the first half of the nineteenth century, when the Empire State claimed one in seven

Americans (the last New Yorker elected president was Franklin D. Roosevelt in 1944; the first Californian, a transplanted one, was Richard M. Nixon in 1968). But the golden bubble, while far from bursting, is beginning to stretch perilously thin in places as California ponders the impact of recession, riots, droughts and tremors that have provoked pause for rare self-doubt in a state that Remi Nadeau mythologized three decades earlier as a "secular Kingdom Come." Defense industry economies, the commercial maturation of Silicon Valley, and the influx of illegal aliens from Mexico were all blamed for a malaise that manifested itself in unfathomable gaps in the state budget and a growing deficit of potable water and unpolluted air. "Thank God for the earthquakes and the fire — maybe it will help keep people from moving here," said Corky Matthews, a native Californian who fears that the lifestyle that became synonymous with the state is being threatened by a declining economy and a deteriorating environment.

They do keep moving there, but maybe more slowly. California, the Census Bureau says, may be "moving into migration equilibrium" with the rest of the nation. Between 1987 and 1988, the state plummeted from seventh in net migration to forty-seventh — still finishing the 1980s in a respectable fifth place, but, perhaps, signaling that America's migration westward — and to California in particular — was slackening. During the last half of the 1980's, three times as many people moved from California to Montana, Idaho, Utah, Arizona, Nevada, Washington and Oregon as arrived in California during an entire generation in the Great Migration of the mid-nineteenth century on the Oregon Trail. Another one fourth of the nation's increase was concentrated in eight other states — Arizona, Colorado, Georgia, Maryland, Nevada, North Carolina, Virginia and Washington. Florida leapfrogged over Ohio, Illinois and Pennsylvania to claim the rank of fourth largest.

Arguably, states outlived their rationale long ago. They exist today largely as political contrivances, neat receptacles for statistics and fonts of shrinking chauvinism. But they rarely define economic, social or political values to the extent that broader regions do. Joel Garreau makes a compelling case that North America can be better understood as a conglomerate of nine nations: New England; the Foundry, stretching west from the Middle Atlantic; Dixie; the islands of the Caribbean; the Midwest breadbasket; MexAmerica, including Texas and southern California; Ecotopia, along the Pacific Coast; the mineral-rich Empty Quarter, which stretches from the Mountain States into Canada and Alaska; and Quebec. Regional perspective also helps explain the political realignment that produced a Democratic ticket in 1992 headed by two southerners. Of the eight states that gained congressional representation, all are in the South or West. California alone picked up seven seats, boosting its delegation to fifty-two, or as many congressmen as New York and Pennsylvania have combined (and the first time any state cornered more than 12 percent of Congress since New York in 1860). Florida gained four and Texas three to grow to within one seat of the New York delegation, which shrank by three members to thirty-one. Of the thirteen states that gave up congressmen, all but four are in the Northeast and the Midwest. The West and South gained fifteen seats lost by the Northeast and Midwest.

Much of the realignment results from restlessness. Since 1960, nine in ten American households packed up for another home. Interest rates, housing costs and recessions have caused the rate to fluctuate since 1948, when the census first measured mobility and one in five Americans moved annually. The rate has generally declined since then. And, barring a postrecession spurt, the relatively stable population of couch potatoes may increase because the proportion of prime movers — people in their twenties and thirties — is smaller than in any period recorded by the Census Bureau. When the 1990s began, about one in six Americans, or more than 40 million people, moved from one residence to another in any single year. Of those, only about one in six moved to another state.

Incredibly, nearly half the people in the United States said they had moved from one home to another in the last half of the 1980s alone. That degree of mobility is unique in the developed world. Most people moved within their community or metropolitan area. The West, where more people have moved from other parts of the country, was the most mobile region, if for no other reason than its residents were used to moving. About one in four westerners pulled up stakes in the closing year of the decade, compared to about one in five in the South, one in six in the Midwest and one in ten in the Northeast. Renters—who are disproportionately young, black or Hispanic—were nearly five times more likely to move than homeowners.

Where did they go? Most moves were within the same county. The South was the destination of choice for people from other regions—from the Northeast and the Midwest, in particular, whose residents gravitated mostly to the Atlantic seaboard from Maryland to Florida. Net migration was the major impetus for population change in California, Florida, Texas, Arizona, Nevada and New Hampshire. Net outmigration accounted for Iowa's losses. A Census Bureau study of movement within the United States—exclusive of immigration—found that Florida grew as a result of three times the net migration as the second-ranked state, Georgia. New York lost twice as many people to migration as the second biggest loser, Illinois.

Proportionately fewer people followed Horace Greeley's advice in the 1980s than in the last century. From New York, the farthest west many got was New Jersey. From the Northeast, 1.6 million people moved south—five times the number who went west. The disparity was smaller from the Midwest, where 1.7 million surged to the south and another 920,000 headed west. Every year, more than 65,000 New Yorkers moved to Florida—

or, over the entire decade, a number equivalent to the combined 1990 population of Albany, Buffalo and Rochester. Sections of the Sunshine State were transformed into distant suburbs of New York. The New York-to-Florida flow was the largest between two states every year except in 1985, when New Jersey absorbed more expatriate New Yorkers than Florida did. Florida, California and Texas actually lost more residents to neighboring states than they attracted from those states — suggesting, again, that states like Georgia and Nevada were absorbing spillover from the magnet states. Still, Nevada would have been first in the rate of net migration even without the influx of Californians, who accounted for one third of that migration. Between 1980 and 1990, the Northeast and Midwest would have lost population without the influx of immigrants from abroad. The South drew the greatest number of people from other parts of the country, but was edged out by the West in net migration when immigrants were counted.

More than half the residents in each of eight states were born in some other state. In Nevada, more than three fourths were. In Pennsylvania, Louisiana, New York, Iowa and Wisconsin, though, fully four fifths of the residents were born in the state in which they now live. Fully two thirds of the people who lived in the nation's metropolitan areas were born there (and only half of all metropolites were living in the same house for more than five years). The percentage of people born in the state where they now live was highest in the Northeast and Midwest — 87 percent in Pittsburgh, 73 percent in Detroit, 72 percent in New York and Boston. It was lowest in Washington, D.C., where fewer than a third of the residents were born in the place where they now lived. In Phoenix, 33 percent were; in Miami, 38 percent.

Even with the migration, differentials in population density among regions remain stark. Nationwide, the United States has 70.3 persons per square mile, still not very dense, but much more crowded than the 4.5 persons per square mile recorded within much narrower boundaries in 1790, 17.8 a century later, 37.2 in 1940, and 64 in 1980. (A suburban tract with one-acre zoning and three people per house would accommodate more than 1,800 people per square mile.) The Northeast is home to 313 persons per square mile, compared to 98 in the South, 79 in the Midwest, and only 30 in the West. New Jersey is the most congested state, with 1,042 persons per square mile. Rhode Island is second, with 960.3. New York, with 381, trails well behind Massachusetts and Connecticut. Alaska is the most sparsely populated; if its people were spread evenly across the state's 570,000 square miles, a resident would be fully a mile from his nearest neighbor. Florida, which had only 91.5 people per square mile in 1960, more than doubled its density to 239.6 three decades later. In California, density nearly doubled during the same period, from 100.4 to 190.8. The densest central city in the United States is Hoboken, the blue-collar Hudson River hometown of Frank Sinatra — and also of the horticulturist who introduced the chrysanthemum to America. Rediscovered by single people and young families priced out of Manhattan, Hoboken is home to 25,690 people per square mile — edging out New York City, with 23,705.3. Both cities are about double the density of Boston, Chicago and Miami Beach, more than three times as crowded as Los Angeles and eight times more dense than Houston, which encompasses more than ten times the land area of Boston.

The nation's population density has increased for still another reason: The United States is shrinking. Collectively, the expanse of land and water is the largest ever. But officially, the nation's land mass — 3,536,342 square miles — is the smallest in well over a century, since before the purchase of Alaska. The census now measures bodies of water more precisely and subtracts their mass from land area. Until 1990, lakes and ponds were counted as water only if they covered at least forty acres. To qualify, streams and rivers had to be at least one eighth of a mile wide. In 1990, a computerized hydrographic analysis allowed the Census Bureau to identify and reclassify smaller bodies of water, including reservoirs (but not all those suburban swimming pools). Another reason for America's declining land mass is more ominous, though: coastal erosion. "They're tryin' to wash us away," Randy Newman warned in his mournful ballad "Louisiana." That is precisely what has happened where bayous course through parishes that are partly below sea level. In 1970, Louisiana's land area was 49,000 square miles. By 1990, it had contracted to 44,500.

America, where everyone came from someplace else, has always been a nation of shallow roots. "An American will build a house in which to pass his old age and sell it before the roof is on; he will plant a garden and rent it just as the trees are coming into bearing," Tocqueville wrote. Americans "broke the ties of attachment to their native soil long ago, and have not formed new ones since," he added, concluding that their "restless spirit, immoderate desire for wealth, and an extreme love of independence" contributed to the stability of the United States compared to more developed European nations. A century and a half later, those emotions still fire America's soul, but have become prone to overheating. "Without such restless passions," Tocqueville wrote, "the population would be concentrated around a few places and would soon experience, as we do, needs which are hard to satisfy."

CHAPTER VII

WHERE
WE DREAM

I f home ownership epitomizes the American Dream, the 1980s
was a particularly fitful decade. For the first time, the nation's
inventory of houses and apartments topped 100 million. But
the goal of owning one of them became increasingly elusive
for young married couples. The fastest growing category of housing was prisons. More than 1 in 250 Americans are housed in a
correctional facility — twice the number living in military housing
in the United States and the highest incarceration rate in the
world. The second fastest growing category during the decade
was mobile homes, which have been emblematic of life at the
margins of American society — geographically, economically and
culturally. The number of mobile homes grew by 60 percent to
comprise more than one in seven of the nation's residences.

Of the nation's 102,263,678 housing units in 1990, 59 million were occupied by their owners; 33 million were rented. As of April 1, Census Day, another 3.3 million Americans lived in what the Census Bureau calls group quarters, which include rooming houses, college dormitories, convents and homes for unwed mothers. And 3.3 million were institutionalized. More Americans lived in college dormitories (1,953,558) and nursing homes (1,772,032) in 1990 than in the nation's jails and prisons, but not many more. In the West, in fact, the census found more prison inmates than college dormitory residents and as many inmates as nursing home patients. In 1990, the average number incarcerated was 1,115,111, or more than the total population of nine states. Fifty years ago, about half as many people were in mental institutions as in prisons. By 1990, advances in pharmacology and civil liberties had virtually emptied mental hospitals; the prison population more than quadrupled. During the 1980s, the nation's overall population grew by 10 percent. Prison occupancy more than doubled. As a consequence, in part, of the changing role of mental hospitals, another housing category registered alarming gains: Americans without their own homes altogether. The 1990 census sought to quantify the homeless for the first time. Counting them was problematic, but there were too many to ignore. The homeless had evolved over the decade into a fixture of the urban streetscape and the nation's most visible symbol of poverty, despair and desperation.

For Americans who do have a permanent place to live, single-family homes continue to predominate. Two thirds of Americans live in them. California alone has 6 million detached single-family houses. Among people who own their homes, the proportion is even higher — 87 percent live in single-family homes, compared to 7 percent who own their mobile homes and 6 percent who own their apartments. Even among renters, one third lives in single-family homes. Generally, the biggest single-family and mobile homes were in the Northeast, where the median size is 2,104 square feet, compared to the national median of 1,688 square feet. New homes are getting bigger. The average size increased 21 percent during the decade, from 1,720 square feet to 2,080, even as the average number of children declined. If many Americans have their heads in the clouds, they still prefer to keep their feet near the ground. The Northeast claimed the biggest share of housing in buildings with four or more stories. But, even there, the proportion was 23 percent, compared with 9 percent in the West, 7 percent in the Midwest and 5 percent in the South. Among owner-occupied housing, the mean number of rooms ranged from 4.4 in Hawaii to 6 in Maryland. The nationwide mean was 6.2. In Miami Beach, the mean was only 2.8; it was 7 or more rooms in suburban Norwalk, Connecticut; Bryan–College Station, Texas; Logan, Utah; and the fringes of Vacaville, California, and Stamford, Connecticut. Rented homes and apartments had a mean 4.1 rooms.

The number of persons per unit — a measurement of crowding — ranged from 1.77 in Miami Beach to 4.3 in the New Mexico portion of metropolitan El Paso and to 5 in Slidell, Louisiana. Housing with more than 1 person per room is usually defined as crowded. Nationwide, the proportion of those units rose from 4.5 percent in 1980 to 4.9 percent in 1990. That was 40 percent below the 1970 level, but was the first increase recorded since the Census of Housing began fifty years ago, when it was 20 percent overall. Among families with children, the share in which density exceeded 1 person per room reached 12 percent in apartments or houses rented by married couples and as much as 38 percent among Hispanic families living in rented quarters.

Collectively, all of the houses and apartments in the United States are younger than the people who live in them. For the past fifty years, the median age of housing occupied year-round has fluctuated between twenty-three and twenty-eight years. In 1990, the median was twenty-six years. Nearly eight in ten houses or apartments were built during the past fifty years. About one in three were built since 1975. The 1990 census found that one in five was less than ten years old — about the same proportion that was more than fifty years old. In Nevada, an astounding 40 percent of the housing was built during the 1980s alone. In contrast, only 9 percent of the housing in New York State was less than ten years old. Massachusetts has the highest share of housing built before 1940 — 39 percent. Nevada was lowest, with 3 percent.

Among homeowners, 94 percent say they have washing machines, 73 percent have garages or carports, 58 percent have dishwashers, 45 percent have air-conditioning and 41 percent have a fireplace. Renters reported fewer such amenities by far: Only 43 percent have washing machines, 30 percent have garages or carports, 33 percent have dishwashers, 32 percent have air-conditioning and 13 percent have a fireplace. Nearly one in ten houses or apartments had what its occupants described as a moderate or severe physical defect — problems that were more prevalent among renters than owners, among black and Hispanic people, among poor people (18 percent of whom reported those problems), and among residents of the South. The percentage of housing with moderate or severe physical problems was about the same in central cities and in rural areas. More than 12 percent of the homes or apartments in Alaska lacked complete indoor plumbing — well above the next ranked states, Maine, New Mexico and West Virginia, where the proportion was 3.5 percent or lower. About one in eight dwellings in Arkansas lacked complete plumbing. Connecticut boasted the most complete plumbing, though not as complete as on Nantucket where a census sample found no one without hot and cold piped water, a bathtub or shower and a flush toilet, compared to Hancock County, Tennessee, where three in ten homes were missing at least one of those amenities. In New Mexico, Mississippi, Arkansas, West Virginia and Maine, more than one in ten homes or apartments have no telephone. Massachusetts is the best connected state, with only about one in fifty homes where E.T. would have to improvise (although Lake Buena Vista, a central Florida resort community controlled by Walt Disney World, is one of the rare places where every resident reported having a telephone). Natural gas predominates as the home heating fuel of choice. It's used in about half the nation's homes. One fourth use electric heat. Solar energy may be a comer, but it hasn't caught on yet, even in the Sunshine State. Florida ranks second, after Hawaii, in the number of people who heat their water with solar power. But thirteen times as many Floridians heat with wood as with solar energy.

The South, where most people live, has the most houses and apartments. Nearly half are in the suburbs, about one third in central cities and fewer than one fourth outside metropolitan areas. The South also has half the nation's 8.5 million mobile homes, most of which are in rural areas. The federal government has urged states to remove legal barriers to mobile homes as a vehicle for more affordable housing. About two dozen states have done so. Many trailers, as they were once called, aren't really mobile anymore. Nor are they really homes, at least according to the banking industry. Mobile homes typically lose value as they age; worse, still, they are considered personal property, so borrowers are subject to higher interest rates than for houses. The mobile home industry prefers to call its product "manufactured housing" — though the factories don't make either basements or garages. About one in sixteen Americans lives in a mobile home. The average resident is 50 years old. South Carolina and Wyoming have the highest proportion — about one in six housing units. Mobile homes constitute about one third of all the housing on the outskirts of Las Cruces, New Mexico, and of Myrtle Beach, South Carolina. Incredibly, the census found 51,135 "mobile homes, trailers or other" residences somewhere in New York City, a figure that is astounding in its magnitude, but not as anomalous as it may first seem. Only 635 were actually mobile homes or trailers. The remaining 50,500 are "other" residences, which can be a car, a tent, a misunderstanding by someone filling out the form, or, as Census Bureau demographer Bill Chapin explains, "anything you say is your home that doesn't fit another category."

The Census Bureau goes to great lengths to define what constitutes housing and what doesn't. Recreational vehicles, boats, vans, tents and railroad cars count only if they are occupied as someone's usual place of residence. Vacant mobile homes don't count if they are on a dealer's parking lot, but do count if they are intended for occupancy on the site where they are parked. The government's definition of what constitutes a room would appall any apartment broker. "Do not count," census instructions caution, "bathrooms, kitchenettes, strip or pullman kitchens, utility rooms, foyers, halls, half-rooms, porches, balconies, unfinished attics, unfinished basements, or other unfinished space used for storage."

None of those definitions was of much value in counting two other categories of people: persons away from their usual residence on Census Day and the homeless. The first group includes migrant workers. If they didn't report a usual residence elsewhere, they were counted as residents of wherever census takers found them. People displaced by a natural disaster that had destroyed their usual residence were also counted wherever they were found. Counting the homeless was another story entirely. Increasingly, compassion and self-interest had parted company in legal battles to reconcile society's responsibilities with the rights of the homeless, who demanded, as one man did in New Jersey, access to a local library where his body odor was deemed offensive, and, as others did in Miami and Reno, freedom to sleep in public parks. Responding to lawsuits and to political pressure, cities like New York found a financially costly but politically correct solution that had been insufficient in the 1890s, much less the 1990s. They focused on physical shelter, investing heavily to fill a vacuum left by the federal government's virtual abandonment of housing programs, but pumping much less into vital social services. Nobody had to sleep outdoors, but some people chose to because the National Guard drill halls and welfare hotels provided by government were often less inviting and often less safe. Without the socializing institutions of family, religion or settlement houses, though, physical shelter didn't suffice. An influx of formerly homeless tenants jeopardized the tenuous social stability of the city's public housing stock, many of whose residents are the working poor. Overwhelmed, even New York redefined its policy of shelter on demand when the supply of housing could not keep pace. While other cities are dynamiting public high-rises, by the end of 1992, the waiting list for an apartment in New York's 324 projects reached a record 240,000 applicants — nearly as many people as the number of occupied apartments managed by the Housing Authority. Given the average turnover, a prospective tenant might have to wait twenty years.

The Census Bureau was wary even about defining who was homeless, preferring to characterize them only as displaced people without a usual residence. In 1980, the bureau had conducted what it called a casual count or Mission Night operation — surveying street corners, pool halls and welfare offices in what was described as "a coverage-improvement operation." Whatever the number of homeless people then, as the decade progressed they became more obvious everyplace from Manhattan, which was dubbed a new Calcutta (a metaphor that offended civic boosters in New York as well as in old Calcutta), to the beaches of Santa Monica, California, to highway underpasses in Connecticut, where a judge ruled that police could not legally search a homeless person's makeshift accommodations without a warrant.

In 1990, there were no pretensions that the overnight Shelter and Street Enumeration had found all the people who lacked a conventional residence. In fact, the Census Bureau made a point of explaining that it had defined locations where the homeless are likely to congregate, not to count the homeless, per se, but to include homeless people in its overall count. Enumerators were armed with explicit instructions: "Not to ask who was homeless; rather, they were told to count all persons [including children] staying overnight at the shelters and everyone they saw on the street except the police and other persons in uniform, and persons engaged in employment or obvious money-making activities other than begging and panhandling [presumably, prostitution and drug dealing]. At both shelter and street sites, persons found sleeping were not awakened to answer questions. Rather, the enumerator answered the sex and race questions by observation and estimated the person's age to the best of his or her ability." No attempt was made to count people doubled up with other families in houses or apartments. Nor were inmates of prisons and mental hospitals asked whether they had a regular home someplace else. Census Bureau demographers acknowledged that their street count was fuzzy: "There is a general sense from some census takers familiar with the homeless population that fewer seemed to be in their customary spots than usual. It was not a typical night." With military and bureaucratic precision, the elaborate S-Night was conducted March 20, 1990, at emergency shelters and at "open locations in streets or other places not intended for habitation." Predesignated street sites included parks, subway stations, and abandoned buildings from which people were counted as they emerged between four A.M. and eight A.M. Emergency shelters included all hotels and motels costing $12 or less (before taxes) per night, regardless of whether people living there defined themselves as homeless, and pricier hotels and motels that were used exclusively for homeless individuals and families. Enumerators, including some homeless people themselves, received a $50 bonus for successfully completing their assignment. However incomplete, the tally was sobering. The Census Bureau found 168,309 people in emergency shelters, 10,329 in shelters for runaways, and 11,768 in shelters for abused women. Another 49,734 — a number nearly big enough to qualify as an "urban place" peopled entirely by the homeless — were discovered "visible in street locations." In a separate count of people who reported that they had "no usual home elsewhere," the census found 1,682 in homes for unwed mothers, 52,038 in group homes for drug or alcohol abusers, 35,289 in dormitories for migrant farm workers, 32,348 in group homes for the mentally ill, and 97,727 in what the census blandly described as "other non-household living situations." Together, the number of displaced or misplaced persons totaled 459,224 — or more than the entire population of Wyoming.

That New York had become emblematic of homelessness may have been as much a consequence of density and obtrusiveness as actual numbers. Nearly as many were counted in California's emergency shelters as in New York's; the tally of street people in California — 18,081, or more than one third of all those found in the nation — was nearly double that of New York State (where they may merely have been wilier in evading government interviewers and less willing to endure the March night outdoors). But no other city even approached New York in the two biggest categories: The census found 23,383 people in emergency shelters and another 10,447 on the street — more than four times the total recorded in second-ranked Los Angeles. If all of them were piled head to toe, they might look pretty much the way they did on S-Night. "There is no generally agreed-upon definition of 'the homeless' and there are limitations in the census count that prevent obtaining a total count of the homeless population under any definition," the Census Bureau said. As a result, it offered neither its own definition nor a total count, adding, with atypical imprecision, "the number missed will never be known."

Prison inmates are easier to count because they are easier to find (even if some itinerant inmates had had no other usual residence until they were incarcerated). Prison construction was the leading response to rising crime in the 1980s, although it seemed to be neither an antidote nor a preventative approach.

Instead, it was largely intended to stanch the flow of felons through the court system back to the street by warehousing them before recycling. Referring to their current residence as a "correctional" institution is usually a misnomer. Generally, except for some prisons with intensive drug treatment, about all they correct are the mistakes of judges who had decided in previous cases that jail was either an unacceptable or unavailable alternative. Fifty years ago, the census counted 312,423 inmates of correctional institutions, a figure that remained fairly constant for nearly a half century. In 1980, it was 315,974. By 1990, it had grown to 1.1 million, or more than the entire population of Detroit. Growth was greatest for drug offenses — a category in which arrests and convictions were often open-and-shut. About one third of state and federal inmates are drug offenders. The highest rates of prisoners under federal and state jurisdiction were recorded in Nevada, Alaska, Michigan, Delaware, Maryland, South Carolina, Georgia, Florida, Alabama, Louisiana, Oklahoma and Arizona. In the course of two decades, the public authority that Governor Nelson A. Rockefeller had established within days of Dr. Martin Luther King Jr.'s assassination to provide affordable homes for poor New Yorkers largely maintained its mission, but with one major difference to the occupants: The authority had begun building or buying more prison cells than apartments.

However dramatic, prison construction was still outpaced by housing construction overall, even though the pace slowed considerably during the 1980s, to about 1.7 million units a year — down from an annual increase of about 2.1 million in the 1970s. In 1991, 700,000 single-family homes were built, the smallest number in forty-five years. During the last decade, almost half the new houses, and nearly two thirds of the newly placed mobile homes, were in the South. The South was also home to the highest housing vacancy rates. The nation had enough vacant houses and apartments — 12 million, or one in ten of the entire housing stock — to comfortably shelter the entire population of Somalia. About 4.5 million were on the market. Another 4.5 million were occupied occasionally or by persons whom the census classified as having their usual residence elsewhere. About 2.9 million were vacation or weekend homes. Overall, the growth in the inventory of vacant homes and apartments outpaced the growth in occupied ones — 29 percent compared to 14 percent.

During the 1980s, the number of renters increased by 17 percent compared to a 10 percent rise in the number of homeowners. Among Baby Boomers, the disparity was even starker: The ranks of homeowners grew 12 percent; the number of renters increased at twice that rate. Among householders between the ages of 35 and 44, the number of owners rose 30 percent; the number of renters rose 60 percent. Homeownership rates had risen every decade since 1940, when the rate was 44 percent. But they dropped from 66 percent of all households in 1980 to 64 percent in 1990.

Still, the actual number of homeowners increased in every region except the Midwest. Generally, the most expensive regions have the lowest rates of home ownership. The proportion also varies by state, from about 53 percent in California — where, in Los Angeles alone, the rate ranged from 6 percent in immigrant-flooded Westlake to 88 percent in affluent Bel Air — to about 74 percent in Pennsylvania and Maine. Married-couple families were more likely to own a home than non-married-couple families, men in those households were more likely to own than women, but women living alone were more likely to be homeowners than men living alone.

One dramatic exception to the ownership trend was in New York City. Because of the quick-buck investment in cooperatives and condominiums during the 1980s, the proportion of New Yorkers who own their homes topped 25 percent probably for the first time in a century or more. Fifty years ago, only 14 percent of New York City householders owned their own homes or apartments. The surge of co-op conversions and construction boosted the percentage of homeowners in the city to 28 percent — transforming many residents of what is still unabashedly a tenant town into that most reviled of species: the landlord. "It has taken a while to realize that the landlord is us," said Mary Ann Rothman, executive director of the Council of New York Cooperatives. Manhattan, hardly known as a bastion of home ownership, gained 73,993 homeowners during the decade. (Overall, though, New York City still had a considerable 258,015 detached single-family homes; and, in contrast, the home ownership rate in neighboring Nassau and Suffolk counties was nearly three times higher, 77 percent.) The shift had profound consequences. Paralyzed by plunging prices for cooperative and condominium apartments, the proliferation of owners halted what might have been another hemorrhaging of the middle-class from the city. "The simple fact of home ownership does not mean people will put up with severe deprivation in their quality of life," said Kathy Wylde, vice president of the New York City Housing Partnership, a nonprofit builder of affordable homes, "but it does have a stabilizing influence." That stability extended well beyond the "Prisoners of Second Avenue" in Neil Simon's Manhattan to white, black and Hispanic communities that might otherwise have been vulnerable to middle-class flight. Also, the metamorphosis from tenant to owner prompted city officials to revisit what they finally acknowledged was a hidden middle-class subsidy: disproportionately low property taxes that had historically been levied on one-and two-family-home owners.

What caused the ownership slump? "Not all who want to buy a home can afford to do so," the Census Bureau concluded. If the prose in the analysis by the bureau's F. John Devaney was tempered, the figures themselves offered a rude awakening from the American Dream: In 1988, 57 percent of families could not afford to purchase the median-priced home in the very region where they lived. That proportion included 36 percent of current owners in their own region and an astonishing 91 percent of the renters. Even a modestly priced house was beyond the reach of 48 percent of the nation's households. The median-priced home was unaffordable to 43 percent of prospective white buyers, 77 percent of blacks and 74 percent of Hispanic households. Sadly, younger families qualified least. Fully 94 percent of families headed by a person younger than 25 couldn't afford the median-priced house. Nor could 27 percent of families headed by someone between the ages of 55 and 64. Among first-time home buyers, nearly half needed government assistance in the form of an insured mortgage or low-cost loan. More than one in ten managed to afford only a movable version of the dream: a mobile home.

The Census Bureau's dismal assessment was based on 1988 prices, but economists suggested that the subsequent plunge in interest rates might only raise false hopes. "The decade of yuppie spending is over," said James W. Hughes, a professor of urban planning at Rutgers University in New Jersey, where the median cost of a house soared from $61,000 in 1980 to $162,000 a decade later. In California, median home value more than doubled, to $195,500 — the nation's highest. In 1980, the census counted 275,000 homes in the state that owners said would sell for more than $200,000. By 1990, the number had soared to 2.2 million. During the 1950s, median value of owner-occupied one-family homes rose nearly one third faster than inflation. In the 1960s and the 1980s, the national increase barely kept pace. The average sales price of all detached, single-family homes more than doubled during the decade, from $71,800 to $148,800 — driven entirely by the jump to $188,600 in the Northeast, which was the only region where average prices, in constant 1989 dollars, increased. The median value of owner-occupied homes increased 71 percent in current dollars but only about 5 percent after inflation to $79,100 — and even less for older homes. (During the 1980s, median monthly rent jumped 19 percent to $374.) Homes with a mortgage were worth more than those without one, reflecting the higher cost of new housing. Of all homes sold during the decade, those with the highest median price were in the West. Suburban Stamford, Connecticut, boasted the highest home valuation — a median of more than $500,000. Median values ranged from $457,000 in Palo Alto, California, to $22,200 in Monessen, Pennsylvania. Median home value was highest in Hawaii, California, Connecticut, Massachusetts and New Jersey — all above $150,000. It was lowest in Mississippi and South Dakota and four other states where median home value was less than $50,000. In constant dollars, Wyoming registered the steepest decline in home value — 35 percent — trailed by Oregon and Utah. What happened in some states was a reversal of fortune from the 1970s. During that decade, Wyoming had had the largest increase in home value — 96 percent. Home values in New York increased only 1.7 percent in the 1970s, but 82 percent in the 1980s.

Collectively, the nation's homeowners spend 18 percent of their income on housing. But housing costs rose twice as fast as income during the decade, to the point where two in ten homeowners and four in ten renters were spending more than 30 percent of their income on housing — above the government's own guideline. Wealthier owners and renters spent a smaller percentage of their income for housing. Among homeowners with incomes below $5,000 (overall, nearly 5 million households reported that they made less than $5,000), housing consumed a median 62 percent of their income. Owners who make $120,000 or more spent only a median 8 percent on housing. Similarly, renters who make less than $5,000 spent 75 percent of their income on housing. Renters with incomes over $120,000 spent 7 percent.

Los Altos Hills, near San Jose, California, has the highest median household income in the area — $115,851. But it also ranks highest locally in the percentage of homeowners who make more than $50,000 but spend more than 35 percent of their income on housing. In Broward County, Florida, median household income rose $2,783, adjusted for inflation. But median housing costs, including mortgage payments, increased by $2,856. (Sometimes, though, those costs may be inflated because they include interest and principal on second mortgages or home equity loans taken out to consolidate debt or to increase indebtedness by financing anything from a new car to a face-lift.) The number of mortgaged homes increased much more slowly than the number of nonmortgaged ones — another consequence of the rising proportion of older homeowners. The number of homeowners below the age of 35 dropped 5 percent; the number 65 and older swelled by 20 percent. Fully 83 percent of elderly homeowners had paid cash for their homes or had paid off their mortgages. New Jersey was first in monthly homeowner costs for mortgaged houses — $1,105 — with West Virginia last, at $498.

Tenants spent a median 27 percent of their income on rent, although nearly two in ten spent more than half of their income for housing. One in ten lives in public or subsidized housing. Among the rest, tenants in California, Maryland, Massachusetts, New Jersey and New York receive an indirect government subsidy in the form of rent control — regardless of income. Hawaii got bragging rights to the highest median rent — $650 a month — while West Virginia claimed the lowest — $303. Monthly median rent topped $800 in Palo Alto, California; Kailua, Hawaii; and in Stamford, Connecticut, where it was $911.

Northeasterners pay the highest property taxes — an annual median of $1,500, or double the national median of $756 and more than triple the levy in the South. Still, while the national median was 67 percent higher than it was a decade earlier in current dollars, in constant 1989 dollars the median tax had not increased at all. The West boasted the highest median housing costs for homeowners with a mortgage, in part because of the high sale prices during the decade, but also the lowest median cost for homes without a mortgage, because of relatively low real estate taxes and smaller heating and air-conditioning bills. Housing costs for mortgaged homes climbed 108 percent in current dollars and 24 percent in constant 1989 dollars, outpacing the consumer price index. More than a third of the median monthly cost of $702 went for taxes, utilities and insurance. Rents, meanwhile, increased 95 percent in current dollars and 16 percent in constant 1989 dollars. Nonetheless, median monthly housing costs for renters ($424) was higher than median monthly housing costs for owners ($399), except for owners under 45 years old with mortgages. The disparity was greatest for people living alone. Their median rent was $368. Their median cost as owners was $241. Most owners living alone are elderly and have already paid off their mortgages. And owners, overall, were richer than renters. The median income of owners was $33,000; of renters, $18,100. Poor people constitute 8 percent of the homeowners and 22 percent of renters.

Typically, the greatest disparities in the place people call home are a reflection of race and ethnicity as well as of income.

Among white householders, 67 percent own their own homes. Half are in the suburbs; one third are in the South, more than any other region. The median size of detached single-family houses and mobile homes owned by whites is 1,754 square feet, or 699 square feet per person. The median value of that home is $75,000. Mortgaged homes cost their owners 24 percent of income. Seven percent of white homeowners are poor. White renters paid a median 26 percent of their income for housing. About 11 percent are tenants of public or subsidized housing; 19 percent are poor.

Disproportionately few blacks are homeowners. Only 43 percent of black households own their own home — 60 percent of which are in central cities and 53 percent of which are in the South. The median size is 1,483 square feet, or 562 square feet per person. The median value is $51,000, which, in a mortgaged home, cost the owners 24 percent of income. Twenty percent of black homeowners are poor. Black renters pay 29 percent of income, though rent consumes half or more of the income for 22 percent of them. Nearly three times as many black renters as white ones live in public or subsidized housing — 29 percent — and 37 percent of the black renters are poor.

Homeowners account for 40 percent of Hispanic householders. Their homes have a median size of 1,434 square feet, or 446 square feet per person, and a median value of $76,000 — about the same as for whites. Mortgaged homes cost Hispanic homeowners, 12 percent of whom are poor, about 25 percent of income. Overall, renters paid out 31 percent of their income for housing, but 24 percent of them spent 50 percent or more of their income on rent. Sixteen percent of the renters live in public or subsidized housing; 30 percent are poor.

No group had a higher proportion of homeowners than the elderly, reflecting their accumulated wealth and resulting in disproportionate space in empty nests. Among elderly householders, 76 percent owned their own homes, which have a median size of 1,576 square feet, or 965 square feet per person. In homes with mortgages, householders paid 29 percent of their income for housing. Among elderly renters, 30 percent spend more than half their income on rent, 30 percent live in public or subsidized housing, and 30 percent are poor.

Among the poor, fully one fourth of homeowners are 75 years old or more. Four in ten live in the South. Their homes are worth $43,600, which is five times their annual income. For most, the home in which they live is the only one they had ever owned. Their homes are smaller than those of owners overall, but poor people who owned their own homes were less likely to bump into each other: They had 713 square feet per person compared to 688 for all householders, reflecting, perhaps, the high proportion of poor homeowners who are elderly and preside over depleted households. Housing costs accounted for 41 percent of their income, a startlingly high figure surpassed only by the median 53 percent of income that poor tenants spent on rent.

The 1980s witnessed a marked increase in spending on home improvements, which reflects economic common sense: Renovating is usually cheaper than moving. Renters are typically more mobile than homeowners. In 1989, 36 percent of the renters had moved within the past year alone; so had only 8 percent of owners. Northeasterners are considerably less mobile; fully 55 percent live in the first home they owned. In the West, 54 percent of homes changed hands during the decade; in the Northeast, only 43 percent did. Among rental properties in the West, only one fifth were occupied by the same tenants at the end of the decade as when it began. The census found few regional differences among homeowners by age, but sharp disparities among renters. That the Northeast was home to 30 percent of elderly renters and 17 percent of renters under age 35 suggested an exodus of younger renters. One consequence of the declining proportion of renters was an increase in the proportion of home ownership, which the Northeast was the only region to record.

Where people live often is a consequence of where they work. If, for most Americans, a home represents their biggest asset, most also managed to accommodate their second largest investment: the car, which remains the nation's foremost means of commuting. In the 1980s, even more than during the decade before, their credo became: Don't leave home without it.

CHAPTER VIII

HOW WE COMMUTE

If getting there were half the fun, Americans would have had 2.5 million hours a day more time to enjoy it by the end of the 1980s than when the decade began. That's the cumulative increase in mean time that commuters spent traveling to work. The trip got forty-two seconds a day longer between 1980 and 1990, to 22.4 minutes. The number of subway and railroad commuters also increased, but the car was king. More than half the nation's households have two or more vehicles available; only one in ten households has none.

Fewer commuters used car pools or public transportation during the 1980s than in the decade before. The percentage of America's 115 million workers who drive alone to work rose from 64 percent to 73 percent, or another 22 million drivers. Car pooling declined from 20 percent to 13 percent. And overall mass transit ridership dipped from 6 percent to 5 percent. Eight times as many people walk to work — 4.5 million — as ride a railroad. Another 470,000 say they commute by bicycle, 240,000 by motorcycle, 180,000 by taxicab (one third of them in New York), and 40,000 by ferry.

The 1990 census revealed vivid contrasts not only in how Americans get to work and how much time they spend getting there, but in their historic love affair with cars. Most people surveyed separately by the Census Bureau didn't even seem to mind what any objective observer would consider the liabilities of motor vehicles. Yes, more than one third of the households acknowledged, street noise or heavy traffic is commonplace in their neighborhoods. In urban areas, 32 percent of homeowners and 45 percent of renters said so. Even in rural America, 27 percent of owners and 32 percent of renters agreed (although their threshold for intolerable noise and congestion may be lower). But a majority of the households that acknowledged the noise or traffic said they weren't bothered by it. Owners and the elderly said they were least bothered. For all the complaints about congestion, parking, pollution, horn honking and the high cost of purchasing or repairing a car, nine in ten American households have at least one. The proportion of households with two or more vehicles ranged from 67 percent in Idaho to 38 percent in New York State, where 30 percent had no vehicle available at all — twice the rate of the next car-deprived state. Even in oversaturated suburbia, the number of cars is increasing. Frustrated planners blame the increase on more two–wage-earner families, more jobs located in suburbs with inadequate mass transit, more young adults still living at home, and abundant gasoline. Young and old are more dependent on cars, particularly in suburban areas poorly served by public transportation. While one third of households headed by someone 75 or older have no car, nearly half have one car and one in five have two or more cars. Half the heads of households under age 25 have two or more cars; only

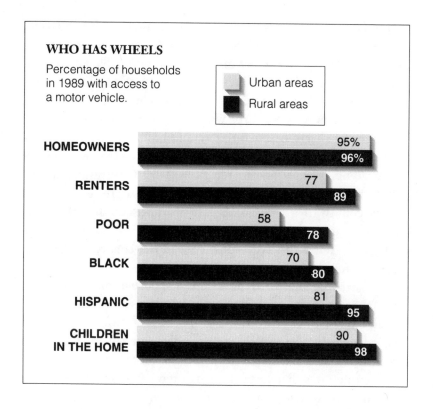

WHO HAS WHEELS

Percentage of households in 1989 with access to a motor vehicle.

Urban areas
Rural areas

	Urban	Rural
HOMEOWNERS	95%	96%
RENTERS	77	89
POOR	58	78
BLACK	70	80
HISPANIC	81	95
CHILDREN IN THE HOME	90	98

about one in seven don't have any. Wyoming, by one count, has more cars than people — .99 persons per motor vehicle, compared to the high of 1.82 in New York.

On average, the commute in metropolitan New York was longest: 30.6 minutes, compared to a national metropolitan area average of 23.2. (By county, the longest was 41 minutes in Park County, Colorado; the shortest, 9 minutes, in Mitchell County, Kansas.) Washington, D.C., was close behind New York at 29.6 minutes. Los Angelenos, defying the freeway stereotype of urban crawl, actually took 4 minutes less. The average commuting time was 24 minutes or so in Boston, Philadelphia, Dallas and Miami and a mere 21 minutes in Minneapolis. In uncongested nonmetropolitan areas it was even shorter: 19.2 minutes. Long Island, which is synonymous with suburban congestion, also defies the stereotype of traffic-choked highways and unreliable railroads — compared to neighboring New York City, anyway. The average commute was 28.5 minutes in Suffolk County, 31.5 in Nassau, and 36.5 in New York City where, on many midtown streets, average speeds are below 4 m.p.h. and motorists are easily out-paced by pedestrians. More striking was where the commuters were going. Nearly one in ten New York City residents now work in the suburbs. And fewer suburbanites are leaving their home county to work. Commuting patterns vividly affirm the economic maturation of many suburbs. In Westchester, more than six in ten adults with jobs work in the county. In Suffolk, seven in ten do.

Car ownership is by no means a suburban obsession only. In Manhattan alone, where three in four households have no car at all, 2,000 families own three or more cars — twice the number recorded a decade earlier. Presumably, some were parked in weekend homes outside the city or other places and not garaged at monthly rates that surpass median rents in many cities. More than half of America's households care enough about their cars to shelter them in a garage or in that partially enclosed suburban counterpart, a carport. Another third park them in their driveway or on an adjacent lot. Only one in twenty homeowners, but one in five renters, had to fend for themselves on public streets where the hazards of alternate-side regulations and of smash-and-grab radio thieves can make parking perilous.

When cars aren't parked, they are often moving in the same direction at the same time. Consequently, the Census Bureau says, "the impact on local road systems of this regular large-scale movement of people going to and from work is intensified." Most motorists describe the self-inflicted impact more concisely: traffic, that is, their collective movement. Within the three hours beginning at six A.M., 70 percent of American workers leave for wherever they work. Between seven-thirty and eight A.M. alone, 17 percent leave home. But gregariousness goes only so far. Of the nearly nine in ten Americans who drive to work, only 12 percent avail themselves of car pools — much lower than the government's goals for energy conservation but, still, twice the proportion who choose subways, buses, commuter trains and other forms of mass transit or who have no practical or affordable alternative. Carpooling was most popular in Hawaii and least appealing, or available, to South Dakotans.

Unless the cost of driving alone becomes prohibitive, though, and other alternatives are made more appealing, the emotional attachments to private cars and the marriages of convenience seem unlikely to be severed. The percentage of commuters who drive to work by themselves is smallest in the Northeast, but even there as many as 70 percent do. Seventy-five percent do so in the West, 78 percent in the Midwest (more than eight in ten in Ohio and Michigan), and 79 percent in the South. Northeasterners commute by public transportation more than residents of any other region. Fully 11 percent use subways, buses or trains to get to work (23 percent in New York State). In the West, which ranks second, only 4 percent do, although highways saturated with vehicles are oversaturating the air with pollutants. In 1992, Los Angeles opened the 4.4-mile first leg of the Metro Red Line, a subway system that local officials hoped would persuade as many as one in five commuters to give up their cars by 2020. Yet the government subsidizes motor vehicles much more than mass transit, justifying the interstate highway system in the 1950s less as a transportation program than as a national defense project to speed access for troops and supplies. By one estimate, a range of benefits from road repair to tax deductions for parking fees costs public treasuries $300 billion a year. Mass transit receives less than 1 percent of that amount.

Renters are about three times more likely as homeowners to ride subways, buses or commuter trains at least once a week.

Two reasons explain why one in five depends on public transportation. First, it is more likely to be available where renters live. About seven in ten, compared to fewer than half the homeowners, said it was there for the taking. Another variable makes mass transit an even more compelling alternative: the fact that 22 percent of renters, but only 5 percent of owners, don't have a motor vehicle. The proportion without cars is highest among rural households with children — 98 percent — and among homeowners, and lowest among the poor — 58 percent — and among blacks. Often, the working poor face the toughest commute. Because they are more prone to rely on public transportation, they are likely to leave home earlier and spend more time commuting. In Washington Park, just west of Fort Lauderdale, more than four in ten families are poor and one fourth of working commuters have no car. They depend more on public bus service than do any other commuters in Broward County. In Parkland, where the poverty rate is 2 percent, one third of the families own three or more cars and 87 percent of commuters drive to work alone.

That contrast underscores a principle of economics and of spatial mobility. The means by which people commute is generally a consequence of a larger end: where, or whether, they work.

CHAPTER IX

WHAT WE'RE WORTH

For fifty years, Americans weaned on the Depression were spoon-fed a fundamentally optimistic philosophy: Rising prosperity would improve almost everybody's lot and the next generation would surely be better off than the preceding one. But after the nation's largest economic expansion since the 1920s, most of America began the last decade of the century reeling from harsh reality. Many of the gains had been illusory. Paper improvements were often achieved because wives were working and because couples had fewer children to support. Much of the benefit has been eroded by inflation. The yuppie was succeeded by what Marissa Piesman, co-author of *The Yuppie Handbook*, branded the "schleppy." One demographer, Frank Levy, found that the 35- to 44-year-olds were half as wealthy as their parents had been at that age.

The census affirmed what the majority of Americans had already suspected: that F. Scott Fitzgerald's maxim about the very rich is even truer today than it was in the 1920s. During the 1980s, the rich got richer, the poor got poorer, and the middle class contracted for the second consecutive decade. The percentage of income received by the top 20 percent zoomed to the highest ratio recorded by the Census Bureau since it began counting in 1949. The middle-class glue that joins both ends of the economic sandwich has been shriveling since 1969. So has confidence in the future. A college degree is still the greatest determinant of higher earnings as the gap between the salaries of low-skilled and higher-skilled workers grows. But as the 1990s began, many students wondered what kind of world they were graduating into. Their uncertainty was reflected not only in what they earn but in how they and the rest of America live. One American family in twenty-five was making $100,000 or more when the 1980s ended. But half the nation's families could not afford the 5 percent down payment and monthly payments on a thirty-year mortgage for a median-priced house in the region where they lived.

The 1990 census may have captured the economy nearly at its best, the final frame before the smile faded for many Americans. Nationally, median income was up for the decade; the proportion of people living in poverty was down. But those broad trends masked vast contrasts between regions, by race and ethnicity and, above all, by the income category people had been in when the decade began. One year after the 1990 census measured income, the average income of the nation's households declined about $525 to $29,943, adjusted for inflation. For individuals, it receded by 3.6 percent to $14,387 — the first decline in personal income since 1983. While the earnings ratio of women to men reached a record high — women earned seventy-one cents for every dollar earned by men — the disparity narrowed in part because men's earnings had declined for the third consecutive year.

Black married couples where the wives worked have edged closer to white families since 1967, from $72 for every $100 earned by white couples to $85. Despite those gains, though, in nearly a quarter century the ratio of median income between all black and white families declined from 59 percent to 58 percent (or 58 cents for every dollar earned by white families). Similarly, the vast differences in net worth between blacks and whites were smallest among the upper-income group, but even at that level the median net worth of whites was more than twice that of blacks.

Inequities charted by the Green Book issued annually by the Democratic-dominated House Ways and Means Committee were dismissed by one conservative congressman as "a database for demagogues." But the Census Bureau itself found "a fairly substantial increase in inequality": The share of income received by the bottom fifth had stagnated since 1973 while the share amassed by the highest fifth swelled. The shifts, three Census Bureau economists concluded, produced perhaps the greatest disparity between rich and poor of any major Western nation. The Congressional Budget Office also found that despite a decade marked by tax revolts and promises of "no new taxes," panglossian euphemisms like the Tax Equity and Fiscal Responsibility Act of 1982 and the Omnibus Budget Reconciliation Act of 1990 actually increased the average American's tax burden. Reductions in income tax rates were more than made up by higher payroll and Social Security taxes. Total federal taxes did drop for one group: the very richest 1 percent. The Treasury Department's Office of Tax Analysis insisted, though, that "the poor grew much richer and the rich only a little richer." And Michael J. Boskin, President George Bush's economic adviser, suggested: "It's much more important for economic policy to promote growth in family incomes than to redistribute it." Yet by all accounts the incomes that grew the most were those of families among the top 20 percent and what trickled down merely dampened the aspirations of the other 80 percent. Even the Republican White House conceded that there had been "some increase in inequality." Kevin Phillips called the 1980s a second Gilded Age, paralleling earlier epochs of excess in the late nineteenth century and again in the 1920s. *Architectural Digest* and television's *Lifestyles of the Rich and Famous* celebrated arrivistes. Tom Wolfe's fictionalized *The Bonfire of the Vanities* and Lewis Lapham's stinging *Money and Class in America* vilified them.

The 1990 census found that median income — the point at which half the people were making more and half were making less — was $37,152 for a family of four (a category that includes a single mother with three children). High income was defined as at least twice that, or above $74,304; low income was considered less than half the median, or below $18,576. By that measure, the proportion of affluent households increased by well over one third, from 10.9 percent to 14.7 percent, during the decade. The share of low-income households rose by more than one third, from 31 percent to 42 percent. The middle-income share shrank, from 71 percent to 63 percent. Among the wealthiest 5 percent of families, average income rose from $120,253 in 1979 to $148,438 in 1989 — the only group whose earnings easily outpaced inflation. Measured another way, the top 20 percent collected 44 percent of money income in 1970, 44 percent in 1980, and 47 percent by 1990. Figuring in taxes on the rich and the value of food stamps and other benefits for the poor, the top income group still amassed a hefty 44 percent of all income. If capital gains from the sale of homes, cars, stocks and bonds were included, the share amassed by the richest one fifth of Americans would have risen to 51 percent, or more than the poor and middle class collected combined. Meanwhile, the share of aggregate income collected by the poorest one fifth of Americans declined from 4.2 percent in 1980 to 3.9 percent. The middle fifth's share slipped from 16.8 percent to 15.9 percent. While the average pretax family income, adjusted for inflation, grew slightly — from

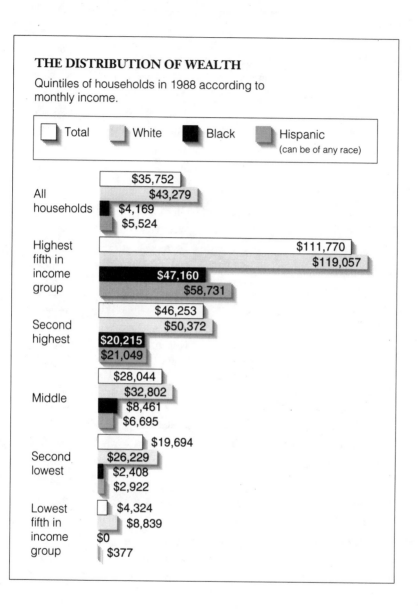

THE DISTRIBUTION OF WEALTH

Quintiles of households in 1988 according to monthly income.

☐ Total   ◻ White   ■ Black   ◻ Hispanic
(can be of any race)

All households
- $35,752
- $43,279
- $4,169
- $5,524

Highest fifth in income group
- $111,770
- $119,057
- $47,160
- $58,731

Second highest
- $46,253
- $50,372
- $20,215
- $21,049

Middle
- $28,044
- $32,802
- $8,461
- $6,695

Second lowest
- $19,694
- $26,229
- $2,408
- $2,922

Lowest fifth in income group
- $4,324
- $8,839
- $0
- $377

HOUSEHOLD INCOME, STATE BY STATE

Median income in 1989.

Connecticut	$41,721	Ohio	$28,706
Alaska	41,408	Maine	27,854
New Jersey	40,927	Arizona	27,540
Maryland	39,386	Florida	27,483
Hawaii	38,829	Kansas	27,291
Massachusetts	$36,952	Oregon	$27,250
New Hampshire	36,329	Wyoming	27,096
California	35,798	Texas	27,016
Delaware	34,875	North Carolina	26,647
Virginia	33,328	Missouri	26,362
New York	$32,965	South Carolina	$26,256
Illinois	32,252	Iowa	26,229
Rhode Island	32,181	Nebraska	26,016
Washington	31,183	Idaho	25,257
Michigan	31,020	Tennessee	24,807
Nevada	$31,011	New Mexico	$24,087
Minnesota	30,909	Alabama	23,597
District of Columbia	30,727	Oklahoma	23,577
Colorado	30,140	North Dakota	23,213
Vermont	29,792	Montana	22,988
Utah	$29,470	Kentucky	$22,534
Wisconsin	29,442	South Dakota	22,503
Pennsylvania	29,069	Louisiana	21,949
Georgia	29,021	Arkansas	21,147
Indiana	28,797	West Virginia	20,795
		Mississippi	$20,136

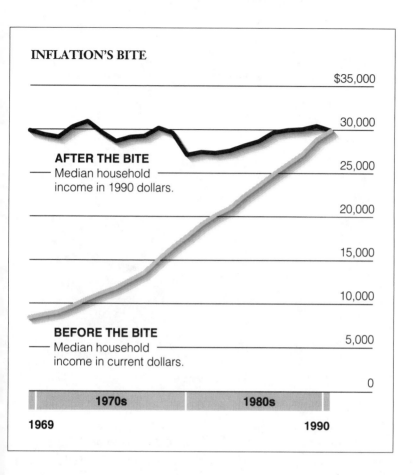

INFLATION'S BITE

$35,000

30,000

AFTER THE BITE
— Median household
income in 1990 dollars.

25,000

20,000

15,000

10,000

5,000

BEFORE THE BITE
— Median household
income in current dollars.

0

| 1970s | 1980s |

1969   1990

$33,400 in 1983 to $35,700 in 1989 — because of big gainers at the high end, the Federal Reserve Board found that median family income — the middle of the middle class — hardly increased at all, by only .4 percent. Among American households, the gap between perceived and real median income was even greater. Between 1947 and 1973, median family income, adjusted for inflation, doubled. During the next seventeen years, it rose only 6 percent — depressed by the proliferation of single-parent families, although the median grew by just 11 percent for married-couple

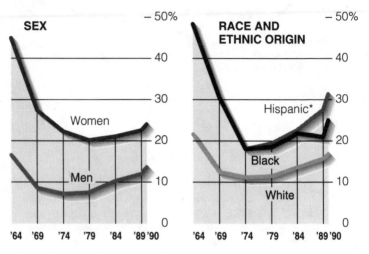

LOWER WAGES

Percentage of full-time, year-round workers with low earnings, or $12,195 in 1990 ($6.10 an hour, 40 hours a week for 50 weeks).

SEX

Women

Men

RACE AND ETHNIC ORIGIN

Hispanic*

Black

White

'64 '69 '74 '79 '84 '89 '90

* Can be of any race. Figures only compiled since 1974.

families between 1973 and 1990. In current dollars, the median rose from about $8,000 to $30,000 since 1969. Adjusted for inflation, though, the median never really budged above $30,000 in constant 1990 dollars during the entire two decades.

In America's putatively unpedigreed culture, the middle class has always occupied a special place not usually afforded a group that might otherwise be dismissed as merely average. It has achieved mythic status as a historical bulwark of economic growth and of social and political stability, although, in reality, the encompassing middle class that we lionize today is largely a post–Second World War phenomenon. By no means patrician but not quite plebeian either, the middle class is a vaguely defined

EDUCATION'S LINK TO WAGES

Average weekly earnings for working adults under age 65, in constant 1989 dollars.

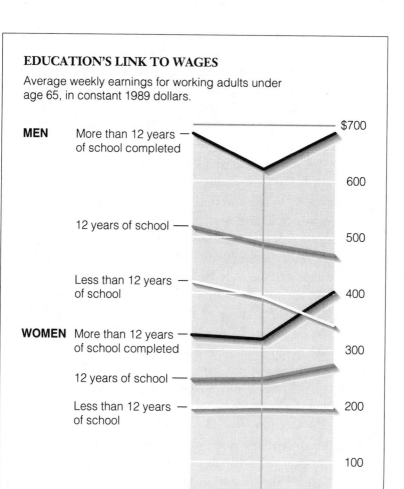

MEN More than 12 years of school completed

12 years of school

Less than 12 years of school

WOMEN More than 12 years of school completed

12 years of school

Less than 12 years of school

$700

600

500

400

300

200

100

0

Source: Rebecca M. Blank, Northwestern University

1969   1979   1989

group that Democrats began to court vigorously again only belatedly in 1992. Four years earlier, the blocs that voted heaviest and that provided George Bush with an insurmountable base had been the biggest beneficiaries of the 1980s boom: executives, professionals, and retirees, whose Social Security benefits had increased. As a result, Bill Clinton's rallying cry resonated: "The rich get the gold mine and the middle class gets the shaft." In the 1992 election, the typical middle-class suburban family — two cars and probably two workers to produce two incomes — was the bellwether. "When working and middle-income people vote against poor people and blacks, Republicans win," said Victor Fingerhut, a political consultant to organized labor. "When they vote against the super-rich and big corporations, the Democrats win." Clinton was the first Democrat in a generation to win a plurality among white voters. Suburbia, Kevin Phillips concluded, "now held a majority of the U.S. population, but the Republicans no longer held a majority of suburbia."

A century and a half ago, Tocqueville proclaimed the "general equality of condition" among Americans. That perceived economic equilibrium overlooked a glaring exception: slavery. But even among other Americans, the scales began to grow increasingly lopsided in favor of the wealthy almost without interruption until the stock market crashed in 1929. Some Americans were always more equal than others and no decade dealt those people a better hand than the 1980s. The number of billionaires more than tripled to an estimated 71 by 1991, or one for every 3.5 million plebeians. In 1979, the top 1 percent of households held less than 20 percent of the nation's net worth, Claudia Goldin and Bradford De Long of Harvard and Edward Wolff of New York University found. Ten years later, the share of net worth held by the top 1 percent had nearly doubled, to 36 percent — or as much as it had been during the century between Tocqueville's observation about equality and the Depression. Wealth had been redistributed by the New Deal and by wage and price controls during the Second World War. With the stock market collapse in the mid-1970s, the share of wealth held by the superrich sank to under 18 percent, about the lowest since the Northwest Ordinance parceled out vast tracts of land in relatively small lots in 1787 rather than as feudal fiefdoms. The wealthy scored an impressive comeback, sparked by a deep cut in the top tax rate from 70 percent to less than 30 percent, the Federal Reserve's anti-inflation strategy, and hefty interest rates. During the 1980s, wages were barely keeping pace with inflation but stocks and bonds appreciated significantly. Home ownership and pension plan membership dipped; pay and productivity for average workers was virtually frozen. Return on labor trailed the return on wealth. But the recession that struck white-collar workers with unusual severity when the decade began may have produced an unexpected side effect. "Inequality in the distribution of household incomes, after rising slowly in the 1970s and accelerating in most of the 1980s, changed very little between 1987 and 1991," said Paul Ryscavage, a Census Bureau economist. "These developments raise a question as to whether or not the long-run trend towards greater inequality in the income distribution has come to an end."

What was the likelihood in the 1980s that a hard-driving Horatio Alger hero would metamorphose into Michael Milken or Donald Trump? Treasury Department analysts maintained that the chances of moving from the bottom 20 percent in income distribution to the top 40 percent were one in four. In a largely contradictory study, the Urban Institute rated the odds at one in ten. Moreover, it concluded that the top 20 percent, which had been four times richer than the bottom 20 percent twenty years earlier, was five times richer by the end of the decade. The middle class, meanwhile, was running in place, trapped on a treadmill during a decade when it was as easy to slide back to a lower income category as it was to inch forward into a higher one.

Why so many people were shortchanged by the boom is arguable. To varying degrees, economists blame the disparity in pay between poorly educated and better-educated workers, the importation of goods that could have been produced by low-skilled American workers, and the influx of immigrants who expanded the low-paid pool. Still another cause was the decline of organized labor and one consequence of that decline: pay hikes were subordinated to job security as a goal of collective bargaining. As a consequence of recession-induced labor cutbacks, productivity and competitiveness improved. But industries vulnerable to foreign imports warily regarded the free trade agreement negotiated with Canada and Mexico in 1992 and muscle-flexing by the European Community. Unions had been blamed for the nation's declining competitiveness, but as Dennis Rivera, the head of New York's hospital workers union and an emerging power in labor and Hispanic politics, said: "If 84 percent of all American workers do not belong to a labor union, labor is not the problem. Labor is irrelevant." The convergence of two sociological trends was very relevant, though, and conspired against equality: More married women were working, but proportionately fewer families — including newly impoverished middle-class families — were headed by married couples. "There are two things driving these numbers," said Douglas J. Besharov, a resident scholar at the American Enterprise Institute. "First is the economy. But there is a second, underlying trend which is much more powerful. That is the breakdown of low-income families, and not just black families. Murphy Brown notwithstanding, it's all but impossible for a high school dropout who gives birth to her first baby at 19 to be anything but poor."

The Census Bureau defines net worth as the value of savings and checking accounts, real estate, cars, stocks and bonds, and other assets — excluding pension plans, jewelry and home furnishings — minus debt. Household net worth is held in disproportionately few hands, in part because home ownership accounts for nearly half of net worth nationwide. Net worth typically increases with age until retirement, when more of it is consumed and less is accumulated. Vast disparities exist not only between rich and poor, but among the poor themselves. Fully half of the lowest income blacks had no net worth at all or a negative net worth — meaning that they owed more than they owned. White households were worth about ten times as much as black households — $43,279 compared to $4,169 — in part because whites have benefited from differentials that have endured for generations. The median gap in income between blacks and whites is narrowing, but the disparities in wealth will shrink more slowly. Even among married couples, whites still reported a median wealth three and a half times that of blacks. Among whites, home ownership accounted for about 40 percent of all net worth, and earnings from interest nearly 20 percent. Among blacks, home ownership constituted more than two thirds of net worth. Among white households, 29 percent reported net worth of $100,000 or more (the same percentage of blacks that reported no wealth at all). Only 5 percent of black households and 12 percent of Hispanic households said they were worth that much.

Worth is a reflection of two factors: earnings and spending. In 1990, the Census Bureau found that consumers spend the largest proportion of their budgets on housing, 20 percent — the most in four periods surveyed since 1917. On average, food and alcohol consume 19 percent, a proportion that has been halved since the century began. Spending on apparel and related services, like dry cleaning, declined by two thirds to 6 percent. Health care, entertainment and utilities remained roughly the same, at 4 percent, 6 percent and 8 percent, respectively. How people apportion their spending depends on their age, what they make and where they live. Food, housing and health care accounted for 66 percent of spending by people 75 years old or more, but 48 percent in households headed by people under 25; 59 percent of spending for consumers who earn under $20,000 and 48 percent for those making more than $50,000. Among metropolitan areas, housing consumed 36 percent of household budgets in San Diego but 28 percent in Cleveland. Food ate up 19 percent of household budgets in Buffalo and 12 percent in Atlanta. And health care ranged from 7 percent of household budgets in Kansas City to 3 percent in San Francisco.

Who's worth the most? Generally, people who make the most money. The 20 percent of people who had the highest incomes also held 44 percent of household net worth; their median net worth was $111,770. The 20 percent of people with the lowest incomes held 7 percent of household net worth; their median net worth was $4,324. Typically, married couples of all races were in the best shape financially. In 1990, median income for a married-couple family was $39,895 — 42 percent higher than for a female householder with no husband present. The disparity widened even more among families with children: $41,260 for the married couple and $13,092 for the single-mother household. Less predictably, households headed by women reported a slightly higher median wealth than households headed by men without a wife at home. Many of those women householders are elderly, including widows, who have had more time to accumulate wealth — some of it from their late husbands.

In 1910, 17.5 percent of "working-class wives" with no children were employed, compared to only 4.4 percent of those with children under age seven and 8.4 percent of those whose children were seven or older. Another 16.8 percent of the women with no children, 17.9 percent of women with younger children and 14.3 percent of women with older children kept boarders. Among blacks, even then, nearly one in four with younger children and almost one in three with older children worked outside the home. By 1940, 25 percent of women over age 14 were in the labor force, a figure that might have been understated by the indeterminate number who took in paid boarders or did sewing and other piecework at home. By 1960, the proportion of working women had climbed to 37 percent. By 1990, the proportion appeared to have plateaued at about 57 percent overall and at 73 percent among women age 25 to 34. The surge of women into the work force slowed, perhaps as a result of the recession and of rising birthrates, which, according to the Bureau of Labor Statistics (appropriately enough) were temporarily keeping some women at home. Today, as many as three in four mothers with school-age children work outside the home. In 1990, the mother was in the labor force in 61 percent of families with children under 18 — a proportion that ranged from 53 percent for families with children under 6 and 68 percent when the youngest child was 6 or older. Nearly one in six women — black and white — were in the labor force. Nearly the same proportion of women — 62 percent — worked in families maintained by a single mother. A female householder with no husband present worked full-time in 8.5 percent of white households, 7.8 percent in black ones, and 9.2 percent in Hispanic households.

The labor participation rate among men, while slipping, remained around 75 percent, but with staggering disparities among whites, blacks and Hispanic men and among young men in particular. Both the husband and wife worked in 60 percent of married-couple families with children under 18 years old. When the wife worked, too, the impact on family income was sizable. When only one partner was in the labor force, the median among whites was $37,840 if only the husband worked and $30,657 if only the wife did. If both had jobs, their combined median income was $50,064. Among blacks, the median was $43,273 when both were employed but $28,827 if only the husband had a job and $24,471 if just the wife did. Among Hispanic people, the median for a dual-earner couple was $37,659, and about $23,000 for a single-earner couple — regardless of whether the sole breadwinner was the husband or wife.

That women closed their earnings gap with men was a mixed blessing — in 1990, the narrower gap was less a reflection of progress by women than of a decline in men's earnings. The ratio between what women and men make working full-time, year-round soared 18 percent over the decade to a record high. Still, male executives reported median earnings 57 percent higher than females, male professionals made 41 percent more, men in technical occupations got 53 percent more, and even men in clerical occupations had a 42 percent higher median income. Some gains were wiped out by the rising cost of child care. A Census Bureau analysis found that during the mid-1980s, child-care expenses jumped 17 percent over less than three years. Those costs consumed about 7 percent of average family income but more than one fifth of the family incomes among mothers at or near the poverty level.

Gains were also recorded by minority groups, though with sharp variations. Median income for blacks rose faster than for others, particularly in the Northeast and on the West Coast. In the Midwest, though, the gap with whites widened. Nationally, one in seven blacks reported family incomes of $50,000 or more — more than 1 million, or double the number a decade earlier. The comparable proportion for whites was one in three. Since 1967, the proportion of black households making $100,000 or more (in 1990 inflation-adjusted dollars) also more than doubled, to 1.1 percent (compared to 4.7 percent among whites). But the proportion of blacks making under $5,000 increased, too, if slightly, to 14 percent (while it declined among white households).

Blacks are the only group in which women outnumber men in the labor force. Black women, who were more likely to work year-round and full-time than white women, raised their median earnings to 92 percent of the median earnings of comparable white women, compared to only 79 percent in 1969. Black men working full-time still lagged behind white men. In 1989, they made seventy-two cents for every dollar earned by a white man, compared to seventy-three cents in 1979 and sixty-seven cents in 1969. Overall, black households hardly gained any ground compared to whites. In 1979, a black household, on average, brought in fifty-nine cents for every dollar that a white household made. A decade later, the typical black household was still making the same fifty-nine cents. The median income of black families was about the same in 1979 and 1989, adjusted for inflation. Among married couples, though, the income gap in 1990 between blacks and whites had narrowed to 14 percent – a record low. Black married-couple families earned eighty-four cents for every dollar earned by whites, compared to seventy-six cents in 1975 and sixty-eight cents in 1967.

The income disparity between white and Hispanic married-couple families is actually widening, to just about where blacks and whites had been a quarter century earlier. Hispanic median income trailed that of Asians, non-Hispanic whites, and blacks. Typically, Cubans fared better than Mexicans and Puerto Ricans. Hispanic women are least likely among the major racial and ethnic groups to work outside the home.

Education may be the best barometer of earnings, but the results during the 1980s were mixed. Black women logged the most impressive gains. In part, that was a consequence of changing jobs. Only about four decades ago, a majority of black working women were domestics. Today, perhaps 2 percent are (or 163,000, according to the Bureau of Labor Statistics). By 1990, more than half were in managerial, professional, technical or administrative jobs. Educational attainment and income usually rose in tandem, although the gap in median earnings between men and women actually grew with more schooling. Among high school dropouts, the disparity was $5,009; among college graduates, it spread to $15,162. Earnings of black men actually fell during the 1980s, even though their educational levels rose. So did earnings of white men, but not as much. The median income for a black man working full-time was $20,426 in 1989, off 6 percent from 1979. The comparable decline for a white man was 4 percent, to $28,540. Moreover, black men with college degrees still made only about three quarters the pay that white college graduates collected – $31,380 versus $41,090.

"Education is often touted as the ticket out of this quagmire," the Population Reference Bureau said of the prospects for a class of permanently poor blacks. "However, the economic returns for educational attainment are not as lucrative for blacks as they are for whites. Furthermore, jobs requiring highly educated workers will contribute only a small proportion of the total number of new jobs in the near future. This does not argue against improving educational levels among blacks, but it does suggest that education may not be a sufficient condition for achieving better jobs and higher incomes." Or, as Andrew Hacker has written, more education may only move a black person ahead of other blacks.

The extent to which people participated in the labor force also varied widely by state, ranging from 75 percent in Alaska to a startlingly low 43 percent in West Virginia. Among white men, the rate was highest in Alaska — 85 percent. Among black men, it was highest in Hawaii — 74 percent. And among Hispanic men, the rate was highest in Virginia — 89 percent. The percentage of women participating in the labor force trailed men by about 10 percent uniformly. A smaller proportion of elderly men are in the work force. More are retiring early, even without full benefits. Between 1950 and 1990, the proportion of men 65 and over in the work force shrank from nearly half to one in six; the proportion 55 and older contracted from two thirds to two in five. Nearly one in four women 55 and over are in the work force, a bigger proportion than in 1950. But the proportion 65 and over declined to about half the men's share. Still, nearly one in ten women 65 and over were working.

If the opportunity to retire early signifies social progress, the lack of opportunity for teenagers just beginning to look for jobs suggests something else entirely. Automation and foreign competition have conspired to foreclose alternatives for entry-level jobs, much less job security and a career, in industries ranging from the mills that manufacture steel in Indiana to those that weave textiles in North Carolina. Making a quick buck can be as much a goal in the ghetto as on Wall Street, except that corporate raiders generally don't carry guns. Jobs may be scarce, but so, among some teenagers, are commitment and vision. In 1990, half of America's teenagers were not even looking for work. The combination of fewer available jobs and less inclination to find them reduced the employment rate among black teenagers to less than one in four.

Despite the staggering proportion of blacks living in poverty, the 1980s witnessed some promising growth of a black middle class. That not everyone makes it, though, is evident from the lingering gaps between blacks and whites elsewhere. In Maine, Vermont and Montana, states with tiny black populations, the median household income for blacks and whites was virtually identical — in contrast to Ohio, Wisconsin, Alabama, Mississippi and Louisiana, where whites made about twice as much as blacks. In Connecticut's affluent Fairfield County, median income was $53,300 for whites and $30,600 for blacks. In Manhattan, white median income was $42,100. The median for blacks was $18,100. The Census Bureau found that between 1967 and 1990, the proportion of black families making more than $50,000 more than doubled, from 7 percent to 15 percent. The proportion earning less than $5,000 increased by half, from 8 percent to 12 percent. The middle group shriveled, from 85 percent to 73 percent. But in Queens, New York City's largest middle-class borough, with 700,000 households, an astonishing statistic was personified by people like Winston St. Kitts, a subway car maintainer; and families like the Grimsleys of Cambria Heights, a schoolteacher, an auditor, and their two children; and the Cooks of Far Rockaway, a retired nurse, a computer operator, and their three children. In 1989, the median income for black households in the borough virtually matched the median income of white households. Over ten years, the median income of black households in Queens rose 31 percent, adjusted for inflation, compared to 19 percent for white households. As a result, the gap between the median incomes of black and white households narrowed dramatically. It was 10 percent in 1979, but only .2 percent in

1989. Progress was exemplified by people like thirty-five-year-old Sybil Burnett, who conserved her salary as a paralegal to pay for an apartment and for law school tuition. "When I went to college, you could see so many things you could acquire, you felt you could achieve whatever you set your mind on," she recalled. But Andrea Rattray, a thirty-one-year-old single mother, graduated to the middle class only because she shared the rent with her mother, who works in the personnel department of the United Nations. "With two of us together, we're surviving," she said. "If we went our separate ways it would be rough."

Statistical equality can be chimerical. The gains may be a greater reflection of immigration from the Caribbean than of progress by American-born blacks; many black families graduated to the middle-income category only because more members of the household were working than in a white household; some wealthier whites left the borough during the decade and the median income of the rest was probably depressed because Hispanic people and elderly widows were included in the count of those whites who remained. And, while median income for blacks rose faster than for whites citywide, the black median was still about 40 percent less. Still, the figures signal the latest phase, if a more protracted one, of an evolution that has lifted every other minority group into what is commonly called the middle class. Blacks, who constitute about 20 percent of the borough's population, make up 18 percent of Queens households with income of $35,000 or more. Blacks who make at least $35,000 constitute 49 percent of the black population; whites earning that amount make up 49 percent of the white population. The nation's most ethnically and racially diverse county has also reached income equilibrium. "They make it to Queens," said Frank Vardy, a demographer with New York's Department of City Planning, "because they want the American Dream."

Disparities in median income elsewhere revealed a profoundly stratified nation and vividly uneven prosperity. The median in Mississippi, the lowest of any state, was less than half of what it was in Connecticut, the highest. Median income declined by 10 percent or more during the decade in Iowa, Louisiana, Montana, North Dakota, West Virginia, Wisconsin and Wyoming — states ravaged because there was too little water or too much oil. In 1989, the only major gains were registered by Kentucky, where the economy was invigorated by new Toyota plants and by their suppliers, and by New Mexico, which was being resuscitated by a new General Mills cereal factory and by renewed oil and gas exploration. Virtually every state was riven by vast income differentials. Median income, adjusted for inflation, contracted in twenty-four states — from Arizona and New Mexico through the Farm Belt to the Midwestern notches in the frayed Rust Belt. In South Carolina, median income rose in the 1980s, but none of the increase lined the state's deep poverty pockets. The poverty rate was 12.3 percent in nine suburban counties, 13.7 percent in the three urban counties, and 19.2 percent in the thirty-four rural counties — with a high of 35.8 percent in Allendale. The engines that had traditionally driven the South's economy — cotton, steel, tobacco and textiles — played relatively minor roles in the region's resurgence during a decade in which per capita income rose in every southern state except Mississippi. North Carolina remained the nation's largest textile producer, but the state lost 43,000 jobs in that industry during the 1980s — to 208,000 from a peak of 290,000 in 1973.

In New Hampshire, where rivers and major highways run longitudinally, the income divide split the state latitudinally. Coos, the northernmost county, reported an average median income $16,000 lower than the wealthiest one, Rockingham, in the south. In 1979, the average household in suburban Bloomfield Hills, Michigan, made seven times as much as the average household in Highland Park, which is surrounded by Detroit. Within ten years, the disparity had more than doubled. The legendary miracle of high technology that catapulted Massachusetts' median income 19 percent in the 1980s bypassed places like Brockton and Quincy. In 1990, about one in four unemployment claims was being filed by Massachusetts residents with a college degree and technical or professional credentials. The proportion was even higher among those skilled workers whose last job was along the East's version of Silicon Valley, Route 128. A 24 percent increase in median income, to $41,721, elevated Connecticut past Alaska to claim the highest per capita income. But as the 1990s began, Connecticut, one of the last holdouts, begrudgingly imposed an income tax; Bridgeport, the state's largest city, declared bankruptcy; and Greenwich voted to maintain the state's last almshouse — actually a residence for elderly women.

For all of its spectacular growth, California, too, is scarred by contrasts. Median household income soared 21 percent. But the percentage of low-income families also rose, from 34 percent to 37 percent. In Florida, only the sunshine was dispensed equally. Broward County's highest median household income was reported in Sea Ranch Lakes — an astonishing $86,507. Yet in Broward's Pembroke Park, a community composed largely of mobile homes, nearly one fourth of the residents were living below the poverty level. In New York City, more jobs were created in the 1980s than there are people in Buffalo. But the economic snapshot taken by the 1990 census was a posed portrait. People were striving to put the best face on an emerging recession that lowered the boom on the greed-is-good ethic of the '80s. "When the census was taken, most of the bad news was still to come," said Samuel Ehrenhalt, the New York regional commissioner of the Federal Bureau of Labor Statistics. "After that, the deluge came and New York City was the center of the storm."

When the clouds parted after what had been a bicoastal recession, a fundamental shift in the work force had taken place. During the second half of the 1980s, the biggest job growth was in executive, administrative and managerial jobs, 22 percent; technicians, 18 percent; and professionals, 16 percent. Among the four largest gainers, only protective services, which grew 16 percent, generally was not dependent on education. Three of every four jobs created in the late 1980s were in service industries.

The number of health-care workers rocketed by 50 percent — in response to the growing number of elderly people, the AIDS epidemic, and the introduction of new technology that generated demand for home health aides, X-ray technologists, medical secretaries, doctors' assistants, physical therapists, surgical technicians and countless clerks to nitpick reams of insurance forms. In 1990 alone, medical employment jumped by 8 percent — the greatest increase in two decades and the biggest in any major job category. During the 1980s, the number of Americans working in the retail trade, health, finance, insurance, real estate, entertainment and recreation rose. More people worked as technicians, in sales, and in protective services when the decade ended than when it began; fewer were employed as private household help or as machine operators. In 1990, more people worked in finance, insurance and real estate than in construction; more were employed in health services than in manufacturing nondurable goods.

Among white men and women, about 27 percent were counted as managers and professionals, compared to 13 percent of the black men and 18 percent of black women. About 19 percent of white men and 7 percent of white women were factory workers, compared to 33 percent of black men and 12 percent of black women. One occupation in which blacks face extinction is farming. Mechanization drove blacks from the South decades ago. As recently as 1960, 11 percent of the people running farms were black, about the same proportion as their share of the general population. By 1990, the proportion of black farmers had plunged to 1.5 percent of the nation's 4.5 million farmers.

Most Americans worked in farming or related occupations when the census began asking about employment in 1820. Precisely 150 years later, the number of blue-collar employees among men was exceeded by white-collar workers for the first time. That same year, the census bowed to the computer revolution: Computer programmers, systems analysts and computer specialists were enumerated for the first time, foreshadowing — or belatedly responding to — a phenomenon that would change the way Americans worked, where they worked, and the education they needed to escape poverty. Even welfare caseworkers were supplanted by computers, but technology can only go so far: Despair cannot be quantified in the magnetic strips on newly issued charge cards that further routinize welfare.

The Waverly Income Maintenance Center on West Fourteenth Street in Manhattan was not on any candidate's itinerary during the 1992 presidential campaign. Nor did pollsters conduct any voter surveys there. But just one visit before the election suggested why George Bush would lose. This place of broken dreams and of dreams that had never been dreamed recalled Plutarch's cautionary precept two millennia ago, an enduring truth that applied to government *and* to politics: "An imbalance between rich and poor is the oldest and most fatal ailment of republics." At the Waverly Center, the shabby second-floor waiting area evokes the apprehension and pain of a hospital emergency room. Forms come before substance (one asks welfare applicants whether their assets include a burial plot). Brian Pierce, a thirty-year-old unemployed hairdresser, was seeking a $2,500 loan to avoid eviction from the apartment he shares with his girlfriend, who was also out of work. John Riley, a forty-seven-year-old consulting engineer, had been burned out of his apartment. Michael Mathew, a thirty-four-year-old costume jewelry maker, was looking for a loan after the company for which he had worked laid off two of its five employees. These three men were among the applicants who defied two enduring stereotypes: None had ever applied for public assistance before or even envisioned that they might need to; all three are white. In 1990, for every household and individual receiving unemployment benefits, two households were receiving welfare. Whatever the impact of economic policy on reapportioning income, even the prerecessionary period had succeeded in redistributing poverty. The burden shifted most vividly from the old to the very young and to more and more wage earners who were working full-time but still struggling.

CHAPTER X

HOW
THE OTHER
HALF LIVES

The New Testament prophesied "the poor always ye have with you," but that was two millennia ago — before advanced civilization invented welfare, food stamps, Medicare and Social Security. Yet as another millennium looms, America has more poor people with — or against — us than ever before. Even after their proportion of the population dipped in the mid-1980s, one in seven Americans was living below the official poverty threshold in 1990. Two years later, the ranks of America's poor had swollen to nearly 36 million — the most since 1964, when President Lyndon B. Johnson boldly declared war on poverty. The poverty rate rose for the second consecutive year, to 14.2 percent — the highest since the recession a decade earlier. The rate climbed even among white married couples — considered the most economically secure family group — to one in twenty, compared to more than one in ten among black married couples. And average income for all American households, adjusted for inflation, declined to diminish purchasing power below the 1979 level.

As the final decade of the century began, welfare rolls in New York City broke the 1 million mark for the first time since the 1970s. At no time in the city's history was the proportion of people receiving public assistance higher. In neighboring Connecticut, the nation's richest state, the number of people receiving food stamps nearly doubled from 1989 to 1991. In ten counties that pockmark the nation's midsection from the Rio Grande to the Canadian border, more than half the residents are classified as poor. In south-central Los Angeles, ground zero of the deadly riots in 1992, nearly one third of all black teenagers were unemployed. And, for the first time, a majority of all poor families were maintained by a woman with no husband present.

Poverty's chief victims have been children and *their* victims. *Delinquency* now seems too quaint a term to describe juvenile crime, which has more than doubled since 1960. Teenage suicide and homicide rates have more than tripled. The proportion of children born to an unmarried mother exploded from one in fifteen to one in four. "The evidence is strong and growing," the ideologically diverse Council on Families in America concluded, "that the current generation of children and youth is the first in our nation's history to be less well-off — psychologically, socially, economically and morally — than their parents were at the same age."

Separate nations live side by side in Dickensian contradiction. Only sixty blocks south of the Harlem census tract with New York City's lowest median household income, $5,092, is an old-money tract in Carnegie Hill on the Upper East Side where the median presses $147,000. One study found that the ratio between black and white family income pretty much stalled by 1970, after having risen considerably from 41 percent in 1940 to 61 percent. One reason is noneconomic. The Census Bureau estimated that had it not been for the decline in married-couple families, black household median income would have been about 15 percent higher if households in 1989 mirrored the pattern that existed in 1969 (the median income of white households would have been higher, too, but by about 10 percent). Sometime in 1970, though, the racial trend lines denoting the percentage of married-couple families with two working spouses intersected. The percentage among whites rose and median income climbed correspondingly; among blacks the percentage of working wives declined, and the gap has been widening ever since. Still, even when white social, economic and demographic characteristics were imputed to black households, blacks came up short: They narrowed the gap, but only to seventy-eight cents for every dollar earned by white households.

The contrasts may have become more visible but, like the poor, they are not new. Nor is the notion of an irredeemable underclass. Well over a century before *Time* magazine popularized the term that Gunnar Myrdal had invoked in *The Challenge of Affluence* in 1963, Charles Loring Brace's first report as head of New York City's Children's Aid Society expressed alarm over the growing "ignorant, debased and permanently poor class in the great cities." What's novel is the conspiracy of economic, social, political, racial and spatial factors that have fostered and perpetuated dependency. Concentration and social isolation, the two ecological strains identified by William Julius Wilson, combined with the precipitous loss of semi-skilled factory jobs, the balkanization of cities by racially segregated public housing and by impenetrable ribbons of concrete expressways, and the appeal of the suburbs to produce what the social historian Michael B. Katz calls "an urban form unlike any other in history." An emerging black middle class is narrowing the gap. But progress has a price. "The condition of the urban black poor has deteriorated over the past quarter century," Dean Alan Wolfe of the New School for Social Research has written, "to the point where it threatens all the other gains in race relations that were realized during the same period."

That the poor have always been with us may provide welcome perspective but little consolation to a nation that regards itself as civilized to a fault. "In the fifty years since the Social Security Act was signed," says Senator Daniel P. Moynihan, "we've never had a time that slowly, but suddenly with much greater force, the country is deciding that we're spending too much money on children." Since even before biblical times, though, society has been ambivalent about the poor, periodically, and sometimes arbitrarily, deciding that some are deserving and others aren't. Charity was largely left to individuals or to organized religion until the Elizabethan poor laws transformed social welfare into a secular obligation. In America, that ambivalence had a special dimension: Poverty was viewed as a temporary detour on an individual's deliverance to manifest destiny rather than as the inevitable consequence to which unfortunates in the Old World had been consigned by cruel fate. Tenement reform was left largely to regulation rather than to direct intervention by government. Welfare as we know it began as a Depression-era vehicle to subsidize widows until their children were old enough to work. "Outdoor relief," the baroque term nineteenth-century bureaucrats devised to distinguish welfare recipients from people consigned to poorhouses, was periodically destigmatized with euphemisms like "public assistance" and "income maintenance." Welfare departments were reincarnated as social service or human resources agencies. In 1990, New York City's enlightened commissioner even decided to rename the human resources department's annual statistical yearbook, which, for decades, had callously been known as "Dependency." But no matter how

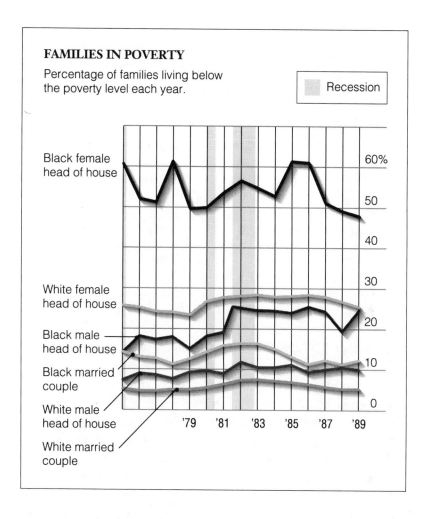

FAMILIES IN POVERTY

Percentage of families living below
the poverty level each year.

Recession

Black female
head of house

60%

50

40

30

White female
head of house

Black male
head of house

20

Black married
couple

10

White male
head of house

'79   '81   '83   '85   '87   '89

0

White married
couple

America spelled relief, regardless of which synonyms were
stricken from the bureaucratic lexicon or whether poverty was
defined as crudely by economists as by popular stereotypes, the
poor have not gone away. As the availability of jobs enabled one
wave of European immigrants after another to graduate into
America's mainstream, poverty was also redefined by race. And
as self-perpetuating poverty festered, its victims became increas-

POVERTY'S UNEVEN GRIP

Percentage of people living below the poverty level in 1990.

LEAST		MOST	
New Hampshire	6.4%	Mississippi	25.2%
Connecticut	6.8	Louisiana	23.6
New Jersey	7.6	New Mexico	20.6
Hawaii	8.3	West Virginia	19.7
Maryland	8.3	Arkansas	19.1

ingly isolated in a world of violence and despair distinguished by guns and drugs from previous eras but subject to familiar misconceptions and totemic myths. Only fifty years ago, more poor people lived in rural America than in its cities. When the prosperous 1950s ended, fully 40 percent of the nation's urban householders were earning too little to avoid poverty. Today, half the nation's poor are either children (four in ten of all poor people) or the elderly (one in ten). The poverty rate for children — nearly 20 percent — was nearly double the rate for the elderly. Despite durable stereotypes, only one in ten poor children was black, urban, and living with a single mother on welfare.

"When a lot of people are out of work," President Calvin Coolidge philosophized, "unemployment results." When a lot of people are poor, poverty results. Poor people have no problem describing poverty: It is a precarious condition in which they cannot afford to fulfill certain basic needs for themselves and for their families. The government's technical definition is more arbi-

IMPOVERISHED SINGLE-MOTHER FAMILIES

Percentage of women-headed families with young children living below the poverty level in 1989.

Louisiana	73.4%	South Carolina	58.4%
Mississippi	72.5	Missouri	58.2
West Virginia	71.5	Massachusetts	58.0
North Dakota	70.2	Washington	57.5
Kentucky	67.7	Georgia	57.4
Montana	67.1%	Kansas	57.3%
Arkansas	66.9	New York	57.2
South Dakota	66.2	Colorado	57.2
Alabama	65.6	Utah	57.1
Oklahoma	65.0	Texas	57.0
Michigan	64.6%	Arizona	56.4%
Iowa	64.1	North Carolina	55.9
Ohio	63.1	Indiana	55.8
Maine	62.8	Florida	53.9
Wyoming	62.4	Vermont	53.6
Rhode Island	62.2%	Connecticut	51.5%
New Mexico	62.2	California	50.3
Wisconsin	61.9	Virginia	50.3
Idaho	61.2	New Jersey	45.9
Oregon	60.9	Delaware	45.3
Nebraska	59.9%	Nevada	44.7%
Tennessee	59.4	New Hampshire	44.5
Minnestota	59.1	Hawaii	41.7
Illinois	58.6	District of Columbia	41.7
Pennsylvania	58.4	Maryland	40.1
		Alaska	39.0%

trary. For bureaucrats, it is impossible to determine who is poor without deciding first what constitutes poverty. The official definition was contrived in the 1960s; it has barely been reexamined since. The poverty level is defined as three times the price of an imaginary market basket of staples conjured up three decades ago by government economists. It is adjusted annually for inflation, but fails to measure regional differences in living costs and changes in family spending patterns. It also has few defenders. In 1990, the threshold varied from $6,652 for a person living alone to $13,359 for a family of four to $26,848 for a family of nine or more.

Critics who say the level is too low argue that as housing and child-care costs have risen, the typical family spends five times its hypothetical food budget these days, not three times. The census found that among low-income households living in rented apartments or homes, 44 percent of married-couple households and 47 percent of one-parent households — including a staggering 62 percent of Hispanic households headed by one parent — spent more than 50 percent of their incomes on housing. (In owner-occupied housing, 6 percent of the married couples and 14 percent of the one-parent households — but 30 percent among blacks — spent that much of their income on housing.) But another chorus of critics says the government formula exaggerates the extent of poverty because it excludes noncash benefits like Medicaid or Medicare, food stamps, and subsidized housing. Among one-parent households in rented apartments or homes, 36 percent received welfare or SSI; 41 percent received food stamps.

When the Census Bureau subtracted all government cash transfers from the official definition of income, the poverty population burgeoned from 32 million Americans to 49 million and the poverty rate rose from 13 percent to 20 percent. Conversely, when noncash benefits were included and taxes were subtracted, the nation's poverty population declined to 26 million — about half the higher estimate, but still one in ten Americans. No formula is foolproof. But one that belatedly revisits typical family spending patterns and how their budgets vary with household size, and assesses the impact of noncash benefits, taxes, and unreported income generated by a flourishing underground economy, would enable economists to quantify poverty more realistically and relevantly. So would a Moynihan tax bill amendment that invoked the Employment Act of 1946, which required an annual calculation of unemployment rates as the model for a national gauge of dependency and an interim goal of reducing it from 13 percent to 10 percent for families with children. Some people may remain unemployable. And America will still have to reconcile the goal of forcing single moms to work with our totemic "family values." But a consensus on the dimensions of poverty might galvanize a broader constituency for dealing with a national affliction that, one way or another, has made everybody a victim. Lawrence Mead, a self-styled conservative political scientist at New York University, likened the latest ferment to a second civil war — a war that, like the first one, the nation cannot afford to lose. "We're trying to prevent a secession of the poor," he said, "from work, school, politics, from mainstream institutions of every kind."

How much deprivation constitutes poverty is in the eye, or the stomach, of the beholder. Caroline Carter, a thirty-year-old Milwaukee widow with two teenage children, makes about $13,800 a year — too much to qualify for food stamps, Medicaid or welfare benefits, but enough to leave her about $60 a month for clothes, medicine and other costs after paying for rent, meals, utilities, a student loan and bus fare. "I am poor," she said unambiguously. Hunger often manifests itself as a shortsighted lack of healthy eating habits rather than of food. Few Americans resemble the horrific images of shriveled Somalian children. "The poor are not hungry and undernourished," Robert Rector of the Heritage Foundation and other critics of the welfare system complain. "In fact, adults are more likely to be overweight than are middle-class persons." How deprived can they be when most have a car, nearly half have air conditioners, and nearly one third have microwave ovens? he said. But to suggest that sheer bulk implies a nutritious diet or that a few plug-in creature comforts compensate for other material and spiritual deficits or that most of the poor are shiftless and homeless willing enrollees in a permanent underclass is merely a reflexive embrace of stereotypes. That those images, like all stereotypes, may have some factual foundation is irrefutable. The fundamental question is whether they represent the exception or the rule and whether or not they are relevant.

The 1990 census counted nearly 32 million Americans living in poverty. Fully half the family householders worked. Poverty rates remain higher among blacks and Hispanic people, but about half of all those Americans classified as poor are non-Hispanic whites. Nearly one in three blacks, about one in five Hispanic people, and fewer than one in eleven whites received cash assistance, food stamps, Medicaid or housing subsidies when the 1980s ended. Still, the actual number of whites receiving benefits in an average month exceeded the number of blacks or Hispanic people. The 1990 rates ranged from 25 percent for children under the age of 3 to 12 percent for the elderly and 11 percent for everybody else between the ages of 18 and 64. Children under the age of 18 accounted for 40 percent of the poor; the elderly constituted another 11 percent. More than half the poor families were headed by a female householder with no spouse. Among blacks, that category accounted for 75 percent of poor families. Fully 60 percent of children under age 6 living in a single-mother family are poor.

The rate for blacks had registered a sharp decline between 1959 and 1979 — from 55 percent to 31 percent. Then it stalled, slipping into a chronic state that seemed resistant to customary remedies like more schooling, which no longer guaranteed commensurate gains in wages, and even work, for which wages had also stopped growing. The proportion of poor people who were white (67 percent) or black (29 percent) stayed about the same during the 1980s, but the proportion identified as Hispanic expanded (from 11 percent to 18 percent). The poverty rate for whites was halved between 1959 and 1979, then remained at about 9 or 10 percent. The proportion of whites with family income under $5,000 remained at about 2.5 percent during the 1980s. Among black families, the proportion swelled to 12 percent. Whatever trickled down had evaporated before it reached the poorest blacks.

But the most striking revelation was how poverty has been redistributed — a testament to what government can help achieve and to what challenges await. During a decade that boomed between two busts, 4.3 million more Americans became poor. One in four of them was a child under 18 years old. In contrast, one in twenty-five of the newly impoverished were 65 years old or older (although black elderly people had the highest poverty rate of any age group; more than half are poor). Overall, the nation's poverty rate has zigzagged from 22.2 percent in 1960 to a low of 11.1 percent in 1973, then up again to 15.2 percent in 1983, when it began declining until the end of the decade. Sometime in the 1970s the poverty rates for children and the elderly crossed paths. For the elderly, the rate dove from 35 percent in 1959 to 11 percent three decades later. For children, it rose from 15 percent in 1970 to more than 20 percent in 1989. In the 1980s, the percentage of black, white and Hispanic poor children increased. Americans 80 and older were among the most likely to be living at the edge of poverty, but only those 85 and over even approached the proportion of poor children under age 5 — nearly one in four. The 1990 census and a follow-up report by the Census Bureau found that children under age 18 accounted for 40 percent of all poor people and only 24 percent of the nonpoor. The elderly represented 11 percent of the poor and 12 percent of the nonpoor. Only in New Hampshire was the rate for children under 5 years old in single digits — 9 percent. In three states — Mississippi, New Mexico and West Virginia — the rate for children under 5 was higher than 30 percent.

"The United States," wrote the economist Sylvia Ann Hewlett, "ranks No. 2 worldwide in per capita income but does not even make it into the top 10 on any significant indicator of child welfare." The Census Bureau's own analysis found that the United States ranked eighth in the percentage of low birth weight babies. In Australia, Canada, West Germany and Sweden, at least 99 percent of poor families with children received some government assistance; in the United States, by one authoritative estimate, fewer than 73 percent did. American children led in another category, though: the proportion whose parents are likely to get divorced. And children of divorced or separated parents are almost twice as likely to be living in poverty than when their parents were together. Researchers found that the percentage of children living in poverty nearly doubled, from 19 percent to 36 percent, within only four months of the break-up — in large part because of the gap left by the father's departure and by his failure to pay child support. The census found that of the 5 million women who were supposed to receive child support payments only half collected the full amount. The rest split about equally between those who received a fraction of what they were due or nothing at all. Another 2.7 million women sought but never received child support awards. More family households with children were headed by a single parent in the United States than in any other major developed country.

"Today," the bipartisan National Commission on Children declared unequivocally as the 1990s began, "children are the poorest Americans." Drawing on the 1990 census, the Children's Defense Fund provided stark specifics on the proportion of children in poverty: half the Hispanic children in Massachusetts, the sixth wealthiest state by median family income; nearly half the Asian children in Wisconsin; more than half the black children in Louisiana; and one in four white children in West Virginia. A black child's chances of being poor were nearly one in two, a Hispanic child's more than one in three (one in two among

Puerto Ricans), an Asian-American child's one in six, and a white child's one in eight. Typically, a poor family had 2.2 children. Nearly two thirds of those families included a householder who was in the labor force, and he or she received more income from that work than from welfare. In 1990, 40 percent of poor people 15 and older worked, 9 percent full-time. Among poor family householders, 50 percent worked, 15 percent full-time. In poor female-headed households, 43 percent of the householders worked, 8 percent full-time. In fully 60 percent of all poor families, at least one person worked, and two people did in 18 percent of those families.

B ut even for people struggling to escape poverty by gainful employment, a job didn't always suffice. "Working poor" is no oxymoron. The proportion of low-paid full-time workers declined between 1964, when it was 24 percent of all full-time workers, and 1974. The rate remained frozen at about 12 percent through 1979. A decade later, though, 16 percent of full-time workers did not make enough to remain in the ranks of the nonpoor. Just one year later, the proportion rose to 18 percent. In 1985, nearly one in ten adults who became poor worked year-round, full time; almost the same proportion also slipped into poverty even though their work load increased. (Still, the largest proportion who escaped poverty had found year-round, full-time jobs or became part of a married-couple family.) The Census Bureau defined low-paid workers as those whose wages totaled less than the poverty level for a family of four, which was $12,195 in 1990. To make even that much, a person would have to earn $6.10 an hour for working fifty forty-hour weeks. In the 1980s, as many as one in five married-couple households in which the husband worked full-time but his wife did not work were unable to avoid poverty. Again, the figures were even more daunting for young people and for black and Hispanic full-time workers. Among 18- to 24-year-olds, 40 percent of the men and 48 percent of the women who were working full-time fit the Census Bureau's definition of low earners (although presumably not all of them were supporting a family of four). Among blacks, 25 percent earned poverty-level incomes even though they worked full-time; among Hispanic people, 31 percent had full-time jobs that did not pay enough to qualify them as nonpoor. The percentage of black males between the ages of 25 and 34 who either had no job or earned less than the poverty threshold leaped from 37 percent to 45 percent. The prospects were grimmest for black high school dropouts; when the decade ended, nearly 84 percent were either jobless or were paid below the poverty threshold.

An optimist — loosely defined as somebody with a job that pays above the poverty level — might exult that the working poor represented only 2.6 percent of all Americans working full-time. Also, because so many were single or members of households with more than one worker, only 13 percent of the people whom the Census Bureau classified as low-paid full-time employees were actually poor themselves. A skills deficit, a surfeit of immigrants and a severe decline in labor union membership each contributed, to a degree, to an inequality in earnings. But global forces that depressed blue-collar wages and polarized Americans economically and socially challenged the Horatio Alger ethic. If hard work is its own reward, it is often not enough of one to survive, much less to succeed.

W here do poor people live? Mostly with other poor people. Nationally, poverty rates ranged from 8.7 percent in the suburbs to 19 percent in the central cities. The rate was 12.7 percent in metropolitan areas and 16.3 percent in rural America, where a larger proportion of poor blacks than nonpoor blacks live. Poor Hispanic people are more likely to live in metropolitan areas — 92 percent of the Hispanic poor, compared to 78 percent of poor blacks and 70 percent of poor whites. Predictably, a majority of the two thirds of poor people who live in metropolitan areas live in central cities; a majority of the nonpoor live in the suburbs. Whites are an exception, though. In metropolitan areas, just under half of poor whites live in the central cities. Still, in 1960, families living in New York City made 93 percent of the median income of their suburban counterparts. Nearly thirty years later, as family composition changed, the city families' percentage of suburban family income had plunged to about half.

America's poor are often concentrated in what the Census Bureau refers to as "poverty areas" and what are colloquially called ghettos — census tracts where 20 percent or more of the residents are poor. About 37 percent of poor people lived in those areas where the poverty rate in 1990 was 33.3 percent, or two and a half times the national average. Among them, 59 percent lived in central cities, 28 percent in rural areas, and only 13 percent in suburbs — just as Jefferson had feared. "The mobs of great cities," he warned nearly two centuries ago, "add just so much to the support of pure government, as sores do to the strength of the human body." Imagine how he would have characterized the great mobs of seemingly obsolete cities. Or, for that matter, how he would have reconciled his dream of "a chosen country, with room enough for our descendants to the hundredth and thousandth generation" with the twentieth-century exodus from a rural America that had also been rendered obsolete by the grim circumstances of many Americans who had grown dependent on land that no longer depended on them.

More than half of all blacks in central cities — 54 percent — live in poor neighborhoods, as do 67 percent of all the poor blacks in central cities. Blacks are more concentrated in those poverty pockets than whites or Hispanic people. Regardless of any other factor, one reason for the segregation is housing discrimination. Among whites, 17 percent of those who live in central cities live in poverty areas; so do 41 percent of poor whites. Among Hispanic people, 44 percent live in poor neighborhoods; 61 percent of the Hispanic poor do, too.

Intensive — and expensive — education and training programs can wean a select if indefinite number of people from welfare. But another major obstacle impedes the welfare-to-work agenda: not enough jobs within reach of the jobless. An Urban Institute consultant, Mark Alan Hughes, suggests that the government invest in systems of reverse commuting in metropolitan Los Angeles, Chicago, Philadelphia, Detroit, Washington, and other places where employment declined and the percentage of people in poverty soared in the central cities while those trends were reversed in the suburbs. "The new metropolis is predicated on mobility, and private automobile travel is how this mobility is realized," Hughes reported. "However, the transportation costs associated with all this mobility are regressive. Participation in work, shopping, schooling and so on requires travel in the modern metropolis. What for most people is a low-density life-style becomes for the poor a set of costly barriers. Some of the most persuasive post–L.A. riot rhetoric says give the poor a greater stake in their communities. That's the right incentive, but the wrong geography."

If *underclass* is defined as adults who are high school dropouts, members of a household that collects public assistance, never-married mothers, or chronically underemployed men, then the number who live in rural America exceeds those who live in the suburbs. And the rural underclass is more than half the size of the more visible group that epitomizes the urban ghetto. Using those criteria, research by William P. O'Hare and Brenda Curry-White for the Population Reference Bureau concluded that a certifiable underclass accounts for 2.4 percent of the rural population, compared to 3.4 percent of central city residents, and, overall, represents 3 million, or 2.1 percent, of working-age Americans. Non-Hispanic whites constitute a majority of that underclass — 55 percent. Blacks account for 32 percent and Hispanic people 8 percent. But nearly 7 percent of black adults were lumped in that category, compared to 5.5 percent of Hispanic adults and only 1 percent of whites. Regardless of where they live, the biggest segment of people with underclass characteristics are young adults between the ages of 19 and 34. They represented about half the rural underclass and six in ten among central city dwellers. Women account for a greater proportion in cities; so do people over age 50 in rural America. Non-Hispanic whites make up only 17 percent of the urban underclass but 55 percent of the rural one. Blacks are 32 percent of the rural underclass but 49 percent of the urban one — although a larger proportion of rural than urban blacks is classified as underclass. Hispanic people make up only 8 percent of the rural underclass but 29 percent in central cities. More than twice as many people who met the underclass characteristics were identified in the South as in the Northeast.

About one in four poor people lives in the South, the highest concentration of any region. Whites had the highest poverty rates in Arkansas and New Mexico. More than four in ten blacks were below the poverty level in Mississippi, Louisiana, Arkansas and Wisconsin (the poverty rate among blacks was below 10 percent in only one state, Hawaii, where it was 8.8 percent). More than half the black children under the age of 5 were poor in a broad swath of the nation's midsection: Ohio, Michigan, Wisconsin, Minnesota, South Dakota, Kentucky, Alabama, Mississippi, Arkansas and Louisiana. In North Dakota, every black person age 75 and older was poor (although the census counted only six of them in all). Massachusetts recorded the highest percentage of poor Hispanic people — 38 percent — and Maryland the lowest — 11 percent. In Massachusetts and Pennsylvania, more than half the Hispanic children under age 5 were poor. The highest poverty rate among Asians was in Wisconsin — 25 percent — which was nearly double the national average.

Ten counties, all of them largely rural, shared a dubious distinction: More than half their residents were poor. The highest poverty rate, 63 percent, was recorded in South Dakota's Shannon County, the Badlands home of most of the Pine Ridge Indian Reservation and the site of the Wounded Knee Massacre, which occurred as the nation's centennial census was being conducted. In the southwestern part of the state, the Pine Ridge Reservation is a 2-million acre rural slum punctuated by arid buttes instead of burned-out tenements. Pine Ridge is home to 16,000 descendants of Crazy Horse and other heroes of the Oglala branch of the Sioux. Fewer than three in ten adults are employed. Most of those with jobs work for agencies of a government whose greed cost the people their pride and whose guilt-edged good intentions have plunged many into a despair so deep that it gives the concept of underclass and the grim reality of dependency a whole other dimension. Alcoholism claims ten times as many lives there as the national average. One in five households lacks a motor vehicle, which is the only means of mechanized transportation within Shannon County or off the reservation to a job. The infant mortality rate on the reservation is three times the national average. "We're a fifth-, going on sixth-generation welfare state," said a leader of the tribe, Leo Vocu.

Starr County, Texas, hard by the Rio Grande, was the second poorest county, followed by East Carroll Parish, Louisiana; and Tunica and Holmes counties, Mississippi. The other six were in Kentucky, Mississippi, South Dakota and Texas.

Only ten counties in the nation recorded poverty levels of less than 3 percent — three of them in New Jersey. Texas won bragging rights for having the least poor county — Loving, population 107, just north of Pecos. Like Yellowstone National Park, population 52, Loving reported no poor people at all. Few places were so insulated. Even in Palm Beach, Florida, a glitzy treasure isle by every gauge, the Census Bureau found 577 residents out of 9,814 who said they made less than the poverty level. "Rather unbelievable," was how the head of the Palm Beach Community Chest/United Way pronounced the bureau's discovery. Elsewhere in south Florida, though, the poor are less anomalous. While the population of Broward, Palm Beach and Dade counties expanded by an impressive 26 percent in the 1980s, it was outpaced by the 29 percent increase in the number of poor people. In Broward, the number of poor families with children under the age of 5 rose 65 percent. In Lake County, almost abutting Walt Disney World, nearly half of Leesburg's preschool children are poor. Leesburg's overall poverty level was 19.6 percent. In Mount Dora, where the poverty rate was 16 percent, 110 residents reported income of $100,000 a year, but another 127 reported making less than $5,000. While California's population grew 26 percent during the 1980s, the number of poor related children grew by 41 percent, the number of poor families by 28 percent, and the number of poor elderly people by 21 percent. Poverty and prosperity expanded side by side to create a precarious economic and social fault line. Single-parent households account for about one fifth of all households with children in California's Orange County, where the overall poverty rate was 5.2 percent. But one fifth of all families there headed by single mothers were poor.

In St. Louis, 24.6 percent of all residents and 39.3 percent of the children were poor — a startling contrast with surrounding St. Louis County, where the rate was 5.6 percent for all the residents and 7.4 percent for children. But even St. Louis looks like a glittering city on a hill from across the Mississippi River in East St. Louis — a city so impoverished that it even had to give its City Hall away to satisfy a court judgment in a suit brought by a prisoner who had been beaten by another inmate in the municipal jail. Mechanization in the meat-packing industry all but relegated East St. Louis into a ghost town that lost half its population since 1960. Three fourths of those remaining are poor enough to qualify for some form of public assistance. If few cities envy East St. Louis, at least misery loves company. It represents, perhaps, the worst case in a litany of ravaged cities, including Camden and Gary, that plunged from vibrant blue-collar economies into small-town, and nearly real-life, versions of a menacing film called *Escape from New York*. In Newark, a concerted effort to revive the city's downtown prompted Mayor Sharpe James to exclaim: "The Phoenix is rising again." But his metaphor also suggested just how far his city had fallen — it lost 52,000 residents, or 16 percent of its population, in the last decade alone. Moreover, it is arguable whether the gleaming office towers, courthouse, college dormitories and Postal Service distribution center will benefit most of the city's remaining residents. "Newark is experiencing one of the biggest inner-city developments anywhere, but the problem is, there's no trickle down," said Norman J. Glickman, director of the Center for Urban Policy Research at Rutgers University. "Go five blocks from the core of the business district and you find some of the worst urban conditions in the United States."

Louisiana, typically ranked among the poorest states, was plunged further into poverty during the 1980s. The overall poverty rate rose from 19 percent to 24 percent. One third of the residents of New Orleans are poor. So are three of every four children under age 5 in households headed by a woman. In Colorado, the census found almost one in six children living in poverty, compared to one in nine a decade earlier. In Tunica County, Mississippi, which was mercifully bumped in 1990 from the nation's poorest county to its fourth poorest, abject poverty is largely unabated. Still, casino jobs sliced the unemployment rate. And the infamous row of shacks that dumped their waste into Sugar Ditch just a half block from the business district has been razed at long last. And Johnnie Mae Milbrooks, in whose home the governor of Mississippi pledged to provide new housing for Sugar Ditch tenants, finally got a federally subsidized apartment — after waiting seven years. "Never get your hopes up," Milbrooks said philosophically. Tunica County may have little else in common with upper Manhattan, but in places like Sugar Ditch or West 162nd Street in Washington Heights, places largely hidden behind facades erected by civic boosters, people share one common emotion: despair. Riots erupted in Washington Heights during the summer of 1992 after a young Dominican immigrant who had dabbled in drug dealing was shot to death by a police officer. The year before, Washington Heights led New York City in murders, with 122, most of them drug related. Of those residents who survived, nearly one third are poor. "This is not a nurturing kind of neighborhood," one disgusted resident said. "It takes, but it doesn't give."

The census's portrait of the poor represents only a rough sketch, rather than a profile, because of disproportionate undercounting. However incomplete, it is not a pretty picture. Blacks were poorer than whites, regardless of whether they had gotten a high school diploma or a college degree. Among the 31 million people classified as poor, 39 percent were in families whose income was less than half of the poverty threshold. Another 400,000 poor families and 800,000 poor unrelated individuals reported annual income that was a precarious $500 above the poverty level. The Census Bureau found that almost one in six Americans received some form of government assistance during at least one month in the late 1980s, even before the recession peaked. The survey of food stamps, Supplemental Security Income, Medicaid, housing assistance and the primary welfare program, Aid to Families with Dependent Children, found that while the majority of recipients were white, blacks and Hispanic people were disproportionately represented: Forty percent of blacks, 29 percent of Hispanic people and 11 percent of whites were enrolled in one or more major assistance programs at some point during 1987–88. A lot of people use the programs as a stopgap. The proportion who participated continuously during the entire two-year period was considerably smaller: 26 percent of blacks, 15 percent of Hispanic people and 5 percent of whites. The census study quantified two eternal truths: Members of families headed by women were five times as likely to have received government assistance as members of married-couple families; 21 percent of high school dropouts, 7 percent of the high school graduates, and only 3 percent of people who had attended college for one or more years had collected public assistance during an average month. Among the officially poor, 28 percent said they had received no benefits at all — whether because they were unaware that they were eligible, because they were disqualified because of some asset they owned, or because the bureaucracy was just too daunting. About the same percentage of poor people said they had no medical insurance, as did 12 percent of nonpoor people. Among the 35 million Americans who had no health insurance, 28 percent were poor. Again, age was a defining factor. Among poor children, 22 percent had no medical coverage. Only 2.5 percent of the elderly were uninsured.

"We have a welfare system that nobody likes," said Michael B. Katz, the University of Pennsylvania history professor who has written extensively about the system. "And we have the conjunction of stale rhetoric with an unprecedented situation in American cities." A dependent class of teenage mothers defies precedent. During a recession, it also defied the indulgence of a public accustomed to spending money on the dole but fed up with subsidizing an "undeserving" underclass and frustrated with the plight of the deserving, if seemingly permanent, poor. Welfare cost states more in 1990 than education, and it cost localities more than they spent on highways. New Jersey draconically barred additional payments to mothers on welfare who gave birth to more children — largely a symbolic gesture that would withhold another $2.12 a day and that appeared likely to penalize the children more than their mothers. The National Commission on Children proposed an experimental child support insurance program and tax credits worth $1,000 for every child — not to shortchange other needy Americans but to rectify an imbalance in which the federal government spent 11 times as much on each person over 65 as on each one under 18. By 1990, Washington was spending $353 billion on Medicare and on Social Security. By comparison, the government's budget for food stamps, school lunches, tax credits, Medicaid and welfare for the nonelderly poor was about $100 billion. Government spends about eight times more on the personal health of people 65 and over than on people under 19. Over one fourth of the Medicare budget — more than the government spends on the health care of all American children, Betsy Dworkin of the University of London has written — is spent on patients in their last year of life. (At the beginning of that last year, though, we don't often know it will be the last.)

The biggest single factor in reducing poverty among the elderly was a calculated decision by government to index Social Security payments to inflation. In 1959, 33 percent of white elderly and 63 percent of black elderly were poor. By 1990, the proportions of poor elderly had been cut by more than half — to 10 percent of white elderly, 34 percent of black elderly (and 23 percent of the Hispanic elderly, who had not been counted separately in 1959). Among those 75 years old and older, the poverty rate ranged from a low of 10 percent in California to a high of 37 percent in Mississippi. Among Americans under 18 years old, the percentage living in poverty has increased, at least since 1975, to 16 percent among whites, 45 percent among blacks and 38 percent of Hispanic people.

For all the nation's diversity, for all that immigration and desegregation have done to dilute the melting pot's lumpy molten mass, the poor have become increasingly isolated at the bottom as more mobile Americans graduate from poverty into the middle class. What's left is society's sludge. When the penultimate decade of the twentieth century ended, poverty was increasing among white and Hispanic people, in the Northeast, in metropolitan areas, and among both children and the elderly. The cloud behind the silver lining for blacks was that more poor black families are headed by an unmarried woman and, therefore, are more likely to be dependent on welfare, which, until states started paring benefits, might be ravaged by inflation but was pretty much recession-proof.

During the final decades of the twentieth century, two presidents vowed to alleviate poverty and largely failed — in one case, perhaps, because the goals were too high and in the other because the commitment was too low. Lyndon B. Johnson declared war on poverty. To which Ronald Reagan later declared: "Poverty won." Not quite. The poverty rate tumbled from 22.2 percent in 1960 to a low of 11.1 percent in 1973. "If Johnson had said, 'We're going to cut poverty in half within ten years,' then he would have been wildly successful," said Sheldon Danziger of the University of Michigan.

"The war we did fight, we won," said Senator Moynihan, contrasting the decline in poverty among the elderly with a reversal of fortune for the young. "The war that wasn't won," he said, "we didn't fight." To lift every American family out of poverty in 1989, the Census Bureau calculated, would have cost $5,138 each. The government described that figure as the families' "income deficit." It was less than what America spent in forty-three days in 1991 on the Persian Gulf War.

CHAPTER XI

ARE
WE SMARTER?

Measured by the census for the first time by diplomas and degrees, Americans are better educated today than ever before. But they are still well below grade compared to citizens of other industrialized nations, and behind the overall rise in schooling are these disturbing trends:

- Growth in educational achievement by young adults has all but stalled. Moreover, the greater number of years spent in school hasn't necessarily meant that Americans are smarter or even better educated.
- Forget about getting by without a high school diploma in an economy that depends decreasingly on unskilled labor. Even a

college degree no longer guarantees
financial success.

• Regardless of degrees and of the parity that
men and women have achieved in college
education, the income of women and blacks
is still outpaced by what white men make,
although the gap is narrowing.

Three fourths of American adults 25 and over have completed high school. More than one fifth have finished four or more years of college. Both proportions are record highs, as were the high school levels attained in 1990 by men, women, and whites. For the first time, at least half the nation's white, black and Hispanic men and women have finished high school. The average American today has gone to college, at least, if not graduated. The smallest proportion of people who had completed college — 11 percent — was among people 75 and older. "In general, the long-term rise in educational attainment for the general adult population is driven principally by the replacement of older less-educated persons by younger persons who have completed substantially more education," Census Bureau demographers Robert Kominski and Andrea Adams concluded, adding this disclaimer: "The increase in attainment among younger persons has slowed considerably, and may be leveling off." Among young adults between the ages of 25 and 29, high school and college completion rates barely budged from the levels recorded a decade earlier.

Between 1970 and 1990 alone, the proportion of people who had not completed high school was more than halved; the proportion who completed four years or more of college doubled (a measure, however, of endurance that does not necessarily mean they received a degree). If the stunning degree to which black students progressed has been largely unheralded, the 1990 census confirmed their educational gains over the last fifty years — gains tempered by how far they have had to come, how far they still remain behind whites, and how stubbornly the pattern of separation and inequality that begins even before kindergarten has endured. If some educators were baffled by the degree of progress, parents and students were less at a loss: They attributed the gains to incentives ranging from the proven value of prekindergarten programs to the growth of the black middle class to the inflexible demands of a job market that would tolerate nothing less than a high school diploma. Black men 25 and older who are not even in the work force — much less have legitimate jobs — constitute nearly a third of the entire black civilian population. Among them, half are high school dropouts and fewer than one in one hundred finished college. Among Hispanic men 25 and older who are not in the labor force, two thirds are high school dropouts. Blacks often begin lagging in the early grades. Then the gaps widen. Coupled with the number of black young adults who are jobless or who are described euphemistically as "outside the labor force," the proportion of often idle high school dropouts balloons to a staggering four in ten.

During the last decade, the economy exacted a severe penalty from high school dropouts, in particular. In 1969, more than four in ten dropouts earned more than the national average income. By 1989, fewer than three in ten did. The proportion of college graduates who made more than twice the average rose, though marginally. But even with all of the caveats, the correlation between higher education and higher income is irrefutable. About one in twenty childless, college-educated couples under age 25 are poor. But among households headed by an uneducated woman, fully nine in ten are living in poverty. Americans with jobs claimed the highest proportion of high school and college graduates, 87 percent and 27 percent, respectively. Among unemployed people, 73 percent had completed four or more years of high school and 12 percent had spent four years in college. Of those who were no longer looking for work or were not in the labor force for some other reason, 63 percent had finished high school and 12 percent had spent four or more years in college — figures that again attest to a job deficit.

Women and black and Hispanic workers continue to trail white men in mean income. But their mean income advanced by 50 percent or more, as did white men's, if they had earned a high school diploma. The income differential between those workers who had graduated only from high school and those who got a college degree was about double. Overall, the mean earned by high school dropouts was $11,045, compared to $17,072 for high school graduates, $31,256 for workers who had completed four years of college, and $42,800 for those who had finished five or more years of higher education. In 1990, high school dropouts earned, on average, one tenth the monthly income of other Americans with professional degrees: $492 for the dropout, $1,077 for a high school graduate, $2,116 for the holder of a bachelor's degree, $2,822 for a master's, $3,855 for a doctorate, and $4,961 for a professional degree. Median household income for the college educated rose 31 percent between 1969 and 1989, to $56,654. For Americans with a high school education or less, median household income rose only 8 percent, to $33,026.

Disparities in prenatal care have led some experts to suggest that a student's academic and professional success may be determined in the womb. Schools are being asked to shoulder a multitude of roles, from doctor to parent. School immunization programs can reach many of the up to 90 percent of youngsters in some ghetto neighborhoods who have not been inoculated, but the school system alone is an insufficient substitute for the nurturing of family. The Committee for Economic Development, a group of business executives motivated by a melding of altruism and self-interest, warned that by the time many poor children start school they have been conditioned by anarchy and chaos. Enrollment in nursery school and kinder-

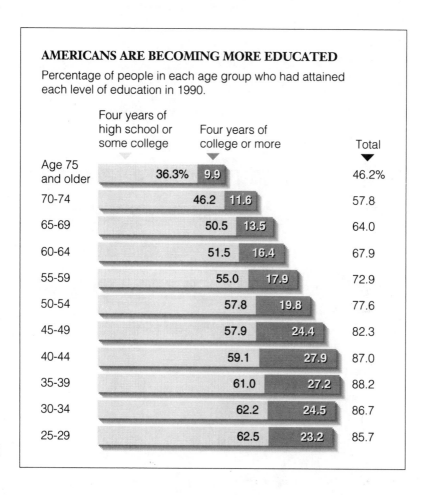

AMERICANS ARE BECOMING MORE EDUCATED

Percentage of people in each age group who had attained each level of education in 1990.

	Four years of high school or some college	Four years of college or more	Total
Age 75 and older	36.3%	9.9	46.2%
70-74	46.2	11.6	57.8
65-69	50.5	13.5	64.0
60-64	51.5	16.4	67.9
55-59	55.0	17.9	72.9
50-54	57.8	19.8	77.6
45-49	57.9	24.4	82.3
40-44	59.1	27.9	87.0
35-39	61.0	27.2	88.2
30-34	62.2	24.5	86.7
25-29	62.5	23.2	85.7

garten has grown, but still lags among poor children and Hispanic youngsters in particular. Overall, 44 percent of the nation's 3- and 4-year-olds are enrolled in public and private nursery schools, which also means that more than half are not. In families whose income is less than $20,000, 30 percent of the eligible children are enrolled. In families that make $40,000 or more, 59 percent of the children attend nursery school or kindergarten. Predictably, family income is a reliable indicator not only of whether children

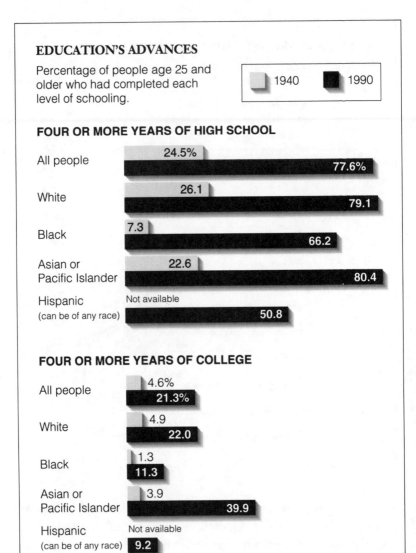

EDUCATION'S ADVANCES

Percentage of people age 25 and older who had completed each level of schooling.

☐ 1940   ■ 1990

FOUR OR MORE YEARS OF HIGH SCHOOL

All people
24.5%
77.6%

White
26.1
79.1

Black
7.3
66.2

Asian or Pacific Islander
22.6
80.4

Hispanic (can be of any race)
Not available
50.8

FOUR OR MORE YEARS OF COLLEGE

All people
4.6%
21.3%

White
4.9
22.0

Black
1.3
11.3

Asian or Pacific Islander
3.9
39.9

Hispanic (can be of any race)
Not available
9.2

UNEQUAL EDUCATION

Percentage of people 25 years and older in 1990 who were
high school graduates.

MOST		LEAST	
Alaska	86.6%	Mississippi	64.3%
Utah	85.1	Kentucky	64.6
Colorado	84.4	West Virginia	66.0
Washington	83.8	Arkansas	66.3
Wyoming	83.0	Alabama	66.9

go to nursery school or kindergarten but which one. Also, of
whether they stay in school long enough to get high school and
college degrees. Among families with incomes under $20,000, 66
percent of the nursery students attend public schools. Among
families with incomes over $40,000, only 15 percent do.

As troubling as high school dropout rates may seem today,
they were substantially higher a century ago as a result of three
factors: laxer compulsory education and child labor laws; the need
to supplement family incomes; and the availability of jobs that
were largely dependent on brawn. Given literacy and technical
skills demanded by the marketplace, today's dropout rate is intol-
erably high because it dooms that proportion of a generation to
joblessness and dependency. The lowest levels of formal schooling are registered by people who live on farms, although the
opportunities for employment in agriculture are declining and
the demand for technological know-how is increasing. Farmers
cannot operate or repair most machinery or keep pace with the

most rudimentary advances in genetic engineering without being able to read. More sophisticated technology has meant that more and more jobs, from newspaper compositors to television cameramen and court stenographers, either are being automated or demand a higher degree of education or, at least, literacy. In the 1990s, more people held skilled white-collar jobs than blue-collar jobs for the first time.

Fifty years ago, American men completed a median 8.3 years of school. One in four people over the age of 25 had finished high school. Among men, 12 percent completed high school; 5.4 percent graduated from college. Women went to school for a median 8.5 years and had a higher high school graduation rate than men (16 percent) but a lower college graduation rate (4 percent). By 1990, Americans were staying in school longer than ever before (although the census still found nearly 2 million over the age of 25 who had never been to school at all). American men were spending a median 12.7 years in school, about the same as the 12.6 years that women were enrolled. Among men, 73 percent had graduated from high school and 21 percent had earned a college degree. Among women, 74 percent had completed high school and 17 percent had finished at least four years of college. For the first time, women accounted for more than half of all college students; the statistical difference had vanished between the proportion of men and women age 25 to 29 with four or more years of college. Yet those overall gains in the paper chase mask vast disparities. And, measured against challenges posed by technological advances and overseas competition, progress is more problematic. The possibility that graduation rates for young adults have plateaued and may even have begun to decline also suggests the challenges posed in meeting a goal set by President George Bush when the decade began: that by the year 2000, nine of every ten high school students will persevere long enough to get their diplomas.

What Jonathan Kozol called "savage inequalities" in per

capita spending permeate a system buffeted by philosophical feuds over the definition of multicultural education and over the lengths to which schools, as surrogate guardians, provide AIDS education or dispense condoms. Most teachers were hobbled by a more prosaic problem, one that confronted Vivian Horn at the Montebello Intermediate School, east of Los Angeles. When she entered her classroom on the opening day of school in 1991, she was confronted by forty-five children — well above the number educators consider a workable, much less an ideal, enrollment. Montebello's budget was drafted during California's seemingly infinite economic boom, which ended abruptly in a recession. Reality was injected in the form of economies that cost the school twelve of its fifty-eight teachers. "We have said we can handle all this if you just give us more money," said Art Revueltas, an assistant principal. "The public is saying that we still want you to do that, but we are going to give you less. Maybe the social contract we've been living under has been canceled." In legislatures and in courtrooms, how to finance local education equitably was debated from New Jersey to Texas, where spending disparities ranged from nearly $12,000 per pupil in the richest districts to $3,200 in the poorest.

Elementary school enrollment fell during the 1970s and early 1980s, reflecting the population decline among eligible youngsters. If current trends continue, enrollment appears likely to increase by the mid-1990s. How that growth will be apportioned may depend on the government's investment in public schools and the flexibility proposed voucher programs give parents in choosing where to enroll their children. Given government's insufficient support for the public school system coupled with the inadequate return on investment, parents who could afford to, like Bill and Hillary Rodham Clinton, rejected public schools — risking condemnation as hypocrites but refusing to sacrifice their daughter's safety and future for their own principles. Nearly four times as many students from families with incomes of $40,000 or more attend private school than do students from families that make under $20,000 — 15 percent versus 4.1 percent (which may suggest that the families have to make that much just to pay the tuition). Private school by no means guarantees a better education. But, at the least, it often means smaller class size and fewer students who pose disciplinary problems, since private and parochial schools can be more selective. That more than one in ten students from wealthier families have abandoned public education suggests another troubling trend: an emerging two-tiered school system divided even more by class than by race or ethnicity. Wealthier Hispanic families are most likely to send their children to private school — about two in ten, although the census doesn't specify whether they go to integrated schools and whether they attend parochial schools, which may not be as prestigious but are often more rigorous than the public school system.

Age differences and when children start school can skew raw figures on how many fall behind grade level. Even so, the proportion of youngsters who are in a grade too low for their years or who have left school altogether is growing. In 1990, 22 percent of all children ages 6 to 8 were enrolled below their expected grade level, compared to 15 percent a decade before. Among 15- to 17-year-olds, 35 percent had fallen behind, compared to 2 percent in 1980. Black and Hispanic students trail increasingly as whites advance into higher grades. "Black students fall behind early in school and stay behind," the Census Bureau found. Among whites, 5 percent more are below their expected grade in the 9- to 11-year-old group than in the 6- to 8-year-old group. Among blacks, the gap between students who have fallen behind in the two age groups grows to 11 percent. Among Hispanic students it is even higher, 14 percent. The gap widens further between the 9- to 11-year-old group and 12- to 14-year-olds. Among whites, it rises only a statistically insignificant 1.4 percent. Among blacks, though, it jumps by 13 percent. By the time students are between the ages of 15 and 17, 32 percent of whites were behind, compared to 48 percent of the blacks and Hispanic students. The proportion who lagged or had dropped out completely ranged from 26 percent among white girls to 53 percent among black males. In the mid-1970s, a horrific 8 percent of 17-year-old black students were reading at what one national test defined as an "adept" level — the third highest of four rankings. A decade later, the percentage had more than tripled. The rate for whites has improved only marginally, but was 46 percent — hardly impressive, either, but fully 20 percent higher than for blacks.

Even a high school diploma is no automatic meal ticket. "African-American education levels are improving, no question about it," John Kasarda of the University of North Carolina said after the 1992 riots in Los Angeles. "But you have to also look at what kind of an education the kids are getting. I would argue that they are getting their education in inferior schools. They may have the diploma, but they really are not well equipped to get that first job." And everyone agrees that not having a high school diploma all but dooms whatever hopes poor youngsters harbor of getting ahead. In south-central Los Angeles, epicenter of the 1992 riots, one third of the young people were jobless. Another 12 percent of black young people were neither in school nor working — nor even looking for a job — meaning that more than four in ten black young adults were largely idle. The proportion of Hispanic and Asian unemployed teenagers also increased during the decade, a rise attributed, in part, to language and cultural barriers.

Computing high school dropout rates is problematic. By most definitions, the overall rate has declined and blacks are more likely to complete high school than ever before. Compared to fifty years ago, the gains are astounding. Among whites, the proportion who completed four or more years of high school tripled, from 26.1 percent to 79.1 percent. Among blacks, the rate rose nearly ninefold, from 8 percent to 66 percent. Among black women between the ages of 25 and 29, only 14 percent had completed four years of high school in 1940 compared to 82 percent fifty years later — not far behind the 88 percent recorded in 1990 by white women. Among men, the gap was even narrower (in part, because white men had not advanced as far as white women). In 1940, only 11 percent of blacks between the ages of 25 and 29, but 39 percent of whites, had completed high school. By 1990, 82 percent of the blacks and 85 percent of the whites had.

Still, the census found that one in ten Americans between the ages of 16 and 19 was neither a high school graduate nor enrolled in school. The proportion was highest among Hispanic teenagers — 22 percent — compared to 14 percent among blacks, 10 percent of whites and 5 percent of Asian-Americans. Between 1989 and 1990, 4 percent of students in the tenth, eleventh or twelfth grade quit school, compared to 6 percent a decade earlier. Again, income was a good determinant. In families that made less than $20,000, 6 percent of the students had dropped out of high school. In families that made more than $40,000, only 1 percent had. Dropout rates were among the highest in seven California cities, led by Santa Ana's 36.7 percent. By still another measure, the rate ranged from 4.6 percent in North Dakota to 15.2 percent in Nevada.

By yet another standard, high school graduation rates, Mississippi fared worst, with 64.3 percent of the residents 25 and older having diplomas; in Alaska, 86.6 percent of the high school students had graduated, followed by Utah, with 85 percent, and California, with 84. Among whites, the proportion with a high school diploma ranges from a low of 69 percent in Arkansas to 89 percent in Hawaii. Among blacks, the gap is greater between the state with the lowest share — Mississippi, with 47 percent — and the state with the highest — Hawaii, with 94 percent. Among Hispanic people, fewer than half — 49.8 percent — have even a high school diploma. The proportion of those who did in Idaho — 43 percent — was about half the proportion in Vermont — 85 percent. Asian-Americans graduated from high school at about the same rate as whites — 78 percent overall — ranging from 60 percent in Rhode Island, which has a large Hmong population, to 89 percent in West Virginia, which has forged partnerships with Japan not only in manufacturing but in higher education. In 1990, a contingent of students from Japan arrived in Salem, a tiny Appalachian town, for the first full-fledged merger between an American and a Japanese college.

In 1990, a slim majority of all college students were women, who now get over half the bachelor of arts degrees. Among all the students, 61 percent were also working — nearly one third of them full-time. Baby Boomers reported the highest percentage among the college educated — 28 percent — as did people who had never married (fully 44 percent of white women who had never married had attended college for four or more years), Westerners, and residents of metropolitan areas (particularly those outside central cities of 1 million or more). Unlike many young whites, college-educated blacks were more likely to live outside the central city, further evidence, perhaps, of the increasing isolation of stragglers left behind in urban ghettos. A closer look reveals a closing gender gap: Men were more likely to be college educated than women. But among young adults between the ages of 18 and 24, 7 percent of the men and 8 percent of the women had completed four or more years of college.

Asian-Americans easily topped every other group in the proportion of those with college degrees — almost twice the rate among whites. Nationwide, 37 percent had completed college, ranging from 19 percent in Hawaii to 63 percent in West Virginia. Whites were next with 22 percent, with a narrower gap between the low of 14 percent in Arkansas and the high of 30 percent in Hawaii. Blacks were third with 11 percent — half the proportion among whites — with the percentage of black high school graduates who go to college declining slightly during the 1980s. The black proportion ranged from 8 percent in Kentucky to 31 percent in Vermont. And among Hispanic people, 9 percent had completed college, including 5 percent in Wyoming and 28 percent in Vermont. In California and Texas, only about 7 percent of the Hispanic adults had a college degree.

Among 24- to 29-year-olds, the proportion of Asians who had completed college was nearly double that of whites (40 percent compared to 22 percent), more than triple the 11 percent share among blacks, and more than quadruple the 9 percent of Hispanic people. Increasing enrollment levels among blacks and Hispanic people suggest they are catching up, but slowly. Among blacks, 25 percent were enrolled in college, compared to 13 percent in 1967. Only 5 percent of blacks over the age of 65 had completed college, compared to 19 percent of the black 41-year-olds. Among Hispanic people, the percentage enrolled in college rose only marginally, from 13 percent in 1972 to 16 percent in 1990. Only 6 percent of Hispanic people 65 and over had completed college, compared to 16 percent of Hispanic 41-year-olds.

Suburbs of New York, Boston and Philadelphia boasted the highest percentage of higher educated people overall — 27 percent who had four or more years of college, most of them between the ages of 25 and 34. The lowest proportion — 11 percent — was shared by people who lived on farms in the Midwest and in the rural South. "Education is the No. 1 obstacle that the South needs to overcome to go to the next phase of economic growth," said Gary W. Tapp, an Atlanta economist, who described the region's educational deficit as an economic Achilles' heel. "Even someone who runs a printing press or a textile loom has to be able to read and understand a fairly complicated manual, and it's bound to be a computer-driven machine. If the South can't respond quickly enough to its educational needs, those jobs are going to go someplace else."

Among men between 35 and 44 who lived in New England, 39 percent had finished four or more years of college. The lowest proportion of people who had completed four or more years of college was 7 percent, among Hispanic people in the west south-central states. Among major metropolitan areas, 40 percent of men 25 and older in Boston finished four or more years of college, as did 28 percent of women. In Washington, D. C., the proportion was even higher — 43 percent of the men and 30 percent of the women. Massachusetts had the highest percentage of adults with a college degree: 82 percent. And Maryland had the largest proportion with an advanced degree: 11 percent.

But a trend line is emerging that suggests another advance: In 1980, only one in four college students was over 25 years old. By 1990, the proportion had nearly doubled, to four in ten. Nearly 18 percent were above age 35 — double the proportion when the Census Bureau began counting two decades earlier. While younger people are taking longer to earn degrees, more older people are completing higher education, which gives a new dimension to a term that couples respect with apprehension: *college senior*.

CHAPTER XII

HOW WE'RE AGING

J erry Rubin, the yippie-turned-yuppie, was never publicity shy. But even Rubin claimed that he would have been happier if one epochal event in his life had been marked in private, not with the elaborate celebration that filled his balloon-festooned apartment on Manhattan's Upper East Side with investment bankers, lawyers, rock stars, former radicals, his infant daughter, and his personal nutritionist. In 1988, just slightly ahead of the Baby Boom generation, the middle-aged man who had contemptuously dropped dollar bills on the floor of the Stock Exchange in 1967 and twenty years later was about to sell $3 million in shares in his career-networking company, celebrated his first half century with a fresh perspective.

"I used to say, don't trust anyone over thirty," Rubin recalled. "Now, I say, don't trust anyone under fifty."

It's arguable whether the Gray Panthers will be reconstituted as a group of aging bomb throwers, but Rubin's gala was just the beginning of a record number of fifty-year birthday parties — and, with them, the mixed blessing of eligibility for membership in the American Association of Retired Persons. A society that reveres virility and reflexively attached the adjective *young* to the noun *nation* is growing older. Get ready for the debut of *sixtysomething* and a Grandparent Boom.

No reference to old people or to the elderly invades the politically correct lexicon. They have been elevated, rhetorically, to the status of senior citizens, the "longer living," or even the "chronologically advantaged" — less pejorative labels that stress the positive dimensions of aging and just begin to suggest their political potential. The proportion of Americans over 65 is larger than ever before, and they are growing faster than any other age group. The pyramid that graphically defines age differentials in the United States is suddenly bulging in the center like a middle-age paunch. Its changing shape has profound implications for the health-care, insurance and recreation industries, for the nation's work force, and for government and politics. That the number of elderly Americans is growing so rapidly fundamentally reflects on two other groups: younger people, for whom the elderly represent a potential burden and possible competition; and the disabled, whom the census counted for the first time in 1990 and who are disproportionately old.

Two hundred years ago, the first census wasn't much interested in how old Americans were, except to quantify the pool of young men available for military service or for the nation's nascent heavy industry. The median age then is estimated to have been about 16, which means that half the population was older and half was younger. By the centennial census in 1890, the median age of Americans had risen six years, to 22. During the next fifty years alone it surged seven years, to 29 in 1940. It has routinely risen since then, except during the 1940s, when the

Baby Boom began; the 1950s, when Alaska and Hawaii were first included in the count; and the 1960s, before the Baby Boom went bust. When the median age did decline, then, it was by less than 1 percent. And while the increase has slowed, the median age reached 32.9 in 1990 — another record high.

Americans are disproportionately old. The world's population is growing older, too, driven by declining fertility and expanding life spans in industrialized nations. But relatively high birthrates and stunted life spans in the Third World have depressed the elderly's share of the global population to 6 percent. In the United States, though, the proportion is already twice as large. Nearly 13 percent of the world's population 80 and older live in the United States — just behind China's 16 percent. Japan has the highest life expectancy — 79 years. But Japan and the United States rank 19th and 20th respectively in the proportion of their population aged 65 and older (just under 13 percent, compared to Sweden's 18 percent). Universally, two variables drive median age: fertility and longevity. Even in the United States, those variables differ fundamentally by race, ethnicity, sex and geography. Whites live longer than blacks and Hispanics. Blacks are three times more likely than whites to die before they are 1 year old, but blacks who reach the age of 85 are then more likely to outlast whites of the same age. The birthrate among Hispanic people is higher than for whites. Women live longer than men.

When the twentieth century began, an average American could expect to live forty-nine years. The chance of surviving to age 65 was 41 percent. An American born in the last decade of this century is likely to live to be at least 75 — a remarkable 50 percent increase in longevity in less than a century. Life expectancy at birth ranged from 64.6 years for black males to 78.9 years for white women. An American who celebrated a 50th birthday in 1990 could expect to live on average to age 79.2 years; someone who turned 65 that year could count on surviving to

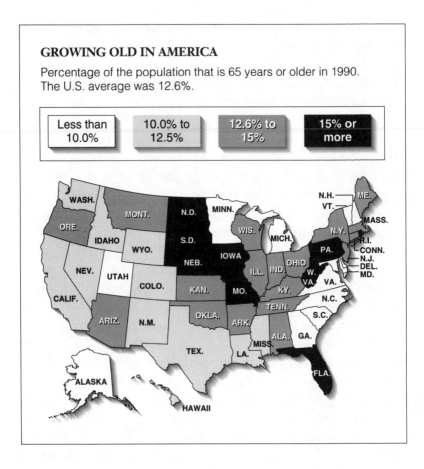

GROWING OLD IN AMERICA

Percentage of the population that is 65 years or older in 1990. The U.S. average was 12.6%.

Less than 10.0%	10.0% to 12.5%	12.6% to 15%	15% or more

82.4 years. The odds of surviving until the customary retirement age of 65 have doubled, to 80 percent. In 1900, Americans 85 and older constituted 4 percent of the elderly. By 1990, their proportion had risen to 10 percent, or 3 million people — more than seven times the number of 85-year-olds who were living fifty years ago. The 85-and-older group is still only 1 percent of the total population. But the number has more than doubled (and their proportion has nearly doubled) since 1970 alone and is

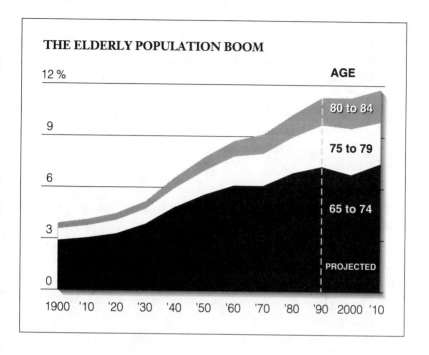

THE ELDERLY POPULATION BOOM

AGE

80 to 84

75 to 79

65 to 74

PROJECTED

projected to nearly double again in twenty years. The 1990 census also counted 36,000 centenarians — amazingly, double the number who were identified only a decade earlier (eight in ten of them were women and white).

The over-65 group grew nationwide by 4 million during the 1980s to 20.5 million, but even that dramatic increase is dwarfed by forecasts for its growth in the twenty-first century. Between 2010 and 2030, demographers predict, the number of Americans 65 and older will mushroom by 30 million as Baby Boomers turn the age pyramid upside down. By 2030, when the youngest Boomers will have turned 65, the number of elderly is projected to be twice what it was in 1990. Already, the number of Americans under the age of 14 roughly equals the number over the age of 60. Within several decades, the number 65 and older may equal the number 18 and younger and deaths may surpass births for the first time in the nation's history.

When will Americans retire and where? Who will care for them? Who will pay for their medical and retirement benefits? And how will they alter the nation's political fabric?

The growing number of elderly people is reshaping the definition and demands of old age. It is creating a legal and ethical gray area for America. That four-generation families are becoming more commonplace implies a benefit and a potential burden. In 1950, there were three persons 85 and older for every hundred people between the ages of 50 and 64 — those most likely to be the elderly's offspring. By 1990, the ratio had tripled, to nine per hundred. The number appears likely to triple again by 2050.

Women live longer, but not necessarily better, lives than men. Elderly women are more likely to be poorer, living alone, and suffering from longer-term, chronic, disabling diseases. As a result, they require more care. But who will provide it? Traditionally, their daughters and granddaughters did. Now more of them are in the work force and cannot afford to risk their own retirement benefits. Half the elderly women in America are widowed — including three in five of those between ages 75 and 84 and fully four in five of the women 85 and over — or, overall, three times the rate among men. Women are less likely to remarry with each passing year. Among widowed women 65 and over, only 2 percent had remarried. More than eight in ten men but fewer than six in ten women 65 and over were living with their spouses or with other relatives. Among people 85 and over, two thirds of the men but only one third of the women were living with family members. Three quarters of the elderly men are still married, but fewer than four in ten women are. Why? More of the men are dead. Their life expectancy is about six and a half years less, usually capped by a short-term, fatal disease.

"It would make demographic sense if women married men at least seven years younger than they are, but they rarely do," one Census Bureau analysis suggested. That shortsightedness will shift the burden increasingly to the sandwich generation, the one pressed simultaneously by the costs of rearing children and of caring for aging parents. Baby Boomers face a different predicament that again may tarnish their golden years. In 1990, one fourth of them had no children to care for, which also means that when they get older they will have to fend for themselves — or are more likely to be institutionalized — sooner than their contemporaries whose adult children offer one buffer against a nursing home. With the number of elderly growing, none of the gauges demographers use to compute what they call support ratios is very encouraging.

In its first such survey in decades, the census found that while about one in ten people between the ages of 16 and 64 said they had trouble moving about or caring for themselves without help, more than three in ten people 65 and over required similar assistance. (In an earlier survey, the census found more than 500,000 Americans were deaf and another 7.7 million had hearing difficulties; 1.7 million were blind and 11.3 million more had visual impairments; 8 million were wheelchair bound and another 11.2 had trouble walking; about 2.5 million had difficulty speaking.) While the results also mean that seven in ten people 65 and over are able to fend for themselves, the trends raise profound questions about the social and economic cost of caring for the elderly and of prolonging life. "Mortality," as the Census Bureau says, "is a limited measure of the health of a population."

Asking elderly people how they feel reflexively prompts a companion question: Compared to what? Compared to the popular perception of a dependent and frail population, the elderly are pretty healthy. Among noninstitutionalized people — admittedly, a more select group — about one fourth of those between the ages of 65 and 74 and one third of those 75 and over described their physical condition as fair to poor. For most people, reality meets perception after they turn 85. One in five Americans 85 and older is institutionalized; one in five of the rest cannot carry on at least one major activity. Women are almost twice as likely to need assistance as men, but nearly half of all people 85 and over need some help with everyday activities. Among those 85 and older, only about two thirds of the people who have trouble walking and nearly one third of those who have difficulty getting outside by themselves receive the help they need.

While Americans 65 and older constitute 13 percent of the population, they account for 44 percent of days spent in the nation's hospitals, 40 percent of visits to internists, and fully a third of the country's health-care spending. Some doctors acknowledge that basic medical education has not kept pace with the aging population. "We don't know the normal lung volume or hemoglobin of someone who's 90 because the charts and research didn't get that far," said Dr. Louis J. Kettel, vice president of the Association of American Medical Colleges. Nor has affordable medical insurance kept pace. Some companies that fled to the Sun Belt were stunned by their bills for employee medical costs — not because the climate is any less healthy but because some doctors and hospitals charge more to private insurers to compensate for reduced Medicare allowances associated with treating large local elderly populations. (Only about half of working women 45 and older have health insurance provided by their employers, which nearly three fourths of working men have — a disparity attributed to the fact that women are more likely to work part-time, that their careers are impeded because they spend more time than men caring for other family members, and because health coverage under their husbands' policies stops when the women are widowed or divorced.) Lack of health insurance for the young and the high cost of medical care for the elderly have prompted the greatest pressure for universal national benefits.

On the basis of income alone, fully one fifth of the elderly are living in or near poverty. While income typically declines after retirement, Americans between the ages of 65 and 69 have the highest household net worth. During the 1980s, more and more retired people returned to work, at least part-time, both to keep pace with inflation and to take advantage of incentives offered by employers whose pool of potential workers had been depleted by the baby bust. Colleges, confronting declining enrollment, tapped the surfeit of senior citizens. Historic havens and emerging planned retirement communities prospered in Florida, Arizona, southern California and — perhaps surprisingly — in places like southern New Jersey, where the "mature market" that retailers were just beginning to woo nationally was already producing a big dividend for local merchants. Demographers dubbed it the "mailbox economy" — a potential buying surge fueled by the influx of Social Security and pension checks that otherwise would have been spent back home. And back home, from the Karen Arms garden apartments in Madison, Wisconsin, to the Penn South middle-income cooperative in Manhattan, Meals on Wheels succeeded tricycles as the vehicles of choice as time transformed housing for young families into naturally occurring retirement communities complete with cost-effective social services.

The marketplace is championing "maturity" and is tailoring its messages to a generation of consumers that used to joke about Geritol commercials. "As people age, they typically become more farsighted," Charles D. Schewe, professor of marketing at the University of Massachusetts, wrote in *American Demographics*. "They have greater difficulty adapting to sharp changes in light. They have a harder time seeing colors at the green-blue-violet end of the spectrum and they lose their ability to hear the high-pitched tones found in a woman's voice. Older people also have greater difficulty coordinating information that is hitting their eyes, ears, and other senses all at once." Schewe recommended simple, familiar messages without deadlines. "When older adults are allowed to process information at their own rate, their learning abilities improve," he said, in a prognosis with profound implications for advertisers and for the advertising vehicles they choose. "Print media let consumers set their own pace; television and radio do not."

Until cryogenics is perfected, problems associated with expanding life spans will become more acute. How acute depends on a fundamental question that neither science nor the Census Bureau can answer conclusively: Is there a biological limit to how long people can live? Even if no magic bullets are invented and the average life span levels off at about 85, the number of Americans 85 and older is projected to increase more than fivefold by 2080 to nearly 19 million. But if a generally healthier population is in good enough condition to lift the longevity ceiling, the number could grow to more than 40 million by 2040 and 72 million in 2080, by one count. "If you assume the death rates among the oldest old will come down," said Dr. James Vaupel, a Duke University demographer, "the numbers will explode." The implications of what he described as "a new paradigm of aging" are immense. An explosion of those proportions could bankrupt private pension plans and the Social Security system. A vast increase in the number of elderly who are able, willing to — and in need of — work could pose yet another threat to young job seekers. With no age cap for full professors, one department at a college of the City University of New York hadn't hired anyone in 15 years."Perhaps in the future," wrote Malcolm Cowley, the essayist who died in 1987 at the age of 89, "our active lives may be lengthened almost to the end of our days on earth; that is the most we can hope for."

The moral implications of prolonging life may dominate debates among doctors, philosophers, advocates for the elderly, and government economists, but more mundane matters preoccupy a public that is increasingly riven chronologically. An American Association of Boomers was established to protect the rights of the elderly-to-be — clashing with the politically mature American Association of Retired Persons over whether wealthier senior citizens deserve benefits that drain Social Security reserves. Retirement communities, challenged by young families, won legal authority to impose age-based residence requirements if, among other things, four in five current residents are 55 or older and the community provides special services for the elderly. Local school budgets, already jeopardized by the recession, face a singular threat as an expanding elderly population flexes its political muscle to guard against tax increases. Boards of education across the country are aggressively enlisting the elderly to vote for local school budgets in which they no longer have a direct stake. In New York's Westchester County, the Pelham schools began issuing gold cards that entitle the elderly to free admission at sporting events. In Riverside, New Jersey, elderly residents are invited to an annual Senior Citizens Day to see firsthand how their tax dollars are invested. But in Kalkaska, Michigan, a retirement haven that hit hard times, officials decided to end the spring semester in March after voters refused for the third time in six months to increase property taxes. "The old people get so angry," said Jill Hillman, a high school senior. "They say, 'I pay too much taxes already.' I say: 'I don't care. I need an education.' " In Arizona, residents of Sun Lake, a retirement complex near Phoenix, emerged as a pivotal voting bloc. "At first, it didn't really affect the district," said Dr. Howard K. Conley, superintendent of the Chandler Unified School District. "But now they can generate 3,000 to 5,000 votes for any issue that comes up, and these votes come in at least 90 percent no." Some, understandably, don't want to see their nest eggs squandered on bloated bureaucracies and dubious spending with little proven value for education. Call others what they are: "selfish seniors."

Political correctness toward the elderly is a consequence of their growing political potency, even if some of their other faculties may be declining. In 1992, Democrats Bill Clinton and Al Gore formed the first all–Baby Boomer ticket, but they never forgot that their generation and the one that preceded it account for the majority of the electorate. Not only are young people the least likely to vote — among 18- to 24-year-olds, the proportion plummeted steadily from 48 percent in 1972 to 33 percent in 1988 then rose in 1992 — but between 1988 and 1992 the number of eligible 18- to 24-year-olds slipped while Americans 45 and older accounted for most of the 3 percent overall increase in the electorate. The elderly, particularly people between the ages of 65 and 74, vote with the greatest regularity. About one in five voters was 65 or older in 1992 — a proportion that is expanding and is already disproportionately large in the Northeast and the South.

Counties with the highest proportion of elderly single people are mostly in the Midwest, where parents and grandparents linger after young adults have fled small towns. In Calhoun County, Iowa, more than 20 percent of the households are headed by someone 65 and older living alone. Statewide, one in fifty people is 85 or older. Iowa and South Dakota also claim the highest proportion of centenarians — .026 percent. In rural Smith County, Kansas, more than one in twenty residents are over 85, the largest share of any county in the country and a proportion that may be mirrored nationwide by 2050. Home health care and state-licensed boardinghouses or hotels are among the promising means of providing low-cost care and preserving the independence that the elderly crave. "Independence is the goal they all will do anything to achieve," said Ellen Davis, director of the Northwest Kansas Area Agency on Aging. "Even if this means moving into a high rise or going into a shared-living arrangement." States with the highest percentage of people in nursing homes — 1 percent or more — form a pistol-shaped region stretching from Montana into the Farm Belt. The greatest increase in the elderly during the 1980s occurred in the South Atlantic States. Nationwide, the nursing home population expanded by 24 percent. In Florida, the number of people in nursing homes more than doubled, to 80,000. In Sun City, Arizona, as it was no doubt intended to be, the median age is 74.3. And in Miami Beach, 30 percent of the population is over 65. In Naples, Florida, the median age is 60.6 — nearly three times higher than the 22.9 median on the outskirts of Logan, Utah. Retirees have made Florida's median age (36.4 — 35 for men, 38 for women) and its percentage of elderly (18 percent, or about the same as Sweden's) the highest of any state. All ten metropolitan areas with the largest proportion of people over 65 are in Florida, topped by Sarasota, at 32 percent.

A net migration of older people to rural America swelled the population of places like Flagler County in Florida. If the trend endures, the elderly will account for at least one in seven people in nearly half of the states. But a survey by the American Association of Retired Persons found that 84 percent of the people over the age of 55 would prefer never to move again. A census analysis found that between 1986 and 1987, 5 percent moved to another house, fewer than 2 percent moved to another county, and less than 1 percent of the elderly moved to another state. Fully 75 percent of the elderly hadn't left their home states after they retired. And when they do move, the aged often return home to be closer to children or grandchildren, perhaps after the death of a spouse, and to more sophisticated medical care. Where the next generation of retirees decides to live out its lives will have an enormous impact not only on local economies but on the demands they place on everything from public transportation to health care. Between 1975 and 1980, Florida gained $1 billion at New York's expense, according to one estimate, as a result of the elderly's net migration south. New York, Ohio, and other states to which the oldest of the old returned, inherited the poorest and frailest people who placed the greatest demand on the health-care system and on other public services.

Very young and very old Americans are the fastest growing groups. The number of children under 18 declined slightly. But the number under the age of 5 expanded by 12 percent. Connecticut exemplified both trends. Overall the state's population increased by 5.8 percent during the 1980s. The number of children under 5 grew by 23.3 percent. And the number of people 65 and older expanded by 22.2 percent. The ranks of graying Baby Boomers between the ages of 25 and 44 increased 27 percent, but they may be the first generation not to replace itself. The boom, from 1946 to 1964, was followed by a baby bust — the result of higher rates of divorce and of working women and of greater availability of birth control and legal abortion — which lasted until 1976. Baby Boomers beating the biological clock and the influx of immigrants reversed the trend again. In 1990, 4,179,000 babies were born in the United States — the most in twenty-seven years.

Younger Americans congregate disproportionately where they attend college, serve in the military, or live as a result of their parents' decision about where to raise a family. In Utah, large Mormon families have kept the state's median age at 26.2, or more than ten years lower than Florida's. The influx of large Hispanic families has lowered the median age substantially in parts of Texas and California. Children under 5 make up 15 percent of the population in Palmdale, California, but only 5 percent in pricier Sherman Oaks. The number of teenagers between ages 14 and 17 dropped 18 percent in the 1980s. Metropolitan Los Angeles and New York had the most, about 5 percent each. In Hidalgo, Texas, teenagers accounted for 9 percent of the population. In contrast, they represented 4 percent of the residents of Pasco County, Florida; 3.5 percent in San Francisco; 3.4 percent in Manhattan; and 3 percent in Pitkin County, Colorado, where Aspen real estate prices discourage large families.

The largest percentages of 18- to 24-year-olds are in college towns and places with military installations (and, probably, prisons). Again, Los Angeles and New York were at or just above the national average, at 12 percent and 11 percent. But in college towns like Harrisonburg, Virginia, those young adults represent 37 percent of the population. Their share is 30 percent or more in Whitman County, Washington; Riley, Kansas; Brazos, Texas; and Montgomery, Virginia. They account for more than one in four residents of Tompkins County, New York — home to Cornell University and Ithaca College. In Sarasota, Florida, only about one in twenty residents is between the ages of 18 and 24, and only 17 percent are under 18, compared to 40 percent in Provo, where the median age is only 22.98 — lowest of any metropolitan area. The lowest median age of any place, as defined by the census, is in Monsey in exurban Rockland County, New York. There the median is just 18.7 — depressed by a Hasidic enclave, transplanted from Brooklyn, with its traditionally large families. In Carrollton, Texas, an influx of immigrants has lowered the proportion of people over 65 to 3 percent, or about one tenth the proportion in Miami Beach.

Disparities in age and birthrates help explain how America's face is changing. While the median age is rising, the black and Hispanic population appears likely to remain younger than non-Hispanic whites. Whites constitute 80 percent of the population — 75 percent if Hispanic people are not included — but 75 percent of Americans up to age 9 and 75 percent of those 10 to 19. By the middle of the twenty-first century, one in four whites may be elderly. Blacks, who represent 12 percent of the total population, account for 15 percent of youngsters 9 and under and 15 percent of those 10 to 19. Hispanic people, who are 9 percent of the population, are 13 percent among those up to age 9.

The twentieth century ends with an unprecedented equilibrium among age groups, a statistical equity that masks a fundamental social, economic and political imbalance. People are stretching the length of their employment and retirement and straining relationships with younger relatives and generations with an altogether different perspective on death and taxes. They'll have to live with it, because, for all its liabilities, old age is still usually preferable to the only alternative now available. Just before he died at the age of 87, Dr. Seuss offered this backhanded diagnosis in his first book directed at grown-ups like himself:

> You're in pretty good shape
> For the shape you are in!

CHAPTER XIII

WHERE WE'RE GOING

Change has accelerated so rapidly that no still cameras wielded collectively by census takers can capture it precisely. The nation does not sit still for a statistical portrait. And even if it did, no picture, however precise, would have currency for very long. Which is why the census is less vital for the blurred profile it sketches on any given day than it is as a vehicle to help explain where we are compared to where we were and where we're going. Our failure to profit from the lessons of history is often self-fulfilling. Our failure to gauge the future and to respond accordingly can be self-defeating. How many nursing home beds will the nation need in the year 2000? Which professions will be most in demand? Will classroom space be adequate to cope with a generation entering kindergarten that is likely to be larger than the one that preceded it and less familiar with

English? Will central cities become even more isolated as middle-class residents of all races and ethnic groups leave, poverty becomes increasingly concentrated, and the suburbs consolidate their political dominance? What will be the impact of shrinking households on home and apartment prices and on real estate development? Will more people leave their cars for Los Angeles' fledgling subway while fewer people use New York's because former commuters are living *and* working in the suburbs? And how will the nation adapt to the most fundamental change in its racial and ethnic composition since "Anglo-Americans," as Tocqueville dubbed them, devolved into a minority more than a century ago? On the basis of current trends, the bicentennial census suggests where we're going:

The surge in immigrants and the surprisingly high birthrate, mainly among Hispanic people, will boost the nation's population by another 50 percent in about six decades — to nearly 400 million in 2050. The number of births is expected to hover around 4 million annually. Immigration during the 1990s is projected to average nearly 900,000 a year. By the middle of the next century, more than one in five Americans will have come to the United States since 1990 or be the children of those immigrants.

By the year 2000, the proportion of whites among America's children will shrink to less than two thirds (it is already half or less in three states: Texas, California and New Mexico). By the middle of the next century, no ethnic or racial group will constitute a majority. The number of Hispanic people will surpass the number of blacks within two decades. Whites will become a minority again around the middle of the twenty-first century.

The decline in household size may have temporarily halted. But unless the birthrate rises even more or housing costs force more people to double up, households with three or more people and families with four or more will remain the exception.

Women may begin marrying earlier again and raising families sooner than Baby Boomers did. But while divorce rates appear to have leveled off, the proportion of unwed women, unmarried couples, and single parents will continue to accelerate.

Spread cities will become denser and their proliferation will further redefine rural America. With California and Florida nearing saturation or beginning to cap unregulated growth, the greatest population increases may occur in spillover states like Nevada and Georgia and in atypical exurban retirement havens in the Northeast and Midwest. The newly designated Washington-Baltimore metropolitan area has already supplanted San Francisco as the nation's fourth largest.

The suburbs will dominate national politics and popular culture. No longer merely bedroom communities adjacent to central cities, suburbs will sprout more satellite centers and sub-suburbs of their own and grow fastest at their increasingly far-reaching fringes. More people will be concentrated in the largest metropolitan areas, but central cities will constitute a smaller share of the population. Suburbs will be more multiclass, but with all-black enclaves.

Without mighty strides in agricultural and medical technology and in political stability, world hunger may emerge as a Malthusian defining issue of the twenty-first century. Bangladesh, with a land mass smaller than Wisconsin, could surpass the present population of the United States by 2025. "Even if by some miracle of science enough food could be produced to feed them," wrote M. F. Perutz of Cambridge University, "how could they find the gainful employment needed to buy it?"

Whether the proportion of poor people in the United States continues to increase will depend largely on how well Americans on the margins survived the recession and on their ability to participate in the economy once conditions improve. The consensus for and success of government programs to wean women off welfare and into work will depend on lowering expectations about how many can be helped and on increasing the opportunities for training and the number of available jobs. No "family values" families for them.

No major job category will be in greater demand than health care. The proportion of women in the work force and of two-earner families will continue to increase, but probably more slowly. The income disparity between college graduates and high school dropouts will grow.

Barring only a startling increase in births and a devastating epidemic that strikes only people over 50, the population will age dramatically for a half century. The percentage of younger children will grow again, the share of middle-aged Americans will implode, and the elderly and very old Americans will swell to unprecedented proportions — changes that pose a profound question: Will an older nation mean a less vital one?

Predictions can be notoriously suspect. Nothing in the 1980 census hinted at the degree to which immigration would reconfigure the country by 1990. And the changes that the census did suggest — that Texas would overtake New York as the second largest state, for one — proved to be valid only if both the direction and the pace of trends detected at the beginning of the decade continued unabated. They didn't. An oil glut stalled a decade of explosive growth in Texas. A vast influx of foreigners, unrivaled since the first decade of the century, reversed what would have been a population loss in New York.

America's first century transformed a fledgling democracy roiled by chasmic differences in commercial and ideological agendas into an enduringly dominant nation. During its second

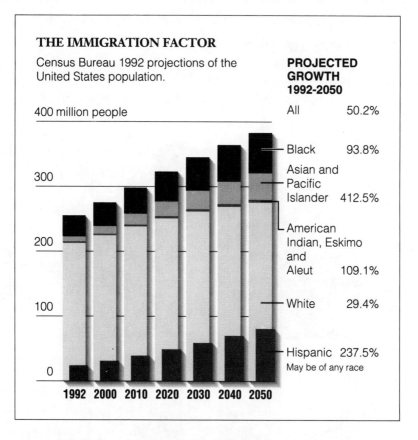

THE IMMIGRATION FACTOR

Census Bureau 1992 projections of the United States population.

PROJECTED GROWTH 1992-2050

All	50.2%
Black	93.8%
Asian and Pacific Islander	412.5%
American Indian, Eskimo and Aleut	109.1%
White	29.4%
Hispanic	237.5%

400 million people

300

200

100

0

1992 2000 2010 2020 2030 2040 2050

May be of any race

hundred years, the United States quadrupled in population; its complexion and culture metamorphosed even more radically. The twentieth century was distinguished by economic and social — but, in a lasting tribute to the country's founders, not political — upheaval as the nation matured into middle age and confronted a battery of mid-life crises that again tested its very rationale and the limits of government.

As recently as the end of the 1980s, the Census Bureau predicted that it would take a half century for the United States to match the population growth of the last twenty-five years. The growth rate seemed to be lower than at any period since the

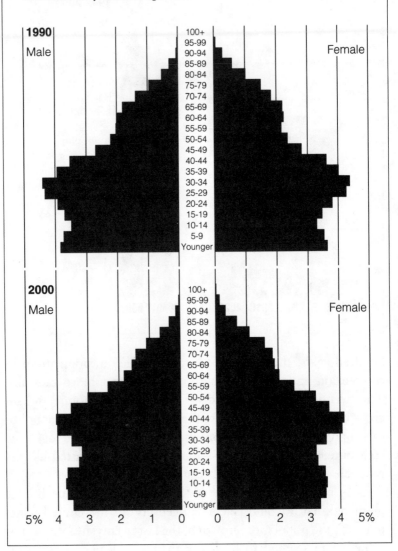

THE AGING OF AMERICA

Actual age distribution in 1990 and Census Bureau estimates for years through 2050.

250

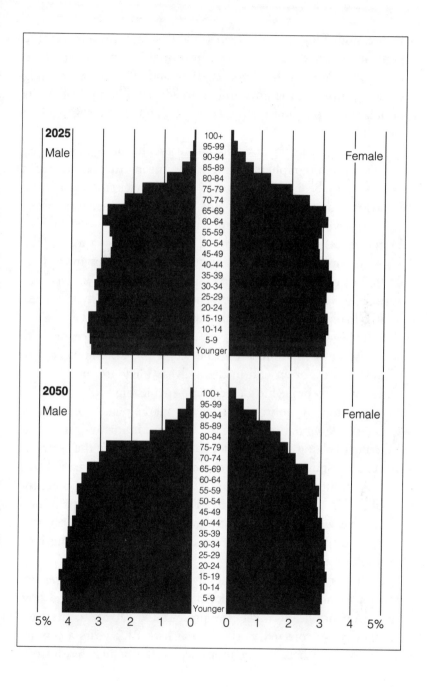

Depression. Under the bureau's middle-range projections, the population would peak in 2038 at just over 300 million and then decline for decades. But between 1988 and 1992 alone, startling growth prompted the government to add 7 million people to its population projection for the year 2000 and another 83 million for 2050.

All of the projections are made on the basis of variables known to demographers today, which means that some trends are likely to be invalidated by events and vicissitudes that are impossible to anticipate. Jobs such as bicycle messengers surged as entry-level vehicles for employment until they were doomed by the recession, the fax machine, and by the mania for cellular phones, which were being activated at the rate of more than 11,000 a day. AIDS, homelessness and crack cocaine, which transformed government priorities and individual lifestyles in the 1980s, had been virtually unknown or unanticipated when the decade began. In that light, the mathematical precision with which some predictions are made seems presumptuous at best. Numbers are not an end in themselves. They are merely tools with which to build life's equations — malleable tools subject to manipulation by politics and by the marketplace. One consequence of deregulation during the Reagan administration was the blurring of sizing formulas adopted in the 1940s by the National Bureau of Standards. A half century ago, a size-10 dress had a 34.5-inch hipline. To accommodate the Baby Boom bulge, the smallest size 10 that Bruno Ferri's Wolf Form Company now makes has a 37-inch hipline. So much for jogging: you can run, but you can't hide. "I hate to say it," Ferri conceded, "but it's a con job on the women."

But if not every individual's figure can be trusted, aggregates form a foundation for vital perspective on the future and how that evolving vision affects the present and relates to the past. Longevity is projected to rise — to at least 81.2 years a century from now. But because the mortality rate for whites has historically declined more quickly, blacks may not achieve the same level of life expectancy as whites until 2080. Rising life expectancy for women outpaced that of men for a half century starting in 1930. It's assumed that the shrinking differential of seven years or so between the sexes will endure, although AIDS – 90 percent of whose initial victims have been men – could become another barrier to parity in life spans. Because Americans are aging, sometime before 2030 the crude death rate (unadjusted for changes in the composition of the population by age and gender) is projected to surpass the crude birthrate, which would mean that only immigration would account for a population increase. All those assumptions might be rendered moot if life expectancy advances indefinitely.

In 1990, the median age of Americans hit an all-time high of 32.9. But in none of the Census Bureau's projections for the next century would the median be even that low again. It would rise to 36 at the turn of the century and to 42.6 in 2040 – the largest increase during any fifty-year period of the nation's history. Driving that increase is the vast pool of Baby Boomers. By the end of the 1990s, the youngest among them will have celebrated his thirty-fifth birthday.

One consequence of the graying of America is a profound shift in what demographers call the dependency ratio – the proportion of children and of elderly to the working-age population. Overall, the ratio is likely to be lower over the next three decades than at any time since the Second World War. But the elderly dependency ratio, already at an all-time high, would inexorably increase. It is now about half the youthful dependency ratio. By 2030, the elderly dependency ratio would surpass the youthful dependency ratio and continue to outpace it for the rest of the twenty-first century.

Predicting the number of the youngest Americans is more problematic because most have not been born yet (and 1.6 million or so won't be each year because of abortions). The number under 5 years old is generally expected to decline, although the most bodacious projections suggest that it could nearly double by 2080. The elementary school population is expected to grow by about 10 percent through the mid-1990s, then fluctuate for several decades. The number of teenagers between 14 and 17, survivors of the mid-1970s baby bust, may decline until 1995, then rebound and remain relatively stable. The number of Americans between the ages of 18 and 24, which has been shrinking since 1980, would continue to decrease until about 1995. But even under the most optimistic projections, it would not exceed the 1980 level for fifty years. Baby Boomers, meanwhile, would swell the ranks of each age group as they sweep through it, leaving a giant gap in their wake. The 25-to-34 group peaked around 1990. By 2000 it probably will contract to 1980 levels. The number aged 35 to 44 will hit a high in 2000; the 45-to-54 contingent will peak a decade later.

Low birthrates during the Depression meant that the population 65 and over would grow only modestly until 2005. But beginning around 2010, that group will begin to grow enormously. By 2030, its ranks will double. By 2040, the percentage of Americans 65 and over will be nearly double what it was in 1990; nearly one in four Americans might be over 65 then. The first Baby Boomers will just begin to turn 85 in 2030. By 2050, at present rates, the number of people 85 and over will, for the first time, exceed the number under age 5. The 85-and-older group will swell to nearly 13 million — five times the number in 1990, when that group accounted for about 1 percent of the population. The percentage is expected to quadruple in fifty years. Projected increases in life expectancy are likely to benefit elderly people most immediately. By 2005, only half the people over 65 will be younger than 75. In 1990, less than 10 percent of Americans 65 and over were older than 85. The proportion will nearly double by 2010, then plateau until it rises again to more than 22 percent in 2050.

The white population is projected to peak in 2027 at 235 million, after an increase of just over 11 percent. By 2030, the black population is likely to be 50 percent larger than it was in 1990. No groups are growing as rapidly as Asians, Pacific Islanders and American Indians. Since 1970, their population has more than tripled. It may double by 2015 and triple again by 2040. Swollen by higher birth rates, the Hispanic population is projected to grow from nine percent of the total to 14 percent in 2010 and 23 percent in 2050.

Census Bureau demographer Gregory Spencer also analyzes population growth another way, by rates of change. The annual growth rate among whites is about .75 percent, or about the same as the total growth rate for the nation during the Depression. Even that rate is expected to fall precipitously. The black population has been growing at about twice the rate for whites and is expected to continue to do so until at least 2030. Since 1970, the growth rate of "other races" (primarily Asians and American Indians) has been four times that of blacks and eight times the rate for whites. Not until 2030 is it likely to decline even to 1.8 percent annually — the recent peak that the whole nation hit at the height of the Baby Boom. As a result, the percentage of Americans of other races is projected to nearly triple to 11 percent by 2080. The proportion of whites, including Hispanic people who identify themselves by choice as white, would steadily decline from 73 percent to 68 percent in 2010 and 53 percent in 2050. The percentage of blacks would inch up to 16 percent.

Those figures reflect sharp variations in birthrates among all three groups. In the 1990s, births are projected to decline by 14 percent among whites as Baby Boomers turn 40 (nearly nine in ten births are still to mothers between the ages of 18 and 34). Black birthrates are likely to remain about the same, as a decline in the fertility rate is balanced by an increase in the number of women 18 to 34. Again, the most striking increases are projected for the "other race" group — growing to double the present number in less than forty years. They now represent about 4 percent of all births, a share that will nearly triple by 2080.

Children having children, a sociological phenomenon that erupted again in the 1970s and 1980s, may begin to decline, but not for reasons that should prompt any claims of victory by advocates of traditional family values. Most of the projected decline can be attributed to the shrinking proportion of women of childbearing age who are teenagers rather than because fertility rates among teenagers are receding. In 1980, 16 percent of all births, 14 percent of white births, and 28 percent of black births were to teenage mothers. Ten years later, those percentages had already shrunk significantly, to 12 percent of all births, 10 percent of white births, and 21 percent of black births (although, overall, out-of-wedlock rates are rising). If future black families evolve to mirror white ones, the percentage of black children born to teenagers will steadily shrivel by about half, or the same percentage as for whites, in 2050. The reverse has been true for births by older women. In 1980, they accounted for 5 percent of all births, which may have been the lowest level ever. In the second half of the 1990s, though, the proportion of births to women 35 and older is likely to double, to about 10 percent among whites and about 9 percent among blacks. Women of other races who are over 35 have had historically high birthrates; they represent the only group in which a new mother over 35 is more common than a teenage mother. Among all three groups, though, the percentage of older mothers is projected to decline again, beginning with the new century.

In 1983, for the first time, 2 million Americans died — a consequence of the growing and graying population. Baby Boomers will begin to turn 65 in the 2010s, pushing the number of deaths annually to 3 million by 2020. Before the end of that decade, a phenomenal change is projected to take place: Every year, the number of deaths might exceed the number of births. That happens now only in retirement communities, but could become routine nationwide. As longevity grows, the proportion of deaths that occur at age 85 and over will double in the next half century from 20 percent in 1990.

If birth and death rates conform to those projections, immigration may not influence age distribution as much as the nation's growth in the twenty-first century. With no net immigration, the population would probably expand to about 260 million by the turn of the century, peak at 270 million by 2030, and then decline to 220 million by 2080, or about where it was in 1980. If America greets about 500,000 immigrants a year, the population would rise to nearly 270 million in the year 2000 and peak at 300 million in 2030 before beginning to decline. If the number of new immigrants is higher, say 800,000 a year, the population would pass 300 million before 2020 and continue to grow for the rest of the twenty-first century. The government claims that the net increase in illegal immigrants will be halved in the 1990s. But, even so, at least 100,000 undocumented aliens would enter the country every year by the government's own acknowledgment. The volume is likely to depend even more on events overseas than on the inclinations, by the United States, to set quotas or to contain illegal immigrants, though. Latin Americans and Asians will probably continue to account for most new immigrants, but other groups — Kurds and refugees from Hong Kong and from Eastern Europe, for example — may change the mix.

If late twentieth-century trends continue, immigration will reshape the nation's racial composition. Since 1960, whites — including people of Hispanic origin — have plunged as a percentage of total net immigration, from nearly 93 percent to about 55 percent. Most of the proportional increase has come in the "other race" category, which multiplied tenfold, from 3.7 percent in 1960 to nearly 40 percent in 1990, and appears likely to remain in the 30 percent range. That rate would guarantee further dramatic growth in the "other race" population, which in 1990 represented about 3 percent of the total.

Despite its use of precise numbers, the Census Bureau is circumspect about its own projections. Nearly as many pages in its volume of forecasts are devoted to the caveats as to the projections themselves. The most problematic categories are the very young and the very old. Figuring out how many children under age 5 and how many aged Americans over 85 will be around decades from now depends on variables beyond the scope of any prudent demographer. Those are the only two age groups for which the difference in high and low estimates of population growth is greater than 5 percent. Even given those disparities, demographers unswervingly embrace two assumptions: that even the high range of fertility projections still would not be high enough to swell the younger proportion of the population; and that while there are now about double the number of Americans under age 18 than over 65, within about half a century the elderly will outnumber the young.

The 1990 census was a single frame in a moving picture. It doesn't pause to accommodate futurists. Spliced onto the twenty frames that were photographed at ten-year intervals since 1790, the bicentennial portrait can only hint at what's to come. In 1890, it was assumed that the world might be devoid of trees within a few decades as wood was devoured for cooking and heating. Instead, forests have survived to face another unimagined threat entirely: acid rain. When the twentieth century began, the otherwise sage Henry Adams declared that the world might last only another fifty years. It has survived nearly twice as long so far, in spite of itself. About the same time that Adams predicted that the planet had a half century left, Wilbur Wright cautioned his brother, Orville, that it would take human beings a half century to create flying machines. Two years later, Wilbur helped prove himself wrong at Kitty Hawk.

What we do know is that the world will be a more crowded and complicated place as it marks a millennium for only the second time since, the New Testament says, Caesar Augustus ordered a census be taken in the year that Jesus Christ was born in Bethlehem. Americans will be even more diverse in the twenty-first century than they became in the one that preceded it. We will be older and more schooled, but not necessarily wiser. For no matter how many Americans there are a century from now or what they look like or how or where they live, one characteristic that cannot be quantified but has defined civilization will be constant. Increasingly, that timeless characteristic will be put to the test as the planet gets more crowded. "Human nature," wrote Aristotle, who counseled a world leader before an earlier Gulf War, is everywhere the same, just "as fire burns the same here and in Persia." You can count on it.

APPENDICES

RACE AND HISPANIC ORIGIN

Race	1990 census		1980 census		Number change	Percent change
	Number	Percent	Number	Percent		
All people	248,709,873	100.0%	226,545,805	100.0%	22,164,068	9.8%
White	199,686,070	80.3	188,371,622	83.1	11,314,448	6.0
Black	29,986,060	12.1	26,495,025	11.7	3,491,035	13.2
American Indian, Eskimo or Aleut	1,959,234	0.8	1,420,400	0.6	538,834	37.9
Am. Indian	1,878,285	0.8	1,364,033	0.6	514,252	37.7
Eskimo	57,152	0.0	42,162	0.0	14,990	35.6
Aleut	23,797	0.0	14,205	0.0	9,592	67.5
Asian or Pacific Islander	7,273,662	2.9	3,500,439	1.5	3,773,223	107.8
Chinese	1,645,472	0.7	806,040	0.4	839,432	104.1
Filipino	1,406,770	0.6	774,652	0.3	632,118	81.6
Japanese	847,562	0.3	700,974	0.3	146,588	20.9
Asian Indian	815,447	0.3	361,531	0.2	453,916	125.6
Korean	798,849	0.3	354,593	0.2	444,256	125.3
Vietnamese	614,547	0.2	261,729	0.1	352,818	134.8
Hawaiian	211,014	0.1	166,814	0.1	44,200	26.5
Samoan	62,964	0.0	41,948	0.0	21,016	50.1
Guamanian	49,345	0.0	32,158	0.0	17,187	53.4
Other Asian or Pacific I.	821,692	0.3	na	na	na	na
Other race	9,804,847	3.9	6,758,319	3.0	3,046,528	45.1

Hispanic Origin

	1990 census		1980 census		Number change	Percent change
	Number	Percent	Number	Percent		
Hispanic origin	22,354,059	9.0%	14,608,673	6.4%	7,745,386	53.0%
Mexican	13,495,938	5.4	8,740,439	3.9	4,755,499	54.4
Puerto Rican	2,727,754	1.1	2,013,945	0.9	713,809	35.4
Cuban	1,043,932	0.4	803,226	0.4	240,706	30.0
Other hisp.	5,086,435	2.0	3,051,063	1.3	2,035,372	66.7

POPULATION OF THE STATES

State	1990 census	1980 census	Number change	Percent change	1990 rank By pop.	1990 rank By percent change
All United States	248,709,873	226,542,203	22,167,670	9.8%	—	—
Alabama	4,040,587	3,894,025	146,562	3.8	22	33
Alaska	530,043	401,851	148,192	36.9	50	2
Arizona	3,665,228	2,716,546	948,682	34.9	24	3
Arkansas	2,350,725	2,286,337	64,368	2.8	33	34
California	29,760,021	23,667,764	6,092,257	25.7	1	5
Colorado	3,294,394	2,889,735	404,659	14.0	26	14
Connecticut	3,287,116	3,107,564	179,552	5.8	27	26
Delaware	666,168	594,338	71,830	12.1	46	17
Dist. of Columbia	606,900	638,432	−31,532	−4.9	48	50
Florida	12,937,926	9,746,961	3,190,965	32.7	4	4
Georgia	6,478,216	5,462,982	1,015,234	18.6	11	8
Hawaii	1,108,229	964,691	143,538	14.9	41	13
Idaho	1,006,749	944,127	62,622	6.6	42	23
Illinois	11,430,602	11,427,409	3,193	0.0	6	46
Indiana	5,544,159	5,490,214	53,945	1.0	14	38
Iowa	2,776,755	2,913,808	−137,053	−4.7	30	49
Kansas	2,477,574	2,364,236	113,338	4.8	32	29
Kentucky	3,685,296	3,660,324	24,972	0.7	23	40
Louisiana	4,219,973	4,206,116	13,857	0.3	21	44
Maine	1,227,928	1,125,043	102,885	9.1	38	20
Maryland	4,781,468	4,216,933	564,535	13.4	19	15
Massachusetts	6,016,425	5,737,093	279,332	4.9	13	28
Michigan	9,295,297	9,262,044	33,253	0.4	8	43
Minnesota	4,375,099	4,075,970	299,129	7.3	20	22
Mississippi	2,573,216	2,520,770	52,446	2.1	31	36
Missouri	5,117,073	4,916,766	200,307	4.1	15	30
Montana	799,065	786,690	12,375	1.6	44	37
Nebraska	1,578,385	1,569,825	8,560	0.5	36	41

POPULATION OF THE STATES

State	1990 census	1980 census	Number change	Percent change	1990 rank By pop.	1990 rank By percent change
Nevada	1,201,833	800,508	401,325	50.1%	39	1
New Hampshire	1,109,252	920,610	188,642	20.5	40	6
New Jersey	7,730,188	7,365,011	365,177	5.0	9	27
New Mexico	1,515,069	1,303,302	211,767	16.2	37	11
New York	17,990,455	17,558,165	432,290	2.5	2	35
North Carolina	6,628,537	5,880,095	748,542	12.7	10	16
North Dakota	638,800	652,717	−13,917	−2.1	47	47
Ohio	10,847,115	10,797,603	49,512	0.5	7	42
Oklahoma	3,145,385	3,025,487	120,098	4.0	28	31
Oregon	2,842,321	2,633,156	209,165	7.9	29	21
Pennsylvania	11,881,643	11,864,720	16,923	0.1	5	45
Rhode Island	1,003,464	947,154	56,310	5.9	43	25
South Carolina	3,486,703	3,120,729	365,974	11.7	25	18
South Dakota	696,004	690,768	5,236	0.8	45	39
Tennessee	4,877,185	4,591,023	286,162	6.2	17	24
Texas	16,986,510	14,225,513	2,760,997	19.4	3	7
Utah	1,722,850	1,461,037	261,813	17.9	35	9
Vermont	562,758	511,456	51,302	10.0	49	19
Virginia	6,187,358	5,346,797	840,561	15.7	12	12
Washington	4,866,692	4,132,353	734,339	17.8	18	10
West Virginia	1,793,477	1,950,186	−156,709	−8.0	34	51
Wisconsin	4,891,769	4,705,642	186,127	4.0	16	32
Wyoming	453,588	469,557	−15,969	−3.4	51	48

POPULATION OF THE STATES, BREAKDOWN BY RACE, HISPANIC ORIGIN AND SEX

State	1990 total	White	Black	American Indian, Eskimo or Aleut	Asian or Pacific Islander	Other
All U.S.	248,709,873	199,686,070	29,986,060	1,959,234	7,273,662	9,804,847
New England	**13,206,943**	**12,032,983**	**627,547**	**32,794**	**231,656**	**281,963**
Maine	1,227,928	1,208,360	5,138	5,998	6,683	1,749
New Hamp.	1,109,252	1,087,433	7,198	2,134	9,343	3,144
Vermont	562,758	555,088	1,951	1,696	3,215	808
Mass.	6,016,425	5,405,374	300,130	12,241	143,392	155,288
R.I.	1,003,464	917,375	38,861	4,071	18,325	24,832
Connecticut	3,287,116	2,859,353	274,269	6,654	50,698	96,142
Middle Atlantic	**37,602,286**	**30,035,921**	**4,985,675**	**92,354**	**1,103,719**	**1,384,617**
New York	17,990,455	13,385,255	2,859,055	62,651	693,760	989,734
New Jersey	7,730,188	6,130,465	1,036,825	14,970	272,521	275,407
Pa.	11,881,643	10,520,201	1,089,795	14,733	137,438	119,476
East North Central	**42,008,942**	**35,764,043**	**4,817,436**	**149,939**	**572,673**	**704,851**
Ohio	10,847,115	9,521,756	1,154,826	20,358	91,179	58,996
Indiana	5,544,159	5,020,700	432,092	12,720	37,617	41,030
Illinois	11,430,602	8,952,978	1,694,273	21,836	285,311	476,204
Michigan	9,295,297	7,756,086	1,291,706	55,638	104,983	86,884
Wisconsin	4,891,769	4,512,523	244,539	39,387	53,583	41,737
West North Central	**17,659,690**	**16,253,914**	**898,504**	**187,960**	**195,396**	**123,916**
Minnesota	4,375,099	4,130,395	94,944	49,909	77,886	21,965
Iowa	2,776,755	2,683,090	48,090	7,349	25,476	12,750
Missouri	5,117,073	4,486,228	548,208	19,835	41,277	21,525
North Dakota	638,800	604,142	3,524	25,917	3,462	1,755
South Dakota	696,004	637,515	3,258	50,575	3,123	1,533
Nebraska	1,578,385	1,480,558	57,404	12,410	12,422	15,591
Kansas	2,477,574	2,231,986	143,076	21,965	31,750	48,797

State	Hispanic origin	White, non-Hispanic	Black, non-Hispanic	Total males	Total females
All U.S.	22,354,059	188,128,296	29,216,293	121,239,418	127,470,455
New England	**568,240**	**11,765,610**	**583,141**	**6,380,000**	**6,826,943**
Maine	6,829	1,203,357	4,937	597,850	630,078
New Hamp.	11,333	1,079,484	6,749	543,544	565,708
Vermont	3,661	552,184	1,868	275,492	287,266
Mass.	287,549	5,280,292	274,464	2,888,745	3,127,680
R.I.	45,752	896,109	34,283	481,496	521,968
Connecticut	213,116	2,754,184	260,840	1,592,873	1,694,243
Middle Atlantic	**3,186,149**	**28,601,213**	**4,626,430**	**18,055,623**	**19,546,663**
New York	2,214,026	12,460,189	2,569,126	8,625,673	9,364,782
New Jersey	739,861	5,718,966	984,845	3,735,685	3,994,503
Pa.	232,262	10,422,058	1,072,459	5,694,265	6,187,378
East North Central	**1,437,720**	**35,074,700**	**4,774,196**	**20,372,570**	**21,636,372**
Ohio	139,696	9,444,622	1,147,440	5,226,340	5,620,775
Indiana	98,788	4,965,242	428,612	2,688,281	2,855,878
Illinois	904,446	8,550,208	1,673,703	5,552,233	5,878,369
Michigan	201,596	7,649,951	1,282,744	4,512,781	4,782,516
Wisconsin	93,194	4,464,677	241,697	2,392,935	2,498,834
West North Central	**288,789**	**16,100,570**	**890,159**	**8,599,083**	**9,060,607**
Minnesota	53,884	4,101,266	93,040	2,145,183	2,229,916
Iowa	32,647	2,663,840	47,493	1,344,802	1,431,953
Missouri	61,702	4,448,465	545,527	2,464,315	2,652,758
North Dakota	4,665	601,592	3,451	318,201	320,599
South Dakota	5,252	634,788	3,176	342,498	353,506
Nebraska	36,969	1,460,095	56,711	769,439	808,946
Kansas	93,670	2,190,524	140,761	1,214,645	1,262,929

POPULATION OF THE STATES, BREAKDOWN BY RACE, HISPANIC ORIGIN AND SEX

State	1990 total	White	Black	American Indian, Eskimo or Aleut	Asian or Pacific Islander	Other
South Atlantic	**43,566,853**	**33,390,885**	**8,923,558**	**172,281**	**631,133**	**448,996**
Delaware	666,168	535,094	112,460	2,019	9,057	7,538
Maryland	4,781,468	3,393,964	1,189,899	12,972	139,719	44,914
D.C.	606,900	179,667	399,604	1,466	11,214	14,949
Virginia	6,187,358	4,791,739	1,162,994	15,282	159,053	58,290
W. Va.	1,793,477	1,725,523	56,295	2,458	7,459	1,742
N.C.	6,628,637	5,008,491	1,456,323	80,155	52,166	31,502
S.C.	3,486,703	2,406,974	1,039,884	8,246	22,382	9,217
Georgia	6,478,216	4,600,148	1,746,565	13,348	75,781	42,374
Florida	12,937,926	10,749,285	1,759,534	36,335	154,302	238,470
East South Central	**15,176,284**	**12,049,158**	**2,976,704**	**40,839**	**84,464**	**25,119**
Kentucky	3,685,296	3,391,832	262,907	5,769	17,812	6,976
Tennessee	4,877,185	4,048,068	778,035	10,039	31,839	9,204
Alabama	4,040,587	2,975,797	1,020,705	16,506	21,797	5,782
Mississippi	2,573,216	1,633,461	915,057	8,525	13,016	3,157
West South Central	**26,702,793**	**20,142,156**	**3,928,626**	**349,611**	**406,651**	**1,875,749**
Arkansas	2,350,725	1,944,744	373,912	12,773	12,530	6,766
Louisiana	4,219,973	2,839,138	1,299,281	18,541	41,099	21,914
Oklahoma	3,145,585	2,583,512	233,801	252,420	33,563	42,289
Texas	16,986,510	12,774,762	2,021,632	65,877	319,459	1,804,780

State	Hispanic origin	White, non-Hispanic	Black, non-Hispanic	Total males	Total females
South Atlantic	**2,132,751**	**31,820,812**	**8,816,523**	**21,129,141**	**22,437,712**
Delaware	15,820	528,092	111,011	322,968	343,200
Maryland	125,102	3,326,109	1,177,823	2,318,671	2,462,797
D.C.	32,710	166,131	395,213	282,970	323,930
Virginia	160,288	4,701,650	1,153,133	3,033,974	3,153,384
W. Va.	8,489	1,718,896	55,986	861,536	931,941
N.C.	76,726	4,971,127	1,449,142	3,214,290	3,414,347
S.C.	30,551	2,390,056	1,035,947	1,688,510	1,798,193
Georgia	108,922	4,543,425	1,737,165	3,144,503	3,333,713
Florida	1,574,143	9,475,326	1,701,103	6,261,719	6,676,207
East South Central	**95,285**	**11,990,018**	**2,965,889**	**7,300,942**	**7,875,342**
Kentucky	21,984	3,378,022	261,360	1,785,235	1,900,061
Tennessee	32,741	4,027,631	774,925	2,348,928	2,528,257
Alabama	24,629	2,960,167	1,017,713	1,936,162	2,104,425
Mississippi	15,931	1,624,198	911,891	1,230,617	1,342,599
West South Central	**4,538,985**	**17,548,372**	**3,872,054**	**13,061,244**	**13,641,549**
Arkansas	19,876	1,933,082	372,762	1,133,076	1,217,649
Louisiana	93,044	2,776,022	1,291,470	2,031,386	2,188,587
Oklahoma	86,160	2,547,588	231,462	1,530,819	1,614,766
Texas	4,339,905	10,291,680	1,976,360	8,365,963	8,620,547

POPULATION OF THE STATES, BREAKDOWN BY RACE, HISPANIC ORIGIN AND SEX

State	1990 total	White	Black	American Indian, Eskimo or Aleut	Asian or Pacific Islander	Other
Mountain	**13,658,776**	**11,761,851**	**373,584**	**480,516**	**217,120**	**825,705**
Montana	799,065	741,111	2,381	47,679	4,259	3,635
Idaho	1,006,749	950,451	3,370	13,780	9,365	29,783
Wyoming	453,588	427,061	3,606	9,479	2,806	10,636
Colorado	3,294,394	2,905,474	133,146	27,776	59,862	168,136
New Mexico	1,515,069	1,146,028	30,210	134,355	14,124	190,352
Arizona	3,665,228	2,963,186	110,524	203,527	55,206	332,785
Utah	1,722,850	1,615,845	11,576	24,283	33,371	37,775
Nevada	1,201,833	1,012,695	78,771	19,637	38,127	52,603
Pacific	**39,127,306**	**28,255,159**	**2,454,426**	**452,940**	**3,830,850**	**4,133,931**
Washington	4,866,692	4,308,937	149,801	81,483	210,958	115,513
Oregon	2,842,321	2,636,787	46,178	38,496	69,269	51,591
California	29,760,021	20,524,327	2,208,801	242,164	2,845,659	3,939,070
Alaska	550,043	415,492	22,451	85,698	19,728	6,674
Hawaii	1,108,229	369,616	27,195	5,099	685,236	21,083

State	Hispanic origin	White, non-Hispanic	Black, non-Hispanic	Total males	Total females
Mountain	**1,991,732**	**10,642,155**	**356,758**	**6,778,610**	**6,880,166**
Montana	12,174	733,878	2,242	395,769	403,296
Idaho	52,927	928,661	3,211	500,956	505,793
Wyoming	25,751	412,711	3,426	227,007	226,581
Colorado	424,302	2,658,945	128,057	1,631,295	1,663,099
New Mexico	579,224	764,164	27,642	745,253	769,816
Arizona	688,338	2,626,185	104,809	1,810,691	1,854,537
Utah	84,597	1,571,254	10,868	855,759	867,091
Nevada	124,419	946,357	76,503	611,880	589,953
Pacific	**8,114,408**	**24,584,846**	**2,331,143**	**19,562,205**	**19,565,101**
Washington	214,570	4,221,622	146,000	2,413,747	2,452,945
Oregon	112,707	2,579,732	44,982	1,397,073	1,445,248
California	7,687,938	17,029,126	2,092,446	14,897,627	14,862,394
Alaska	17,803	406,722	21,799	289,867	260,176
Hawaii	81,390	347,644	25,916	563,891	544,338

MEDIAN HOUSEHOLD INCOME BY STATE

Some states may have the same ranking because their median incomes
were not statistically significant.

State	1989 Median	Rank	1979 Median (1989 $)	Rank	1969 Median (1989 $)	Rank	Percent change in real income 1979-89	1969-79
All U.S.	$30,056	—	$28,220	—	$26,707	—	6.5%	5.7%
Conn.	$41,721	1	$33,643	4	$34,232	2	24.0	−1.7
Alaska	$41,408	2	$42,586	1	$37,191	1	−2.8	14.5
N.J.	$40,927	3	$33,178	6	$32,640	4	23.4	1.7
Maryland	$39,386	4	$33,984	3	$31,790	5	15.9	6.9
Hawaii	$38,829	5	$34,306	2	$33,596	3	13.2	2.1
Mass.	$36,952	6	$29,450	13	$30,097	8	25.5	−2.2
N.H.	$36,329	7	$28,508	21	$27,230	18	27.4	4.7
California	$35,798	8	$30,569	10	$29,275	10	17.1	4.4
Delaware	$34,875	9	$29,904	13	$29,297	10	16.6	2.1
Virginia	$33,328	10	$29,282	13	$26,100	23	13.8	12.2
New York	$32,965	11	$27,895	26	$29,168	10	18.2	−4.4
Illinois	$32,252	12	$32,376	7	$30,547	7	−0.4	6.0
R.I.	$32,181	12	$26,973	29	$27,119	18	19.3	−0.5
Wash.	$31,183	14	$30,777	9	$28,718	14	1.3	7.2
Michigan	$31,020	15	$32,212	8	$31,463	6	−3.7	2.4
Nevada	$31,011	15	$30,516	10	$29,914	9	1.6	2.0
Minn.	$30,909	15	$29,762	13	$27,548	17	3.9	8.0
D.C.	$30,727	15	$27,164	29	$26,068	23	13.1	4.2
Colorado	$30,140	19	$30,256	12	$26,509	22	−0.4	14.1
Vermont	$29,792	20	$24,783	38	$25,055	28	20.2	−1.1
Utah	$29,470	21	$29,611	13	$26,695	21	−0.5	10.9
Wisc.	$29,442	21	$29,626	13	$28,315	15	−0.7	4.6
Pa.	$29,069	23	$28,285	22	$26,902	18	2.8	5.1
Georgia	$29,021	23	$25,190	37	$23,119	36	15.2	9.0
Indiana	$28,797	25	$29,462	13	$28,076	16	−2.3	4.9
Ohio	$28,706	25	$29,750	13	$29,203	10	−3.5	1.9

MEDIAN HOUSEHOLD INCOME BY STATE

Some states may have the same ranking because their median incomes
were not statistically significant.

State	1989 Median	Rank	1979 Median (1989 $)	Rank	1969 Median (1989 $)	Rank	Percent change in real income 1979-89	1969-79
Maine	$27,854	27	$23,151	47	$23,022	36	20.3%	0.6%
Arizona	$27,540	28	$27,562	27	$25,804	26	−0.1	6.8
Florida	$27,483	28	$24,591	38	$22,559	38	11.8	9.0
Kansas	$27,291	30	$27,417	28	$23,850	31	−0.5	15.0
Oregon	$27,250	30	$28,118	23	$26,109	23	−3.1	7.7
Wyoming	$27,096	30	$33,503	4	$25,288	27	−19.1	32.5
Texas	$27,016	33	$27,997	25	$23,724	31	−3.5	18.0
N.C.	$26,647	34	$24,265	38	$22,109	40	9.8	9.8
Missouri	$26,362	35	$26,109	32	$24,145	30	1.0	8.1
S.C.	$26,256	35	$24,651	38	$21,511	42	6.5	14.6
Iowa	$26,229	35	$28,150	23	$24,800	29	−6.8	13.5
Neb.	$26,016	38	$26,685	31	$23,371	34	−2.5	14.2
Idaho	$25,257	39	$25,613	33	$23,547	33	−1.4	8.8
Tenn.	$24,807	40	$23,697	45	$20,869	43	4.7	13.6
N.M.	$24,087	41	$24,555	38	$22,333	38	−1.9	10.0
Alabama	$23,597	42	$22,905	48	$20,202	47	3.0	13.4
Okla.	$23,577	42	$24,716	38	$20,759	43	−4.6	19.1
N.D.	$23,213	44	$25,626	33	$21,744	41	−9.4	17.9
Montana	$22,988	45	$25,839	33	$23,403	34	−11.0	10.4
Kentucky	$22,534	46	$23,401	46	$20,573	45	−3.7	13.7
S.D.	$22,503	46	$22,045	49	$20,299	47	2.1	8.6
Louisiana	$21,949	48	$25,516	33	$20,576	45	−14.0	24.0
Arkansas	$21,147	49	$20,467	50	$16,856	50	3.3	21.4
W. Va.	$20,795	50	$24,405	38	$20,416	47	−14.8	19.5
Miss.	$20,136	51	$20,269	51	$16,432	51	0.7	23.4

ANCESTRY OF THE POPULATION

Ancestry as self-identified by census respondents. People who reported multiple ancestries were listed in each, so figures do not add up to 100 percent.

Ancestry	1990 total	%	Ancestry	1990 total	%
All U.S.	248,709,873		Swiss	1,045,495	0.4%
			Welsh	2,033,893	0.8
European			Albanian	47,710	0.0
Alsatian	16,465	0.0%	Bulgarian	29,595	0.0
Austrian	870,531	0.4	Carpath Russian	7,602	0.0
Basque	47,956	0.0	Croatian	544,270	0.2
Belgian	394,655	0.2	Czech	1,300,192	0.5
British	1,119,154	0.4	Czechoslovakian	315,285	0.1
Cypriot	4,897	0.0	Estonian	26,762	0.0
Celtic	29,652	0.0	European	466,718	0.2
Danish	1,634,669	0.7	German Russian	10,153	0.0
Dutch	6,227,089	2.5	Hungarian	1,582,302	0.6
English	32,655,779	13.1	Latvian	100,331	0.0
Finnish	658,870	0.3	Lithuanian	811,865	0.3
French	10,320,935	4.1	Macedonian	20,365	0.0
German	57,985,595	23.3	Polish	9,366,106	3.8
Greek	1,110,373	0.4	Rom	5,693	0.0
Icelander	40,529	0.0	Romanian	365,544	0.1
Irish	38,739,548	15.6	Russian	2,952,987	1.2
Italian	14,714,939	5.9	Serbian	116,795	0.0
Luxemburger	49,061	0.0	Slavic	76,931	0.0
Maltese	39,600	0.0	Slovak	1,882,897	0.8
Manx	6,317	0.0	Slovene	124,437	0.1
Norwegian	3,869,395	1.6	Soviet	7,729	0.0
Portuguese	1,153,351	0.5	Ukrainian	740,803	0.3
Scandinavian	678,880	0.3	Yugoslavian	257,994	0.1
Scotch-Irish	5,617,773	2.3	Other European	259,585	0.1
Scottish	5,393,581	2.2			
Swedish	4,680,863	1.9			

ANCESTRY OF THE POPULATION

Ancestry as self-identified by census respondents. People who reported multiple ancestries were listed in each, so figures do not add up to 100 percent.

Ancestry	1990 total	%
West Indian *Non-Hispanic*		
Bahamian	21,081	0.0%
Barbadian	35,455	0.0
Belizean	22,922	0.0
Bermudian	4,941	0.0
British West Indian	37,819	0.0
Dutch West Indian	61,530	0.0
Haitian	289,521	0.1
Jamaican	435,024	0.2
Trinidad and Tob.	76,270	0.0
U.S. Virgin Islander	7,621	0.0
West Indian	159,167	0.1
Other West Indian	4,139	0.0
Hispanic		
Cuban	1,043,932	0.4%
Mexican	13,495,938	5.4
Puerto Rican	2,727,754	1.1
Other Hispanic	5,235,192	2.1
Asian, Pacific Islander		
Chinese	1,645,472	0.7%
Filipino	1,406,770	0.6
Guamanian	49,345	0.0
Hawaiian	211,014	0.1
Indian (Asian)	815,447	0.3
Japanese	847,562	0.3
Korean	798,849	0.3
Samoan	62,964	0.0
Vietnamese	614,547	0.2

Ancestry	1990 total	%
Other Asian, Pac. I.	821,692	0.3%
Pacific		
Australian	52,133	0.0%
New Zealander	7,742	0.0
North African, Southwest Asian		
Algerian	3,215	0.0%
Arab	127,364	0.1
Armenian	308,096	0.1
Assyrian	51,765	0.0
Egyptian	78,574	0.0
Iranian	235,521	0.1
Iraqi	23,212	0.0
Israeli	81,677	0.0
Jordanian	20,656	0.0
Lebanese	394,180	0.2
Middle Eastern	7,656	0.0
Moroccan	19,089	0.0
Palestinian	48,019	0.0
Saudi Arabian	4,486	0.0
Syrian	129,606	0.1
Turkish	83,850	0.0
Yemeni	4,011	0.0
Other North African and Southwest Asian	10,670	0.0

ANCESTRY OF THE POPULATION

Ancestry as self-identified by census respondents. People who reported multiple ancestries were listed in each, so figures do not add up to 100 percent.

Ancestry	1990 total	%
Subsaharan Africa		
African	245,845	0.1%
Cape Verdean	50,772	0.0
Ethiopian	34,851	0.0
Ghanian	20,066	0.0
Kenyan	4,639	0.0
Liberian	8,797	0.0
Nigerian	91,688	0.0
Sierra Leonean	4,627	0.0
South African	17,992	0.0
Sudanese	3,623	0.0
Ugandan	2,681	0.0
Other African	20,607	0.0

Ancestry	1990 total	%
North American		
Acadian	668,271	0.3%
American	12,396,057	5.0
Canadian	560,891	0.2
French Canadian	2,167,127	0.9
Penn. German	305,841	0.1
United States	643,602	0.3
Other North Am.	12,927	0.0

FOREIGN-BORN POPULATION, BY PLACE OF BIRTH

Place	1990 total	%
United States	21,631,601	—
Europe	**4,812,117**	**22.2%**
Austria	94,398	0.4%
Belgium	41,111	0.2
Czechoslovakia	90,042	0.4
Denmark	37,657	0.2
Estonia	9,251	0.0
Finland	23,547	0.1
France	162,934	0.8
Germany	1,163,004	5.4
Greece	189,267	0.9

Place	1990 total	%
Hungary	112,419	0.5%
Ireland	177,420	0.8
Italy	639,518	3.0
Latvia	26,380	0.1
Lithuania	30,344	0.1
Netherlands	104,216	0.5
Norway	46,240	0.2
Poland	397,014	1.8
Portugal	218,525	1.0
Romania	92,627	0.4
Soviet Union	336,889	1.6

FOREIGN-BORN POPULATION, BY PLACE OF BIRTH

Place	1990 total	%
Spain	103,518	0.5%
Sweden	57,166	0.3
Switzerland	43,991	0.2
South America	**1,107,000**	**5.1%**
Argentina	97,422	0.5%
Bolivia	33,637	0.2
Brazil	94,023	0.4
Chile	61,212	0.3
Colombia	303,918	1.4
Ecuador	147,867	0.7
Guyana	122,554	0.6
Peru	152,315	0.7
Uruguay	21,628	0.1
Venezuela	51,571	0.2
Other South Am.	20,853	0.1
North America	**8,524,594**	**39.4%**
Canada	870,850	4.0%
Caribbean	1,986,835	9.2
Antigua-Barbuda	12,452	0.1
Bahamas	24,341	0.1
Barbados	44,311	0.2
Cuba	750,609	3.5
Dominican Rep.	356,971	1.7
Grenada	18,183	0.1
Haiti	229,108	1.1
Jamaica	343,458	1.6
Trinidad & Tob.	119,221	0.6
Other Caribbean	88,181	0.4

Place	1990 total	%
Central America	**5,650,374**	**26.1%**
Belize	31,222	0.1
Costa Rica	48,264	0.2
El Salvador	472,885	2.2
Guatemala	232,977	1.1
Honduras	114,603	0.5
Mexico	4,447,439	20.6
Nicaragua	171,950	0.8
Panama	124,695	0.6
Other Central Am.	6,339	0.0
Other North Am.	16,535	0.1
Not reported	916,046	4.2

POPULATION OF THE LARGEST CITIES

City	1990 census	1980 census	Number change	Percent change	1990 rank	1980 rank
New York, N.Y.	7,322,564	7,071,639	250,925	3.5%	1	1
Los Angeles, Calif.	3,485,398	2,968,528	516,870	17.4	2	3
Chicago, Ill.	2,783,726	3,005,072	−221,346	−7.4	3	2
Houston, Tex.	1,630,553	1,595,138	35,415	2.2	4	5
Philadelphia, Pa.	1,585,577	1,688,210	−102,633	−6.1	5	4
San Diego, Calif.	1,110,549	875,538	235,011	26.8	6	8
Detroit, Mich.	1,027,974	1,203,368	−175,394	−14.6	7	6
Dallas, Tex.	1,006,877	904,599	102,278	11.3	8	7
Phoenix, Ariz.	983,403	789,704	193,699	24.5	9	9
San Antonio, Tex.	935,933	785,940	149,993	19.1	10	11
San Jose, Calif.	782,248	629,400	152,848	24.3	11	17
Indianapolis, Ind.*	741,952	711,539	30,413	4.3	12	12
Baltimore, Md.	736,014	786,741	−50,727	−6.4	13	10
San Francisco, Calif.	723,959	678,974	44,985	6.6	14	13
Jacksonville, Fla.*	672,971	571,003	101,968	17.9	15	19
Columbus, Ohio	632,910	565,021	67,889	12.0	16	20
Milwaukee, Wisc.	628,088	636,297	−8,209	−1.3	17	16
Memphis, Tenn.	610,337	646,174	−35,837	−5.5	18	14
Washington, D.C.	606,900	638,432	−31,532	−4.9	19	15
Boston, Mass.	574,283	562,994	11,289	2.0	20	21
Seattle, Wash.	516,259	493,846	22,413	4.5	21	23
El Paso, Tex.	515,342	425,259	90,083	21.2	22	28
Nashville-Davidson, Tenn.*	510,784	477,811	32,973	6.9	23	25
Cleveland, Ohio	505,616	573,822	−68,206	−11.9	24	18
New Orleans, La.	496,938	557,927	−60,989	−10.9	25	22
Denver, Colo.	467,610	492,686	−25,076	−5.1	26	24
Austin, Tex.	465,622	345,890	119,732	34.6	27	42
Fort Worth, Tex.	447,619	385,164	62,455	16.2	28	33
Oklahoma City, Okla.	444,719	404,014	40,705	10.1	29	31

* Consolidated city.

POPULATION OF THE LARGEST CITIES

City	1990 census	1980 census	Number change	Percent change	1990 rank	1980 rank
Portland, Ore.	437,319	368,148	69,171	18.8	30	35
Kansas City, Mo.	435,146	448,028	−12,882	−2.9	31	27
Long Beach, Calif.	429,433	361,498	67,935	18.8	32	37
Tucson, Ariz.	405,390	330,537	74,853	22.6	33	45
St, Louis, Mo.	396,685	452,801	−56,116	−12.4	34	26
Charlotte, N.C.	395,934	315,474	80,460	25.5	35	47
Atlanta, Ga.	394,017	425,022	−31,005	−7.3%	36	29
Virginia Beach, Va.	393,069	262,199	130,870	49.9	37	56
Albuquerque, N.M.	384,736	332,920	51,816	15.6	38	44
Oakland, Calif.	372,242	339,337	32,905	9.7	39	43
Pittsburgh, Pa.	369,879	423,959	−54,080	−12.8	40	30
Sacramento, Calif.	369,365	275,741	93,624	34.0	41	52
Minneapolis, Minn.	368,383	370,951	−2,568	−0.7	42	34
Tulsa, Okla.	367,302	360,919	6,383	1.8	43	38
Honolulu, Hawaii	365,272	365,048	224	0.1	44	36
Cincinnati, Ohio	364,040	385,409	−21,369	−5.5	45	32
Miami, Fla.	358,548	346,681	11,867	3.4	46	41
Fresno, Calif.	354,202	217,491	136,711	62.9	47	65
Omaha, Neb.	335,795	313,939	21,856	7.0	48	48
Toledo, Ohio	332,943	354,635	−21,692	−6.1	49	40
Buffalo, N.Y.	328,123	357,870	−29,747	−8.3	50	39

METROPOLITAN AREAS, RANKED BY WEALTH AND POVERTY

Top 25 metropolitan statistical areas. Income figures are median household income in 1989; poverty figures are percentages of people living below the poverty line in 1989.

Metropolitan Area	Income
Washington, D.C.-Md.-Va.	$46,884
Anchorage, Alaska	$43,946
Poughkeepsie, N.Y.	$42,250
San Francisco-Oakland-San Jose, Calif.	$41,459
Hartford-New Britain-Middletown, Conn.	$41,440
Boston-Lawrence-Salem, Mass.-N.H.	$40,666
Honolulu, Hawaii	$40,581
New Haven-Meriden, Conn.	$39,113
New York-Northern New Jersey-Long Island, N.Y.-N.J.-Conn.	$38,445
Waterbury, Conn.	$37,378
Los Angeles-Anaheim-Riverside, Calif.	$36,711
New London-Norwich, Conn.-R.I.	$36,691
Burlington, Vt.	$36,691
Minneapolis-St. Paul, Minn.-Wisc.	$36,565
Baltimore, Md.	$36,550
Atlanta, Ga.	$36,051
Worcester, Mass.	$35,977
Chicago-Gary-Lake County, Ill.-Ind.-Wisc.	$35,918
Manchester, N.H.	$35,866
Philadelphia-Wilmington-Trenton, Penn.-N.J.-Del.-Md.	$35,797
Rochester, Minn.	$35,789
Santa Barbara-Santa Maria-Lompoc, Calif.	$35,677
Seattle-Tacoma, Wash.	$35,047
San Diego, Calif.	$35,022
Portsmouth-Dover-Rochester, N.H., Me.	$35,009

Metropolitan Area	Poverty
McAllen-Edinburg-Mission, Tex.	41.9%
Brownsville-Harlingen, Tex.	39.7
Laredo, Tex.	38.2
El Paso, Tex.	26.8
Bryan-College Station, Tex.	26.7
Las Cruces, N.M.	26.5
Monroe, La.	24.7
Pine Bluff, Ark.	23.9
Houma-Thibodaux, La.	23.6
Albany, Ga.	22.7
Gainesville, Fla.	22.7
Visalia-Tulare-Porterville, Calif.	22.6
Alexandria, La.	22.6
Shreveport, La.	22.0
Lafayette, La.	21.7
Corpus Christi, Tex.	21.6
Fresno, Calif.	21.4
New Orleans, La.	21.2
Lawrence, Kan.	20.6
Waco, Tex.	20.6
Athens, Ga.	20.6
Odessa, Tex.	20.4
Huntington-Ashland, W.Va.-Ky.-Ohio	20.3
Pueblo, Colo.	20.2
Yakima, Wash.	20.2

METROPOLITAN AREAS, RANKED BY NON-NATIVE POPULATION

Top 25 metropolitan statistical areas. Figures for residents born in other states and in other countries are percentages of the entire area's population in 1990.

Metropolitan Area	Out-of-state	Metropolitan Area	Foreign-born
Sarasota, Fla.	76.0%	Miami-Fort Lauderdale, Fla.	33.6%
Fort Myers-Cape Coral, Fla.	72.4	Los Angeles-Anaheim-Riverside, Calif.	27.1
Las Vegas, Nev.	69.7	Laredo, Tex.	25.0
Naples, Fla.	69.0	McAllen-Edinburg-Mission, Tex.	24.7
Bradenton, Fla.	68.1	El Paso, Tex.	23.9
Melbourne-Titusville-Palm Bay, Fla.	67.9	Brownsville-Harlingen, Tex.	22.1
Fort Pierce, Fla.	66.8	Salinas-Seaside-Monterey, Calif.	21.6
Daytona Beach, Fla.	66.1	San Francisco-Oakland-San Jose, Calif.	20.0
Anchorage, Alaska	65.5	Merced, Calif.	19.8
Fort Walton Beach, Fla.	65.0	New York-Northern New Jersey-Long Island, N.Y.-N.J.-Conn.	19.6
Reno, Nev.	64.2	Yuma, Ariz.	18.8
Colorado Springs, Colo.	63.7	Fresno, Calif.	17.8
West Palm Beach-Boca Raton-Delray Beach, Fla.	63.3	Visalia-Tulare-Porterville, Calif.	17.6
Jacksonville, N.C.	63.1	San Diego, Calif.	17.2
Tampa-St. Petersburg-Clearwater, Fla.	62.7	Santa Barbara-Santa Maria-Lompoc, Calif.	16.9
Cheyenne, Wyo.	60.7	Stockton, Calif.	16.3
Phoenix, Ariz.	60.7	Honolulu, Hawaii	15.7
Orlando, Fla.	59.8	Las Cruces, N.M.	15.0
Ocala, Fla.	59.8	New Bedford, Mass.	15.0
Medford, Ore.	58.4	Modesto, Calif.	14.3
Washington, D.C.-Md.-Va.	58.2	Houston-Galveston-Brazoria, Tex.	12.4
Fort Collins-Loveland, Colo.	58.1	Washington, D.C.-Md.-Va.	12.3
Portsmouth-Dover-Rochester, N.H.-Mass.	56.0	West Palm Beach-Boca Raton-Delray Beach, Fla.	12.2
Tucson, Ariz.	55.6	Bakersfield, Calif.	12.2
Panama City, Fla.	55.5	Yuba City, Calif.	11.8

SOCIAL CHARACTERISTICS IN 1990

All United States population	248,709,873

Urban and Rural Residence

Urban population	187,051,543
Percent of total population	75.2%
Rural population	61,658,330
Percent of total population	24.8%
Farm population	3,871,583

School Enrollment

Aged 3 and up in school	64,987,101
Preprimary school	4,503,285
Elem. through high school	42,566,788
Percent in private school	9.8%
College	17,917,028

Educational Attainment

People aged 25 and older	158,868,436
Less than 9th grade	16,502,211
9th to 12th grade	22,841,507
High school graduate	47,642,763
Some college, no degree	29,779,777
Associate degree	9,791,925
Bachelor's degree	20,832,567
Grad. or professional degree	11,477,686
Percent H.S. graduate or higher	75.2%
Percent bachelor's deg. or higher	20.3%

Residence in 1985

People aged 5 and older	230,445,777
Lived in same house	122,796,970
Lived in other house in U.S.	102,540,097
Same state	80,954,800
Same county	58,675,635
Different county	22,279,165
Different state	21,585,297
Lived abroad	5,108,710

Children Ever Born, per 1,000 Women

Women aged 15 to 24	305
Women aged 25 to 34	1,330
Women aged 35 to 44	1,960

Veteran Status

Civilian veterans	27,481,055
Aged 65 and older	7,158,654

Disability of Civilian, Noninstitutional People

People aged 16 to 64	157,323,922
People with mobility or self-care limitation	16,105,766
Mobility limitation	12,631,557
Self-care limitation	5,376,803
People with a work disability	12,826,449
Work disability in labor force	5,043,990
Work disability, prevented from working	6,594,029
People aged 65 and older	29,563,511
People with mobility or self-care limitation	10,556,606
Mobility limitation	9,342,076
Self-care limitation	3,524,094

SOCIAL CHARACTERISTICS IN 1990

Place of Birth

Native population	228,942,557
Percent born in state of residence	67.1%
Foreign-born population	19,767,316
Foreign-borns, entered 1980 to 1990	8,663,627

Language Spoken at Home

People aged 5 and older	230,445,777
Speak a language other than English	31,844,979
Do not speak English "very well"	13,982,502
Speak Spanish	17,345,064
Spanish speakers who do not speak English "very well"	8,309,995
Speak Asian or Pacific Island language	4,471,621
Asian or Pacific Islanders who do not speak English "very well"	2,420,355

Ancestry

Total ancestries reported by (more than one could be cited)	296,379,515
Arab	870,738
Austrian	870,531
Belgian	394,655
Canadian	560,891
Czech	1,615,477
Danish	1,634,669
Dutch	6,227,089
English	32,655,779
Finnish	658,870
French (except Basque)	10,337,400
French Canadian	2,835,398
German	57,985,595
Greek	1,110,373
Hungarian	1,582,302
Irish	38,769,200
Italian	14,714,939
Lithuanian	811,865
Norweigian	3,869,395
Polish	9,366,106
Portuguese	1,153,351
Romanian	365,544
Russian	2,951,373
Scotch-Irish	5,617,773
Scottish	5,393,581
Slovak	1,882,897
Subsaharan Africa	506,188
Swedish	4,680,863
Swiss	1,045,495
Ukrainian	740,803
United States or American	13,052,277
Welsh	2,033,893
West Indian (excludes Hispanic people)	1,155,490
Yugoslavian	497,684
Other ancestries	68,431,031

SOCIAL CHARACTERISTICS IN 1990

Commuting to Work

Workers aged 16 and older	115,070,274
Percent driving alone	73.2%
Percent in carpools	13.4%
Percent using public transportation	5.3%
Percent using other means	1.3%
Percent who walk or work at home	6.9%
Mean travel time	22.4 minutes

Occupations

Employed people aged 16 and older	115,681,202
Executive, administrative and managerial	14,227,916
Professional specialty	16,305,666
Technicians and related support	4,257,235
Sales	13,634,686
Administrative support and clerical	18,826,477
Private houshold service	521,154
Protective service	1,992,852
Service occupations, except household and protective	12,781,911
Farming, forestry and fishing	2,839,010
Precision production, craft and repair	13,097,963
Machine operators, assemblers and inspectors	7,904,197
Transportation and material moving	4,729,001
Handlers, equipment cleaners, helpers and laborers	4,563,134

Industry Employment

Employed people aged 16 and older	115,681,202
Agriculture, forestry and fisheries	3,115,372
Mining	723,423
Construction	7,214,763
Manufacturing, nondurable goods	8,053,234
Manufacturing, durable goods	12,408,844
Transportation	5,108,003
Communications and public utilities	3,097,059
Wholesale trade	5,071,026
Retail trade	19,485,666
Finance, insurance and real estate	7,984,870
Business and repair services	5,577,462
Personal services	3,668,696
Entertainment and recreation	1,636,460
Health	9,682,684
Education	9,633,503
Other professional	7,682,060
Public administration	5,538,077

SOCIAL CHARACTERISTICS IN 1990

Class of Workers

Employed people aged 16 and older	115,681,202
Private wage and salary earners	89,541,393
Government workers	17,567,100
Local government	8,244,755
State government	5,381,445
Federal government	3,940,900
Self-employed workers	8,067,483
Unpaid family workers	505,226

Income Types in 1989

Households	91,993,582
With wage and salary incomes	71,174,232
Mean wage and salary income	$37,271
With self-employment incomes (nonfarm)	10,810,605
Mean self-employment income (nonfarm)	$20,218
With farm self-employment incomes	2,020,105
Mean farm self-employment income	$10,064
With Social Security incomes	24,210,922
Mean Social Security income	$7,772
With public assistance incomes	6,943,269
Mean public assistance income	$4,078
With retirement incomes	14,353,202
Mean retirement income	$9,216

Income in 1989

Households	91,993,582
Less than $5,000	5,684,517
$5,000 to $9,999	8,529,980
$10,000 to 14,999	8,133,273
$15,000 to $24,999	16,123,742
$25,000 to $34,999	14,575,125
$35,000 to $49,999	16,428,455
$50,000 to $74,999	13,777,883
$75,000 to $99,999	4,704,808
$100,000 to $149,999	2,593,768
$150,000 or more	1,442,031
Median household income	$30,056
Families	65,049,428
Less than $5,000	2,582,206
$5,000 to $9,999	3,636,361
$10,000 to 14,999	4,676,092
$15,000 to $24,999	10,658,345
$25,000 to $34,999	10,729,951
$35,000 to $49,999	13,270,930
$50,000 to $74,999	11,857,079
$75,000 to $99,999	4,115,468
$100,000 to $149,999	2,259,940
$150,000 or more	1,263,056
Median family income	$35,225

SOCIAL CHARACTERISTICS IN 1990

Income in 1989 (cont.)

Nonfamily households	26,944,154
Less than $5,000	3,311,694
$5,000 to $9,999	5,080,560
$10,000 to 14,999	3,593,796
$15,000 to $24,999	5,577,805
$25,000 to $34,999	3,799,161
$35,000 to $49,999	2,979,107
$50,000 to $74,999	1,685,327
$75,000 to $99,999	482,080
$100,000 to $149,999	274,043
$150,000 or more	160,581
Median nonfamily household income	$17,240
Per capita income	$14,420

Poverty status in 1989

All people for whom poverty status was determined	241,977,859
Living below poverty level	31,742,864
Percent living below the poverty level	13.1%
All people aged 18 and older	179,372,340
Living below poverty level	20,313,948
Percent living below the poverty level	11.3%
People aged 65 and older	29,562,647
Living below poverty level	3,780,585
Percent living below the poverty level	12.8%

Unrelated people living together	36,672,001
Living below poverty level	8,873,475
Percent living below the poverty level	24.2%
All families	65,049,428
Living below poverty level	6,487,515
Percent living below the poverty level	10.0%
With related children under age 18	33,536,660
Living below poverty level	4,992,845
Percent living below the poverty level	14.9%
With related children under age 5	14,250,048
Living below poverty level	2,613,626
Percent living below the poverty level	18.3%
Female head-of-household families	10,381,654
Living below poverty level	3,230,201
Percent living below the poverty level	31.1%
With related children under age 18	6,783,155
Living belowpoverty level	2,866,941
Percent living below the poverty level	42.3%
With related children under age 5	2,532,331
Living below poverty level	1,452,618
Percent living below the poverty level	57.4%

SOCIAL CHARACTERISTICS IN 1990

Housing

Total housing units	102,263,678
Occupied housing units	91,947,410

Year Structure Built

1989 to March 1990	2,169,436
1985 to 1988	9,024,365
1980 to 1984	9,931,917
1970 to 1979	22,291,826
1960 to 1969	16,506,410
1950 to 1959	14,831,071
1940 to 1949	8,676,155
1939 or earlier	18,832,498

Bedrooms

No bedroom	2,366,715
1 bedroom	14,062,917
2 bedrooms	31,502,796
3 bedrooms	38,931,475
4 bedrooms	12,549,082
5 or more bedrooms	2,850,693

Selected characteristics

Lacking complete plumbing facilities	1,101,696
Lacking complete kitchen facilities	1,109,626
Condominium housing unit	4,847,921

Source of Water

Public system or private company	86,068,766
Individual drilled well	13,467,148
Individual dug well	1,664,543
Other source	1,063,221

Sewage Disposal

Public sewer	76,455,211
Septic tank or cesspool	24,670,877
Other means	1,137,590

Telephone

No telephone in unit	4,817,457

House Heating Fuel

Utility gas	46,850,923
Bottled, tank or LP gas	5,243,462
Electricity	23,696,987
Fuel oil, kerosene, etc.	11,243,727
Coal or coke	358,965
Wood	3,609,323
Solar energy	54,536
Other fuel	345,580
No fuel used	543,907

Year Householder Moved Into Unit

1989 to March 1990	19,208,023
1985 to 1988	25,963,818
1980 to 1984	12,844,781
1970 to 1979	17,102,506
1960 to 1969	8,428,066
1959 or earlier	8,400,216

Vehicles Available in Occupied Housing Units

None	10,602,297
1	31,038,711
2	34,361,045
3 or more	15,945,357

SOCIAL CHARACTERISTICS IN 1990

Mortgage Status and Monthly Owner Costs

Owner-occupied housing units, where ownership was known   45,550,059

With a mortgage	29,811,735
Monthly cost of less than $300	1,455,511
$300 to $499	5,711,092
$500 to $699	6,635,180
$700 to $999	7,497,193
$1,000 to $1,499	5,294,990
$1,500 to $1,999	1,847,081
$2,000 or more	1,370,688
Median monthly cost	$737
Without a mortgage	15,738,324
Monthly cost of less than $100	960,802
$100 to $199	6,372,610
$200 to $299	5,058,575
$300 to $399	1,930,923
$400 or more	1,415,414
Median monthly cost	$209

Monthly Owner Costs for Owner-Occupied Units as a Percentage of Household Income in 1989

Less than 20 percent	25,846,744
20 to 24 percent	6,288,395
25 to 29 percent	4,280,439
30 to 34 percent	2,673,820
35 percent or more	6,148,822
Not computed	311,839

Gross Rent

Renter-occupied housing units, 32,170,036 where rental status was known

Gross monthly rent of less than $200	2,815,090
$200 to $299	3,736,190
$300 to $499	11,814,251
$500 to $749	8,471,363
$750 to $999	2,637,755
$1,000 or more	1,276,044
No cash rent	1,419,343
Median monthly rent	$447

Gross Rent as a Percentage of Household Income in 1989

Less than 20 percent	9,647,452
20 to 24 percent	4,453,652
25 to 29 percent	3,664,975
30 to 34 percent	2,562,684
35 percent or more	9,864,161
Not computed	1,977,112

INDEX

INDEX

ABOUT THE AUTHOR

SAM ROBERTS is the urban affairs columnist of *The New York Times*. A graduate of Cornell University, he was city editor of the *New York Daily News* and the coauthor of a biography of Nelson A. Rockefeller. For Times Books and the Twentieth Century Fund, he is revisiting the plight of America's urban poor a century after Jacob Riis chronicled "How the Other Half Lives." He is also the host of a nightly television interview program produced by *The New York Times* and Time Warner on New York 1, the city's all-news cable channel.